British and German Cartoons as Weapons in World War I

Wolfgang K. Hünig

British and German Cartoons as Weapons in World War I

Invectives and Ideology of Political Cartoons, a Cognitive Linguistics Approach

PETER LANG

Frankfurt am Main · Berlin · Bern · Bruxelles · New York · Oxford · Wien

Bibliographic Information published by Die Deutsche Bibliothek
Die Deutsche Bibliothek lists this publication in the Deutsche Nationalbibliografie; detailed bibliographic data is available in the internet at <http://dnb.ddb.de>.

ISBN 3-631-50211-7
US-ISBN 0-8204-6056-7

© Peter Lang GmbH
Europäischer Verlag der Wissenschaften
Frankfurt am Main 2002
All rights reserved.

Printed in Germany 1 2   4 5 6 7

www.peterlang.de

Preface

This book aims to advance cartoon research in two ways. First, it attempts to apply the principles of Cognitive Linguistics to the description of political cartoons, because the cognitive processes involved in cartoon comprehension are similar to those involved in the understanding of metaphors and metonymies in language. In the case of cartoons this means that a theoretical and highly complex phenomenon in a target domain is accessed, depicted and ridiculed via a more concrete and simplified source domain.

Second, it compares two large corpuses of 352 British and German cartoons created during the First World War in a detailed and systematic way so that commonalities and differences can be pointed out. Of specific interest are the relationships between the drawings and the verbal parts of cartoons on the one hand and the invectives they launch against the respective war enemy on the other. The invectives constitute the humorous, ironical or sarcastic 'points' of the cartoons, which in many cases rely on national stereotypes and it is revealing to compare those stereotypes of the second decade of the 20th century to the ones of today.

Since we regard the common practice of presenting comments on only a few arbitrarily selected cartoons as unsatisfactory, we think it essential to present the analyses of all of them and, by doing so, document essential background information as well as a fair amount of samples.

I am indebted to René Dirven, Martin Pütz and Ulrich Schmitz for granting me the opportunity of presenting and discussing some of the results of this research at the 2002 LAUD Conference in Landau/Germany.

I would like to say thanks to Allison Blizzard, Dacia Christin, René Dirven, Kay Engels, Steve Maksymiuk, Oyinkan Medubi and Günter Radden for reading and commenting on earlier versions of portions of this book and to the library teams of the English and German Departments of Bochum University for their helpful cooperation. Special thanks go to Tobias Hünig for translating the headings and captions of the *Simplicissimus* cartoons into English. Remaining weaknesses are due to my own shortcomings.

Last but not least, I would like to thank my students and colleagues at the universities of Duisburg, Hamburg and Kiel. As far as those 'northern brights' are concerned, it was very many miles but much more.

Duisburg, June 2002   Wolfgang K. Hünig

Contents

1. Introduction

According to the *Oxford English Dictionary* the term *cartoon* was first used in 1671 with the meaning: "a drawing on stout paper, made as a design for a painting of the same size to be executed in fresco or oil, or for a work in tapestry, mosaic, stained glass, or the like"[1] Today the term usually refers to "a full-page illustration in a paper or periodical; esp. applied to those in the comic papers relating to current events".[2] This use dates from 1843 when *Punch* introduced it as follows: "*Punch* has the benevolence to announce, that in an early number of his ensuing Volume he will astonish the Parliamentary Committee by the publication of several exquisite designs, to be called Punch's Cartoons!"[3] In addition to the meaning of "a portrait or other artistic representation, in which the characteristic features of the original are exaggerated with ludicrous effect"[4], the term *caricature* can also refer to a verbal description in art, meaning a "grotesque or ludicrous representation of persons or things by exaggeration of their most characteristic and striking features."[5] The German term *Karikatur* has both these meanings whereas the loanword *cartoon* in German is mainly used for animated cartoons.

It is presumed that the terms *caricature* as well as *Karikatur* go back to Agostino (1557-1602) and Annibale Carracci (1560-1609) who ran a workshop for the production of cartoons in Italy. According to *Encyclopedia Britannica* other 'pioneer caricaturists' were Giovanni Loreno Bernini (1598-1680) and Pier Leone Ghezzi (1674-1755). The latter was called the first professional cartoonist because he used serial production which was a necessary prerequisite for the effective denigration of the caricatured person in a cartoon campaign. This art spread from Italy to France and then to England where it fell on the fertile ground of the English humorous tradition. Honoré Daumier (1808-1879) and William Hogarth (1697-1764) are the French and British paragons of their trade and their cartoons have retained their high renown until today. Mass production, publication and distribution of cartoons in periodicals and newspapers has become the hallmark of modern political cartoons and it was the famous periodical *Punch* (founded in 1841) which initiated this tradition in England. Early German publications containing cartoons were *Fliegende Blätter* (from 1844), *Kladderadatsch* (from 1848) and *Simplicissimus* (from 1896).

Although there are no sources which could provide an exact account of the readership of *Simplicissimus* and *Punch* it can be safely said that both periodicals catered mainly to educated middle-class readers and both were

---

[1] Cf. *OED Online.*
[2] *Ibidem.*
[3] *Ibidem.*
[4] *Ibidem.*
[5] *Ibidem.*

critical as far as political authorities were concerned. In the case of *Simplicissimus* the fact that its founder and editor, Albert Langen, had to leave Germany and live in exile from 1898-1903 because otherwise he would have been incarcerated for *Majestätsbeleidigung* (insulting the Kaiser) makes it evident that being critiqued in a satirical way posed a problem for the German authorities.[1] But as will be seen later, both publications refrained from criticizing the authorities and remained very loyal during the war years. In any case, the essential focus of this research lies on how members of the other nation are portrayed.

The usual approach to cartoon analysis originates in the arts and/or the history of ideas where three key processes are described as condensation, combination and domestication.[2] Condensation is the compression of a complex phenomenon into a single image that is purported to capture its essence graphically. Combination refers to the mixing of elements and ideas from different domains into a new composite. "Domestication is the process by which abstract ideas and distant, unfamiliar persons or events are converted into something close, familiar and concrete. It translates what is novel and hard to understand into the commonplace by highlighting mutual elements and masking unique ones and by focusing on repetitive patterns to minimize novelty and mental adjustment."[3] A case in point is the portrait of Saddam Hussein as Hitler, which relies on the older generation's experience and evokes the historical background of Nazism in Germany and of the Second World War. Even if such descriptions are intuitively brilliant, they do not allow systematic comparisons of cartoons from different countries, times and artists.

Another field of research in cartoons has concentrated on three main areas: humor, stereotypes and formal features. The first two areas are clearly connected, because very often humor in political cartoons hinges on the attribution of a stereotypical value to a social or national group, e.g. a minority, which is seen as 'awkward', 'weird' or 'inconsistent'. Formal features are discussed against the backdrop of the history of the arts.

The first question we wish to address in this book is how cartoons can be adequately analyzed and the second is how two corpuses of cartoons from two different countries, which deal with similar topics, can be compared in a systematic fashion. For this purpose we have collected 163 cartoons from *Simplicissimus* and 189 cartoons from *Punch* which were published during the years of the First World War and which dealt with the war enemy, i.e. the British and the Germans. What was their role, their function and their stance during these four years? Did they raise a critical voice to stop the killing, or did they even further the causes of war? What were the differences between the

---

[1] Cf. Abret, H. & A. Keel (1985).
[2] Cf. Morris (1993: 200 f.)
[3] Morris (1993: 201).

British and the German cartoons? What were their invectives, i.e. the targets of castigation, and which stereotypes were used? Did they have any argument structure? Were they funny at all or simply ironical or sarcastic?

It is a weird fact that before the war actually began, there was ample time for premeditation and negotiation which might have prevented the catastrophe. After the assassination of Prince Ferdinand and his wife in Sarajevo, it took a whole month for Austria-Hungary to declare war on Serbia. But once military actions had taken their course, they were to go on for four years, resulting in human suffering and an immense death toll on both sides. There is a hypothesis that it was the dreariness of life and boredom that provoked an unbelievable enthusiasm for war, which is testified on contemporary news reels: crowds on the sidewalks are cheering soldiers marching to the front lines. The most convincing hypothesis seems to be that in the newspapers the war was seen and described as unavoidable. This turned out to be a self-fulfilling prophesy.[1]

2. Cartoon description

Condensation, combination and domestication can be redefined and deepened by analytic tools shaped by Cognitive Linguistics, especially by its research in metaphor and metonymy. Although condensation in its function of compressing complex phenomena into a single image is essentially a pictorial achievement, it involves the same cognitive processes as a metaphor. Domestication is a process by which abstract, distant and unfamiliar phenomena are converted into concrete, close and familiar concepts, i.e. an abstract, distant and unfamiliar target domain is pictorially and verbally presented in terms of a concrete, close and familiar source domain. Sentences such as *The debate team brought out their big guns* or *The other team sent in the cavalry against us* rely on the cognitive metaphor 'COMPETITION IS WAR' which has 'WAR' as its source and 'COMPETITION' as its target domain.[2]

2.1 Metaphors and metonymies

In some cartoons there are pictorial translations of verbal metaphors. Thus in *Simplicissimus* cartoon 117 called *John Bull, Death and the Devil Debating the Welfare of Humankind*, the metaphor 'DEATH IS A PERSON' has been translated into a drawing.[3] In literature and on the stage personifications of this kind have a long tradition. In cartoons it depends on the context, whether such

---

[1] Cf. Rosenberger, B. (1998).
[2] Cf. <http://cogsci.berkeley.edu/metaphors/Competition_Is_War.html> (2/17/2002) and also Lakoff & Johnson (1980).
[3] Cf. the drawing and the analysis of *Simplicissimus* cartoon 117 in section 3.3.

scenarios[1] are taken literally or not. In fairy tales, for example, a cognitive space may be created, in which anthropomorphic or supernatural creatures exist.

A truly pictorial metaphor is given, if an element A in a drawing or a picture is replaced by some other unexpected element B from a different domain. Forceville (1994: 5) provides the following example:

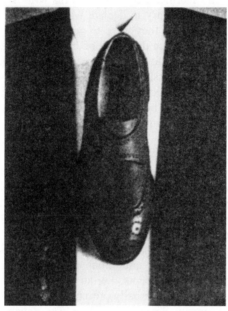

The photo shows the chest of a male person with a white shirt. A shoe is placed where a tie would normally be expected. There is an obvious difference to verbal metaphors which often goes unnoticed: the pictorial context must allow the reader to become aware of the replacement which involves a blending. A mental space in which shoes are worn like ties is blended with a space in which ties are worn in the usual fashion. In this way the meaning of a tie as a decorative accessory is transferred onto the shoe replacing it in the photo and more generally onto the shoes of the firm that launched the advertisement. Since the elements in a cartoon are not processed in a linear order, only the context can determine which element belongs to the source domain and which to the target domain. Pictorial replacements occur when, for example, a human being is drawn with animal features or a human head is put on an animal's body. Such

---

[1] We prefer the term *scenario* to *frame* or *script* to emphasize the compositional, metonymical and often counterfactual character of the referential complexes of cartoons. Cf. Bartlett (1932), Fillmore (1982, 1985), Fillmore, Kay and O'Connor (1988), Lakoff (1987) and Langacker (1987).

combinations can be more precisely described as the conceptual integration of various mental spaces because additional conceptual areas are integrated verbally.

A pictorial metonymy is given in drawings of John Bull who is the stereotypical Englishman and whose image is used likewise by British and German cartoonists of the time. A drawing of John Bull is a metonymy, because it represents, i.e. stands for English people etc., just like the German Emperor represents German people or German authorities etc. These are metonymical mappings from a source domain of a person to a target domain of an abstract political or social entity associated with it. The elements from the source domains are pictorially presented and entail familiar stereotypes, entities derived from emblems such as the British Lion or the German Eagle. Such pictorial metonymies are concept metonymies because one form-concept unit stands for another.

Form $_A$	Concept $_A$		Form $_B$	Concept $_B$
		FOR		
Drawing of John Bull	'prototypical Englishman'		[ɪŋglɪʃ piːpl]	'English people'

The drawn form of John Bull evokes the concept of a prototypical Englishman and this form-concept unit evokes a second one. The contiguity relation is given by the fact that John Bull is a (fictitious) citizen of England, whose persona goes back to a pamphlet by John Arbuthnot, published in 1712.[1] The form concept entity [ɪŋglɪʃ piːpl] - 'English people', can give rise to further metonymies such as 'English army', 'English cricket team' etc.[2] This normally includes further pictorial or verbal hints which indicate domain expansion, reduction etc.[3]

2.2 Sample analyses

A one-panel cartoon is a drawing of a scene with which the verbal elements interact, i.e. the heading and the captions including the legend, speech balloons,

---

[1] The character of John Bull, the typical Englishman, was introduced by John Arbuthnot, 1667-1735, in his John Bull pamphlets (1712), which entailed political satires on the Whig war policy. Arbuthnot was a Scottish author, scientist and court physician (1705-14). Cf.<http://www.encyclopedia.com/searchpool.asp?target=@DOCTITLE%20Arbuthnot%20%20John> (10.6.2001).
[2] Cf. Radden & Kövecses (1999).
[3] Cf. Ruiz de Mendoza Ibáñez & Díez Velasco (2002).

labels on certain entities etc.[1] It typically makes a point which can be humorous, ironical or sarcastic. The reactions of the readers are equivalent to the reactions of people who have heard a joke or an ironical or sarcastic remark. This suggests that comprehension of cartoons can be regarded on a par with discourse comprehension, which is quite flexible and operates at three levels:

1. Speakers, listeners and readers must be clear about what is meant, i.e. they must be clear about the goals and intentions of the interaction.
2. The discourse topic and subtopics must be clear, which include the given mental spaces[2] and relational coherence.
3. The referents must be identifiable, i.e. the entities, processes (including actions) and relations which are given verbally and pictorially.[3]

Since the cartoons under scrutiny deal with the enemies of the First World War there are certain implications involved, e.g. that there are soldiers who fight in trenches, that there are war ships, submarines and mines which have a specific characteristic and which cause a particular type of damage etc. In other words, these cartoons are read against the backdrop of the social, cultural and historical knowledge about wars at land, sea and in the air. In order to understand some of the implications, it is necessary to retrieve information about the technical development. Tanks, for example, were only used in the second half of the war and were not comparable to their versatile modern counterparts. The same does not apply to pragmatic implicatures, which are inferences based on the communicative acts in the given cartoon scenes. They are comparable to modern standards. The discourse topic and the subtopics are inferred from the verbal and pictorial parts of the cartoon and are connected with the point or invective of it. This does not means that there can be only one point or invective for all readers but the analysis shows that the cartoonists ridicule or critique a main point with others being open for consideration as well.
All three structures are necessary to enable recipients or interactants to construct a coherent mental representation of a cartoon. The drawn scene is the starting point for the construction of one or more mental spaces, in which an action is carried out, an event happens or communication takes place. They make up a scenario which is interpreted as deviant or contradictory in a certain way. It is a deviation from or contradiction to a generally accepted or an assumed standard or norm of a certain social or political group. This leads to the goal of political cartoons, which is to level invectives at political opponents. Their actions or

---

[1] Unlike comic strips, which are usually narratives, most political cartoons consist of one panel only.
[2] Cf. Fauconnier (1985).
[3] Cf. Levelt (1989).

character traits are presented in a humorous or ironical way and are thus castigated as politically or morally wrong or at least questionable because they deviate from that assumed norm scenario. A sample analysis of the cartoon, *Fanfares of Victory*, will demonstrate the above description. It shows John Bull, who represents England in this cartoon, sitting in a gravy dish on a cliff overlooking the sea. Further conceptual relations are involved: The cliffs in the cartoon belong to the British Isles, i.e. they represent the white cliffs of Dover. The drawing is a pictorial translation of the German metaphorical expression *in der Soße (Tunke) sitzen (to sit in the stew)*, which is partly given in the caption. It is an example of the metaphor 'DIFFICULTIES ARE CONTAINERS'[1] and more specifically 'DIFFICULTIES ARE CONTAINERS FILLED WITH STICKY FOODSTUFF'[2].

Fanfares of Victory

My victory is as certain as the sun rises tomorrow -
provided someone helps me out of the stew.

---

[1] Cf. http://cogsci.berkeley.edu/metaphors/Difficulties_Are_Containers.html (2/23/2002).
[2] In Dutch there is an equivalent expression, i.e. *to sit in the meshed potatoes.*

In language, metaphors often have a humorous effect when they are taken literally because it is regarded as naïve to do so. The same applies to cartoons when a verbal metaphor is taken literally and translated into a drawing. A second humorous effect is achieved by exploiting the contrast between the pictorial information and the heading or caption. There is a blatant inconsistency between John Bull's verbal claim and his miserable situation. The fact that he fails to notice his calamity also suggests that he has a poor sense of reality. His overly confident assurance that England will win the war is compared to an inalterable fact, i.e. the rising of the sun, which is a general everyday truth. He is ignorant of the fact that by adding a condition to his assurance he invalidates his claim, because the sun rises unconditionally every morning and does not need any helping agent in order to do so. Table 1 shows the inadequacy of the comparison:

In addition, John Bull's aggressive facial expression and his gesture do not render it likely that anybody will volunteer to help him; besides, it will be difficult to get him 'out of the stew' because he is fat and overweight. Another inconsistency is given in the heading. Fanfares are usually played to introduce a special event. In the case of a military victory the fanfares would be played after its completion, e.g. to announce the arrival of the military leader. Thus there is a contrast between this tradition and the premature announcement of John Bull's victory.

Prediction:		Prediction:
The sun rises every morning.		England's victory will be achieved.
	versus	
Condition:		Condition:
None		Provided some other country helps England.

Table 1

2.3 Mental spaces and blends
Cartoons do not have a clear-cut paragraph structure, but they make a point, which constitutes their discourse topic and which can be taken as a criterion of their description. The drawn scene presents a mental space as a starting point. Turner & Fauconnier (1995: 184) define a mental space as "a (relatively small) conceptual packet built up for purposes of local understanding and action." Obviously, mental spaces are conceptual and not locative entities, but in cartoons this may coincide as is exemplified in the following cartoon:[1]

---

[1] Guy Bara: *Tom the Traveller*, in Gombrich (1977[5]: 289).

The mental space of the cartoon scene and the space given in the picture painted by the artist is blurred, because the ape in the picture space frightens the artist in the cartoon space, i.e. for the painter the ape has become part of the latter. The readers find it funny because the painter is naive and obviously lacks the intellectual capacity to differentiate between the two mental spaces - for the humorous effect it does not matter whether the painter is just imagining this. A similar and verbally explicit transgression of two mental spaces is given in the following cartoon:[1]

"Come back into the drawing at once!"

[1] Maurice Henry: *"Willst du wohl gleich in die Zeichnung zurückkommen!"*, in Gombrich (1977⁵: 366). Gombrich gives a interpretation of culture-critique to this cartoon: leaving the framed area of the cartoon equals escaping the narrow framework of the bourgeois family idyll. Techniques like these are comparable to token reflexivity such as *This sentence is not true.* Cf. Levinson (1983: 86).

The contrast between the unframed cartoon area, into which the black cat has moved, and the framed drawing, from which the man is speaking, is exploited. In this case the opposition of the mental space of the framed area and the one of the unframed area functions as a space builder. Further mental spaces may be invoked, either verbally in the heading and captions (including speech and thought bubbles) or pictorially, e.g. by different parts of the drawing. The readers are normally given verbal guidance, which enables them to select and identify the relevant elements and interpret their conceptual meaning and their relational coherence. The boundaries between the spaces are normally clear cut, but may be blurred for humorous effects as was demonstrated above.

The different pictorial elements of a cartoon are not perceived in a definite linear order comparable to the sequential order of sentences, its semantic structure has to be detected by working out the collusion of the heading, the captions and the drawing. The heading suggests the topic framework, i.e. the domain, the participants, their activities and the setting, i.e. location and time. These elements acquire their specific meanings when the reader constructs a mental representation, which has the point of the cartoon as the critical criterion of comprehension. Pictorial-verbal cohesion in single-panel cartoons, which relies on the relationship between the pictorial and the verbal elements, plays an important part in this process, because in this way, the different parts are integrated into the overall conceptual structure.[1]

In the drawing of the cartoon below, *German composer seeking inspiration for melody to a 'song of hate'*, there is only one person. Therefore he is seen as identical to the subject and agent of the caption. Also the note sheet on the window sill suggests that he is a composer. This constitutes pictorial-verbal cohesion and is an anchoring process, which may overrule other hints. The window, for instance, is typically British, because it opens vertically and chimneys like these are not to be found in Germany.[2] The adjective modification identifies the man as German. For an experienced reader of British cartoons of the time the adjective also interacts cohesively with the pictorial part, because the man is drawn like a stereotypical German. The next instance of pictorial-verbal cohesion is given in the part of the caption 'seeking inspiration for melody'. This activity can be seen in the drawing. Holding a pen in the other hand shows that this German composer is willing and prepared to record the

---

[1] Cf. Gernsbacher (1990) and Kintch (1988). Attention can be shifted in image space and it can be manipulated in three dimensions which means that it is visuospatial rather than simply visual. Tactile, auditory and other kind of information can also play a part. Cf. Glass and Holyoak (1986: 132 ff.).

[2] This was most probably overlooked by English readers, because it is not relevant for the point of the cartoon. Had anybody noticed these facts, they might believe that the German composer was working in England as an undercover agent. But this would be an additional point in the cartoon which obviously was not intended.

musical inspiration. The listening activity of the man provokes the readers to search for the source of the sound or noise. It can be identified in the fighting cats on the roof for which there is no direct hint in the caption. For the identification of the items the readers have to rely on their world knowledge, e.g. the circle, which is seen as the moon could also be the sun, but since it is known that cats tend to have their noisy fights at night, it is interpreted as the moon. We will follow Lakoff (1987) and describe world knowledge in terms of idealized cognitive models (ICMs) because they are best suited to cover the processes of conceptual mappings in metonymies and metaphors. In a pictorial as well as a linguistic metonymy one conceptual entity, the vehicle, provides mental access to another conceptual entity, the target, within the same domain or ICM.

The concept of blended spaces has been introduced by Fauconnier (1985) and has been elaborated by Turner & Fauconnier (1995) who have proposed a broader 'many-space model' of metaphor and conceptual projection. In statements such as *If I were in your shoes, I would quit my job*, the speaker takes over the role of the listener and states how he would act in that hypothetical space. A blending process activates at least, four mental spaces: a generic space, the source space, the target space and the resulting blended space or blend. The generic space contains a skeletal structure, which reflects the commonalities of the two input spaces. This very simple verbal example can be analyzed as follows:

Generic space
1. agent
2. takes a decision

Input space 1	**Input space 2**
1. speaker	1. listener
2. quits the job of speaker	2. keeps the job of listener

Blended space
1. speaker
2. quits the job of listener

Table 2

As can be seen, the blended space integrates selected parts of the structure from the input spaces.

The cartoon *German composer seeking inspiration for melody to a 'song of hate'* entails two blends. The noise of the cats is inspiration for the composer and, at the same time, may be seen as the result of his composing efforts, i.e. the orchestra. The first blend has four input spaces and can be verbalized as *instinct driven hatred evoking German composer*. As is normal for cartoons, also this one relies on a contrast between what is given and what should normally be the case: the German composer deviates from what the readers expect composers to do, i.e. to be inspired to compose a piece of music which will please people. This activity is described in input space 3. If this third input space were not given, the cartoon would be neither funny nor sarcastic. In the blended space the result of the invective of the cartoonist is presented: the German composer does not have a normal motivation and inspiration but is driven by a base instinct like mating cats. He does not want to please people but to evoke hatred. This blend is presented in table 3.

German composer seeking inspiration for melody to a 'song of hate'.

Generic space
1. motivation or inspiration
2. causes
3. an entity
4. to perform an activity
5. to reach a certain goal

Input space 1	Input space 2	Input space 3
1. base instinct	1. motivation or inspiration	1. motivation or inspiration
2. causes	2. causes	2. causes
3. cats	3. the German composer	3. a composer
4. to make noise	4. to write a song of hate	4. to write music
5. to procreate	5. to evoke hatred in an audience	5. to please an audience

Blended space
1. base instinct
2. causes
3. the German composer
4. to write a song of hate
5. to evoke hatred in an audience

Table 3: First blend in *German composer seeking inspiration ...*

Generic space
1. a trigger
2. causes
3. a feeling
4. in a person

Input space 1	Input space 2	Input space 3
1. noise of cats	1. an (auditory) experience	1. a positive experience
2. causes	2. causes	2. causes
3. annoyance	3. inspiration	3. inspiration
4. in a person	4. in the German composer	4. in a composer

Blended space
1. noise of cats
2. causes
3. inspiration
4. in the German composer

Table 4: Second blend in *German composer seeking inspiration ...*

Table 4 shows the second blend, which can be verbalized as *cat-noise-inspired German composer*. This blend shows that the German composer also deviates from a normal one in that he takes as an inspiration what usually causes annoyance in people, i.e. the noise which cats produce at night. The two blends lead to the following argument structure of this cartoon:

1. The German composer tries to get his inspiration from the (inharmonious) noise of fighting cats.
2. *The reason for this is* that he does not have ideas of his own and/or that he has used up all his 'hatred reserves'.[1]
3. To a German composer any kind of inspiration is acceptable as long as he can use it against the English.
4. The cats show a behavior driven by an instinctive, sexual aggressiveness. *Since* the German composer gets his inspiration from them, his behavior is of a similar kind.
5. *Instead of* composing music as a creative and joyful activity and thereby achieving a cultural value, he only contributes to the German 'culture of hatred'.
6. The famous German (musical) culture has debased negative roots and is prone to be abused in such a way.

The blending of the two spaces 'nighttime cat fight' and 'German composing music' produces a new negative stereotype of the German composer who writes music in the spirit of aggressiveness and hatred. Since the composer metonymically stands for all German composers or even for German artists in general, all German culture is debased.

This metonymic relation of a German composer metonymically standing for all German artists can be expanded into a metaphor with the German culture as the source domain and German political propaganda as the target domain. As table 5 shows, this metonymic relation can also be seen as metaphorically standing for German political propaganda, thus leveling a very broad-sided invective against the Germans.

---

[1] In other cartoons of the time 'hatred' is conceptualised as an energy that can be spent or that can run out but that can also be replenished. Cf. *Punch* cartoon 26 reproduced and analyzed in chapter 3.4, in which *German soldiers [are] being roused to enthusiasm by the 'hymn of hate'*

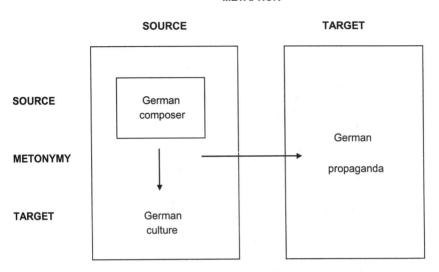

METAPHOR

	SOURCE	TARGET
SOURCE	German composer	
METONYMY		German propaganda
TARGET	German culture	

Table 5

In *Simplicissimus* cartoon 7, *The Headquarters of Lies*, which follows on the next page, metaphorical and metonymic mappings as well as blends can be uncovered. The toad with the top hat vomiting snakes, which crawl along the cables of the British communication network, is an obvious pictorial blend of a toad, John Bull and a news agency. It represents the English government and its propagandistic news management. The snakes constitute a pictorial metaphor enhanced by the caption because moving along the communication cables they represent items of (false) news. The basic meaning is that England churns out masses of false news items, i.e. lies. The meaning conveyed by blending conceptual spaces is that these lies are sly and dangerous like snakes and nauseating like vomit. The cartoon is also a reflection of the German expression *falsche Schlange (false snake)*, which has no idiomatic equivalent in English. In addition, a snake is a Christian symbol of deception and both toads and snakes are at a low level of the conceptual system of the 'Great Chain of Being'.[1] The cartoon contains the invective that the British (try to) mislead the public, that they are abominable liars and that they cannot be trusted.

---

[1] Cf. Lakoff & Turner (1989: 166 f.).

The Headquarters of Lies

Since England's cables are still intact, it is able
to send its major export article all over the world

There is a basic blend shown in table 6. It has a generic space which is a transaction, i.e. one entity transfers an item to another entity via a certain route. The input spaces are given by England sending out news items, by the reproduction of toads and by the deceptiveness of snakes. The reproduction has been blended with vomiting and the offspring belongs to a different species. The meaning of this blend is that British news items are numerous like the eggs of toads and deceptive like snakes.

Generic space
1. an entity
2. transfers
3. an item
4. to another entity
5. via a path

Input space 1	Input space 2	Input space 3
1. a toad	1. a snake	1. England
2. brings	2. brings	2. sends
3. masses of eggs	3. small snakes	3. (true) news items
4. into the world	4. into the world	4. to other countries
5. in water	5. on land	5. via its cables

Blended space
1. England
2. sends
3. masses of deceptive
   news items (lies)
4. to other countries
5. via its cables

Table 6: The British news items are numerous and deceptive.

Further conceptual elements, which represent metaphors in language, may be evoked. They underline the emotional reactions associated with this pictorial rendering of the British news policy: 'THINKING IS GIVING BIRTH', 'DANGEROUS BELIEFS ARE CONTAGIOUS DISEASES' and 'WORDS ARE WEAPONS'.

Two other blends are contained in this cartoon. They concern the dangerousness of the news items on the one hand and revulsion they provoke on the other. They are given in tables 7 and 8.

Generic space
1. an entity
2. has a certain quality

Input space 1	Input space 2
1. news items	1. snakes
2. are not dangerous	2. are dangerous

Blended space
1. English news items
2. are dangerous

Table 7: The British news items are dangerous.

Generic space
1. an entity
2. has a certain quality

Input space 1
1. vomit
2. is nauseating

Input space 2
1. news items
2. are neutral

Blended space
1. English news items
2. are nauseating

Table 8: The British news items are nauseating.

Thus by non-verbal means the cartoonist produces a very negative evaluation. The British news items are numerous like the eggs of a toad, deceptive and dangerous like snakes and nauseating like vomit. These qualifications can be extended to British propaganda as well.

2.4 Humor, irony and stereotypes

When dealing with the humor in cartoons, there are some facts that are important to note. Humor increases when the targeted object is a hated rather than a loved object and also when it belongs to a social, national, ethnic etc. group, which is different from the one of the aggressor and/or the audience.[1] On the other hand, an aggressive act can only be regarded as humorous if the object of the aggression is not seriously injured. Furthermore, a direct aggression as such is not felt to be humorous at all. This means that cartoonists have to strike a balance between downright aggression and humorous insinuation. Three general theories have been put forward to explain humor:

1. Superiority theory
2. Relief theory
3. Incongruity theory

According to the first theory humor arises, when someone feels superior to someone else in a certain field. Freud pointed out that intellectual underachievement and physical overachievement can give rise to feelings of superiority and thus to laughter. This means that too little intellectual and too

---

[1] Cf. Mio & Graesser (1991: 89).

much physical effort can have a humorous effect. The second theory explains that humor is evoked when some psychological or physiological energy can be released after it has been accumulated. Thus a dirty joke can give relief to sexual arousal. The third theory points at the disparity between expectations and reality, i.e. the opposition between an expected scenario and the one given in the joke, cartoon etc.

"Himmel! The All-Highest has the truth spoken – the worst *is* behind us."

Some political cartoons are based on a verbal ambiguity which some or all of the characters fail to comprehend. This failure constitutes an intellectual under-achievement which the political opponent uses as an invective as in the cartoon above.[1] The relevant verbal and non-verbal elements of this cartoon can be summarized as follows:

1. Fearful German soldiers are fleeing from British soldiers and a British tank.
2. The German soldiers are panicking (*"Himmel!"*).
3. They are carrying no weapons and no helmets.
4. One German soldier is lying on his belly, with a staring gaze.

---

[1] *Punch* cartoon 182.

28

5. *... the worst is behind us.* The meaning which the German Emperor intended is: 'we have overcome the greatest difficulties'. The current meaning which is suggested by the drawing is: 'the superior British army is behind us and nothing could be worse'.
6. The speaker uses an incorrect German word order in his English.[1]

The following conclusion is suggested by this cartoon: German soldiers (or Germans in general) are stupid, because, first, they fail to notice the ambiguity in the saying 'the worst is behind us', which is demonstrated to the reader by the drawing. Second, they are stupid enough to hold the naive belief that their Kaiser always tells the truth. Thus they ignore the contradiction between the meaning which was originally intended and the current meaning of the saying. Third, they are stupid, because they cannot speak properly. This alludes to a stereotype that Germans make the same typical mistakes when speaking English. In this case, it is the word order which is ridiculed. Other linguistic targets of ridicule are a lack of linguistic politeness and phonetic mistakes, such as [s] instead of [θ], [z] instead of [ð] and [v] instead of [w].[2]
Cartoons reflect a structured world model with event types, which are either incidental or regular. This means that certain kinds of events are presented as capable of occurring while others do not occur and are thus indirectly judged as highly unlikely or even impossible. The event in the above cartoon could be regarded as incidental, i.e. eight armed British soldiers and a tank chase ten unarmed German soldiers who are fleeing because fighting without any weapons would be suicidal. At a different section of the war frontier, the picture might be reversed. But cartoons present the selected events as regular event types, which are meant to enter the structured world model of the readers. In this case it means: German soldiers – and Germans in general - are ignorant and they are cowards; this is how the world is structured.

The understanding of a cartoon is not an inherent property of the cartoon, but is dependent on the social, cultural and world knowledge of the readers. They establish conceptual links between the various entities, drawn or verbally referred to, and the evoked scenarios, which enable the readers to form mental representations.[3] The conceptual links establish coherence, which is described according to two criteria: The first is a referential criterion and pertains to the drawing, the heading, the captions and their relationship; the second is a

---

[1] Of course, this point is not quite logical, because the German soldier would actually be speaking German. Thus it is a blend of the given situation and one in which a German speaks to an Englishman.
[2] Cf. *Punch* cartoons 5, 8, 16, 25, 27, 40, 54, 121, 162 and 178 in chapter 3.4.
[3] We prefer the term *scenario* to *frame* or *script* to emphasize the compositional, metonymical and often counterfactual character of the referential complexes of cartoons. Cf. Bartlett (1932), Fillmore (1982, 1985), Fillmore, Kay and O'Connor (1988), Lakoff (1987) and Langacker (1987).

relational criterion and pertains to semantic and/or interactional relations between the verbal and the pictorial parts of a cartoon. A cartoon is referentially coherent if a topic, i.e. an integrating higher-order concept, can be detected. In practical terms this means that the description of a cartoon contains a chain of recurring referents. A cartoon is relationally coherent if certain more abstract relationships hold true between clauses, sentences and larger parts of it, e.g. verbal and pictorial parts of the cartoon. Relational coherence is constituted by conceptual relationships between semantic units which can be verbalized as clauses, sentences or even paragraphs. Such relations are for example *contrast, evidence, cause - consequence* etc.[1] Coherence relations may be expressed explicitly or remain implicit.

In the cartoon *Fanfares of Victory* and the other three above, the most important coherence relations are causal ones. They can be paraphrased in such a way that their invectives are elucidated as well:

1. The British are pompous and stupid. Therefore, they can and will not win the war.
2. Germans have no reason to be proud of their culture, because it is a pseudo-culture. – The German war propaganda is aggressive and noisy and is motivated by base instincts. Therefore it is not convincing.
3. The British try to mislead the public in a massive way, because they are abominable and/or militarily inferior. Therefore they cannot be trusted. What they do is extremely disgusting.
4. Germans are stupid cowards. Therefore, they can and will not win the war.

Irony and sarcasm represent a mode of thought.[2] The reader is made aware of the incongruity between a certain claim and reality. Cartoons exploit this ironical mode in order to put forward arguments and invectives against an opponent. Prototypically, irony is constituted when a speaker slips into the role of another person and acts in that role. This explanation covers the mention theory as well as other explanations of irony, e.g. the description of irony as the simulation of a lie.[3] It also explains the ironical or even sarcastic effect, which is brought about by impersonations. Even if the discrepancy between the given state of affairs and an expected state of affairs is obviously exaggerated or presented facetiously – as in the *Punch* cartoon about the German composer above – some of the negative social judgment that is directed towards a critiqued target prevails. Irony and sarcasm differ in that irony can also be used in positive

---

[1] Mann & Thompson (1987 & 1988).
[2] Cf. Gibbs (1994: 365).
[3] Cf. Sperber & Wilson (1986) and Lapp (1992).

social contexts, e.g. in praise or banter, whereas sarcasm always involves a negative criticism. Whether irony has the same effect of muting criticism in complex structures such as cartoons that it has as in face-to-face interaction must remain a hypothesis.[1]

The answer to the question 'What is 20 m long and smells of French fries?' will be 'A bus with Belgians.' if answered by Dutch people and conversely 'A bus with Dutch people.' if answered by Belgians. This type of joke is based on stereotypes, which often apply to minorities such as the Irish or Scots in the British Isles or the Bavarians in southern Germany. They are judged as stupid, miserly, and boorish, respectively.[2] Stereotypes are defined as evaluative judgments of social groups or their members. They take the form of a generic statement, which attributes one or more characteristics to the group or a member of the group in a simplified and overgeneralized manner.[3] They can be either negative or positive.

According to the *realistic conflict theory* of Campbell (1965) and Sherif (1967) negative stereotypes arise, when there is intergroup competition for scarce resources such as money or jobs. The members of one social group see their chances reduced or threatened by a different group. In such cases solidarity within the ingroup grows combined with a sense of identity, whereas the outgroup is denigrated.

But even without intergroup hostilities a general tendency has been observed to have a higher esteem for the ingroup and a lower one for the outgroup. Van Dijk (1984: 29) explains this fact by the tendency to process situations in a selective manner: "... the available cognitive resources are 'biased' towards the interpretation of group category features of social participants, rather than towards the analysis of the situation (setting, other participants, circumstances/or the actual actions of the participant minority members." He assumes that there exists a kind of super schema for the formation of new group schemata in general, and for minority group schemata in particular.[4] Since the acquisition of stereotypes is also part of socialization, they can be formed without any information about an outgroup.[5] This also explains why they are so deep-seated, difficult to change and surprisingly similar in spite of the dissimilarity of the outgroups.[6]

Tajfel's and Turner's *social identity theory* views social stereotyping, i.e. the process of ascribing characteristics to people on the basis of their group

---

[1] Cf. Dews & Winner (1995).
[2] Prejudices have been called *the reason of the fool* (Voltaire) and *the pillars of society* (Gide).
[3] Cf. Wenzel (1978: 28).
[4] Van Dijk (1984: 29).
[5] Cf. Tajfel (1982) and Tajfel & Turner (1979).
[6] Cf. Wenzel (1978: 28). It is striking that in TV series on British television today the stereotype of *the militaristic German* still occurs. Cf. also chapters 4.2 and 4.4.

memberships, as a positive cognitive device, which helps people systematize their social world. They base their theory on the following general assumptions:[1]

1. Individuals strive to achieve or to maintain a positive social identity.
2. Positive social identity is based to a large extent on favorable comparisons between the ingroup and some relevant out-groups: the ingroup must be perceived as positively differentiated or distinct from the relevant outgroups.
3. When social identity is unsatisfactory, individuals will strive either to leave their existing group and join some more positively distinct group and/or to make their existing group more positively distinct.

The basic hypothesis is that pressures to evaluate one's own group positively through in-group/out-group comparisons lead social groups to attempt to differentiate themselves from each other. The aim of differentiation is to maintain or achieve superiority over an out-group on some dimensions. Any such act, therefore, is essentially competitive. This competition requires a situation of mutual comparison and differentiation on a shared value dimension.[2] Social stereotyping also derives from the natural cognitive process of categorization. According to Tajfel, the exaggeration which is commonly associated with social stereotypes is a by-product of the process of accentuation of intragroup similarities and intergroup differences, which in itself is a categorization effect. Social groups compete on continuous dimensions such as extremist-moderate, progressive-conservative, religious-irreligious, etc. It is not difficult to imagine that this competitive principle is adopted for comparison on an international level.

The allocation of attributes such as stupidity or miserliness is one factor, to which exemplars of the targeted group may be added. These may corroborate or weaken the stereotypical pattern. Cartoons, funny everyday stories or jokes about members of an outgroup have characteristic agents who are part of narrative or problem-solving structures.[3] Thus when a story is told about the stupid behavior of a German or English soldier, a prototypical situational model is evoked. In this model aspects of similar experiences or events are added to the features of the particular story or scenario. Since it is regarded as typical of the group, the process of prejudice formation is reinforced. Due to the specific representational means of cartoons, the exaggerated way, in which such scenarios are presented, is comic in itself. Three aspects are important in this process: firstly the outgroup schema can have a very poor knowledge base, secondly the behavior of an outgroup exemplar described in a cartoon is not

---

[1] Cf. Tajfel (1969, 1978) and Tajfel & Turner (1979).
[2] Tajfel & Turner (1979: 40-41).
[3] Cf. Dundes (1965), Hünig (1974) and Propp (1968).

interpreted as an individual behavioral instance depending on a specific situation but as a behavior typical of the outgroup as a whole and thirdly, outgroups receive a higher degree of attention. They are usually members of a minority and thus have a higher profile. In the case of English and German cartoons from 1914 - 1918 the same principles apply. The respective nationals are the outgroup members, who represent the political and military enemy of the war. The fact that there actually was a German minority in Great Britain and a British one in Germany plays only a minor role in the cartoons. Very telling is *Punch* cartoon 117 about a man who a British detective suspects of being a German. True, he has a stout figure, a suit and round glasses like the cartoon stereotype of a German, but because of his behavior he cannot possibly be one: He is considerate and leaves the sidewalk to the two women with the child, his table manners are immaculate, he is patriotic, because he buys a newspaper, which reports about a British military success and he is selfless because he jumps into the sea in order to save a drowning child.

The Detective on the German Spy-trail

Detective. "I'm afraid I'm on the wrong track. That doesn't look like a German."

"I hope I'm after the right man. He doesn't sound a bit like a German."

"He gets less like a German every minute. But perhaps it's his artfulness."

"I'd better go home. This has been a wasted day."

There are many ways in which negative stereotypes are reproduced as reinforced experiences of a culture. They occur and interact in literature, television, film, fashion, and the workplace continuously. But even if the view has gained wide currency that stereotypes are fixed mental representations, which are stored in memory independent of social influences, it is untenable. Stereotypes are flexible social judgments of social groups by others and just as these groups are relative and changing, so are stereotypes. They are the result of social processes and do not form simply because the information processing capacities are limited. A case in point is intermarriage between members of different ethnic groups. In such cases the formerly held stereotypes of an ethnic group are readily changed or adapted.

3. Corpus analysis

For this study we have taken all the cartoons which were published during the war years 1914 - 1918 and which deal with the other side, i.e. we have selected the cartoons from *Simplicissimus* which topicalize and attack the British and those cartoons from *Punch* which topicalize and attack the Germans. The selection comprises 163 cartoons from *Simplicissimus* and 189 from *Punch*. We ignored the cartoons which deal with the German Kaiser and his political role, because this would have doubled the number of the *Punch* cartoons and would have prevented an adequate comparison. In appendix 1 we give an overview of the cartoons which we have selected for this study and which we analyze in the last two sections of this chapter. They are ordered and numbered according to their date of publication and presented with the following information:

1. The volume in which they appeared.
2. The chronological number.
3. The heading or - if there is none - the first part of the caption.
4. The name of the cartoonist.
5. The date of publication.
6. The number of the page.

Some cartoons are taken from the so-called 'Almanack' of *Punch*, which was a section produced for the first volume of each year. It was dedicated to a certain topic and comprised several cartoons. No exact dates and pages are given in the 'Almanacks'.

The analyses follow the same pattern: In the first line the number of the cartoon and the date of publication are given. The numbers correspond to the ones in the list of appendix 1. If there is a heading, this is stated in the following line. In the line below the caption(s) is/are quoted. The German headings and captions of the *Simplicissimus* cartoons are followed by English translations in parentheses. If there is more than one panel, this is also indicated, e.g. *upper left panel* etc. A short description of the contents of the drawing follows. Since the humorous, ironical or sarcastic point of a cartoon is constituted by the contrast of two scenarios, these are described next. The scenario given in the cartoon, which is in some way deviant, is set against a scenario which reflects the normal expectation. In *Simplicissimus* cartoon 2, *The English Business War*, which is reproduced in chapter 3.1 below, members of the British higher military ranks reveal themselves to be cowards. This contradicts the normal expectation that such members should be courageous and prepared to die for their country without any second thoughts. These contrasts pertain to the whole gamut of human behavior. In some cases there is more than one contrast so that a second or even a third pair of scenarios is provided. In many cases we regard the juxtaposition of the (two) contrasting scenarios to be sufficient. In some instances we have provided some additional explanation, e.g. when a specific historical event is alluded to or some other cultural background knowledge seems essential. The explanation is followed by a description of the type of scene that the panel(s) constitute(s). Every panel of a cartoon can be compared to a theater stage because it presents a specific scene, which provides the anchoring ground for the heading and the captions. It also means that every panel of a cartoon presents the source domain of the metonymic and metaphorical processes involved which normally are specified verbally.

The orthographic conventions of the headings and the captions have been retained as far as possible. The periods in *Punch* which are used before direct speech have been changed to colons. Since the headings and the captions are given in the analysis sections in chapters 3.3 and 3.4, they have been left out in the cartoons which have been reproduced as pictorial quotations in this book.

3.1. Verbal-pictorial interaction: scenes
In the given data we distinguish five types of scenes. They allow us to see which situations and events the British and the German cartoonists take as their starting point in order to get their messages across and how the interplay of the verbal and pictorial parts translate into the humorous, ironical or sarcastic conceptualizations:

1. Everyday scenes
2. Non-combatant military scenes
3. War scenes
4. Counterfactual scenes
5. Metonymic scenes (containing pictorial metonymies or metaphors)

An everyday scene is like a photographic replica of a situation that people are used to in their daily lives: A father talks to his son, passengers are traveling on a bus etc. Since the cartoons were published during World War I they include scenes which are connected with the war. There is an important difference between showing members of the military in non-combatant situations or involved in battle activities. In the former they interact without being related directly to the trenches or the sea battles in the latter they are involved in fighting. It is obvious that no cartoon could ever represent the gruesome reality of the trench warfare and neither the British nor the German cartoonists make an attempt at this, i.e. the given cartoons do not show corpses or wounded soldiers in any realistic way. Non-combatant military scenes are realistic scenes in which members of the military are shown without being directly related to the war. War scenes show acts of warfare in a mildly realistic way. Whereas the first three types mirror reality to some extent, there are scenes which are simply counterfactual, e.g. where the cartoonist invents a scene which is far detached from reality. They may represent places such as hell, show zeppelins, which talk, skulls which grow in a field or piglets which are taught how to read. Metonymic scenes are defined by the use of pictorial metonymies or metaphors. Such scenes rely on the pictographic tradition of a country. Apart from John Bull who occurs in British as well as German cartoons with his typical attributes such as a top hat and a stout body, there are other metonymies, which frequently occur, e.g. the British Lion, Britannia and the German Eagle.

Theoretically it may seem that these scenes do not exclude each other but *in praxi* they do. Thus it is obvious that five admirals fooling around in a small row

boat are not part of a realistic war scene or a non-combatant military scene.[1]
Therefore, anything they say will not be taken in the serious but in the humorous
mode. Metonymic scenes are different from counterfactual ones, because the
meaning is established via a stand-for-relationship, i.e. the pictorial elements
such as John Bull or the British Lion do not refer to a person or an animal as
such, but conventionally to the British people, the British government etc.
according to the pictorial and verbal context. In some cartoons the types of scene
can change from one panel to the next. In *Punch* cartoon 71, *The while-you-
wait-school of hatred*, for example, seven of the eleven panels present everyday
scenes and four counterfactual ones. The following figure presents the
relationships of the different scenes:

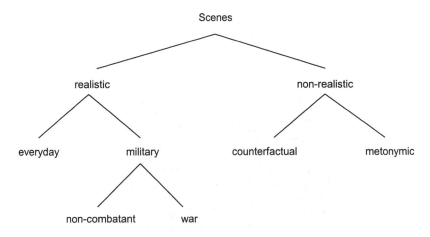

Figure 1

We have subdivided the scenes further into three subtypes according to how the
verbal and pictorial elements interact.[2] This interaction is relevant for the
question of what the point of the cartoon depends on. The first subtype is given
if the scene is constituted solely as a communicative setting. This may include
talking to oneself and voices from off-stage. A second subtype is given when the
heading and the captions interact with the given scene, i.e. when the verbal parts
specify the pictorial elements in some way without communication between
characters taking place. The third subtype is constituted when a communicative
situation is given as well as an interaction between the drawn scene and the

---

[1] Cf. the drawing and the analysis of *Punch* cartoon 92, *Sweeping the North Sea*, in chapter
3.4.
[2] In our corpus there are no cartoons without any verbal elements.

verbal elements. This is thus a combination of the first two types. All three subtypes are listed below:

1. Scene which represents a communicative situation.
2. Scene which interacts with the verbal part.
3. Scene which represents a communicative situation and interacts with the verbal part.

Since these three subtypes can combine with the five types of scenes, there are fifteen possibilities overall. In what follows, we will exemplify the five types of scenes and the three pictorial-verbal relationships.

Ex-Teuton (to landlady): "Ach! madame, eet is all right! I vos Engleesh now! I have to-day mein papers of nationalization to your home office sent off. Dere vos several oaths by half-a-dozen peoples to be svorn: it vos a tremendous affairs!"

The panel of the above cartoon shows an everyday scene, i.e. a scene in a house, with two people communicating.[1] Apart from the communicative situation the captions also specify the speakers, i.e. they interact with the drawing. The identification of the male speaker plays an important role for the point of the cartoon. The use of the non-basic level term *Ex-Teuton* is funny in itself, because the man is obviously German and there is no need to describe him as a speaker of a Teutonic, i.e. Germanic language. But this emphasizes the strong German accent and the linguistic insufficiencies of his language, which are inconsistent with his pride in having become a naturalized Englishman.

The English Business War

"If only we could find someone for each of us who would die vicariously!"

---

[1] *Punch* cartoon 8.

The cartoon above, *The English business war,* is an instance of a non-combatant military scene, which is set in contradistinction to war scenes.[1] Especially in these four years of the war they are similar to everyday scenes. But we found it important to set aside instances, in which members of the military express their opinions. It is similar to the previous cartoon in that it also represents a communicative situation, i.e. the drawing allows the reader to identify the speaker. The heading represents the topic framework, but does not specify any element in the drawn scene.

The next cartoon is an instance of a war scene with the heading and the caption interacting with the drawing.[2] This means that genuine war ships are on their way into 'battle' with the German commercial submarines. The fact that this will not be a genuine battle between equals can only be inferred from the caption and leads to the point of the cartoon, i.e. that the British are cowards and that they will only attack, if their enemy is unarmed and defenseless.

Chasing the German Subs

Since no doubt is left that the German commercial submarines are not armed, the audacious British fleet has left port in order to destroy them.

---

[1] *Simplicissimus* cartoon 2.
[2] *Simplicissimus* cartoon 95.

Facts from the front.

Tactical use, by the enemy, of the more resilient units of the landstorm for negotiating Belgian dykes.

In spite of its heading the above cartoon obviously shows a counterfactual scene far removed from reality.[1] The heading and the caption interact with the drawing, but a communicative situation is not given. *Landstorm* is a calque derived from the German term *Landsturm* which referred to the last category of four types of military service in Germany: active, reserve, *Landwehr* and *Landsturm*. Members of the *Landwehr* and the *Landsturm* were soldiers too old for active service and the reserve.

The next cartoon, *Class of (Draftees) 1917*, is an example of a metonymic scene.[2] The brutal looking butcher with a knife between his teeth and a blood stained apron is John Bull. The calves, which are wearing caps of French soldiers and which are lead by a British butcher to a slaughterhouse, represent young Frenchmen. The obvious meaning is that the British, i.e. their military leadership, cause young French soldiers to die on the killing fields and in the trenches of the war. The heading specifies the timeframe of this scene and thus interacts with it. Since the cartoon was published in 1915 the heading points two

---

[1] *Punch* cartoon 18.
[2] *Simplicissimus* cartoon 65.

years into the future. A detailed analysis and a discussion of the scenes are given in chapter 4.1.

Class of (Draftees) 1917

There is an upheaval in France. People dare to ask into which English slaughterhouse the calves are being led.

3.2 Attacking the enemy: invectives

As was mentioned above, the goal of a political cartoon is to launch an invective against a political opponent by rendering an action and/or a character trait as ridiculous and politically or morally wrong. Since political cartoons are part of the communicative culture of a country, they are also part of the stereotype culture, i.e. on the one hand they rely on stereotypes and on the other they reinforce them. The invectives leveled at the enemy in *Simplicissimus* and *Punch* are surprisingly similar, ranging from a general to more specific levels and from aspects which are independent of the war to those which are directly connected with it. This means that they range from a very general negative characterization that someone is simply abominable to the presentation of more specific traits, e.g. that someone is a bigoted Christian and therefore cannot be trusted, because this is a blatant breach the 'rules'. Thus, if an Englishman or a German misbehaves in a general sense, this constitutes the first type of invective, i.e. X is abominable. In the analyses, the reason why someone is abominable has been specified. It may be greed, clumsiness, ugliness etc. The cartoons normally present specific exemplars of the enemy nation, i.e. a German prisoner of war or a British colonel, but since it is typical of stereotypes that they are undifferentiated, we have not specified the group to which the given exemplar belongs. In some cases such exemplars are so well-grounded in the knowledge structure of the readers that they are easily identifiable, e.g. Tommy, a British soldier, who speaks with a local accent, has a simple, straightforward mind and is, therefore, fearless and cheeky. Whereas the persona of John Bull is used by British and German cartoonists alike, Tommy occurs in British cartoons only.[1] The persona of *der deutsche Michel* is not used at all in the cartoons under scrutiny. William II, the German Kaiser, is used instead. He is the target of more than 160 attacks in the war time *Punch* volumes, but for reasons of comparability we were not able to take these cartoons into consideration. The second type of invective is constituted by instances of intellectual underachievement such as ignorance, naivety and stupidity. Since these are the most common causes of laughter, such invectives could be expected to be the most numerous. Surprisingly this only holds true for the British cartoons, i.e. ridiculing the enemy and depicting him as stupid, ignorant, naive etc. Of course it must not be forgotten that the main aim of political cartoons is not lighthearted humor but a serious attack of denigration. The third type of invective is motivated by the background of the war and attributes characteristics of callousness and cruelty to the enemy, who is blamed for war atrocities. The fourth type of invective presents the enemy as unreliable and not trustworthy, which also implies that a peace is ruled out or not very likely. The fifth type of invective brandishes the enemy as cowardly, which also is a reason why he is likely to commit acts of atrocity and cowardice, i.e. killing civilians, attacking non-military targets such as commercial ships and towns etc. The seventh type of invective shows the difficulties, the enemy is facing, in everyday life, which suggests that victory is within reach. The eighth type of invective is the last which is used by both sides. It is meant to be particularly subversive because it presents the other side as cheats who abuse the press and thus mislead the enemy, the world in general and even their own people.

---

[1] The German name *Fritz* is used as a generic term to refer to Germans, but there is no specific persona with that name.

There are three types of invectives which only the British use against the Germans and one type which only the Germans use against the British. In the eyes of the British cartoonists Germans are militaristic (9), they have no culture or only a pseudo-culture (10) and they harbor an 'irrational' hatred of the British, which seems to be utterly unmotivated (11). The invective in the German cartoons which have no equivalent in the British pertains to the responsibility of the British for (the continuation of) the war (12). The invectives are summarized in table 9:

Simplicissimus	*Punch*
The British	The Germans
1. are abominable.	1. are abominable.
2. are stupid, ignorant, naïve.	2. are stupid, ignorant, naïve.
3. are callous, cruel.	3. are callous, cruel.
4. cannot be trusted, are bigoted.	4. cannot be trusted, are bigoted.
5. are cowards.	5. are cowards.
6. are militarily inferior.	6. are militarily inferior.
7. life is deteriorating.	7. life is deteriorating.
8. mislead the public.	8. mislead the public.
	9. are militaristic.
	10. have no culture.
	11. hate the British.
12. are responsible for (the continuation of) the war.	

Table 9: Types of invectives in *Simplicissimus* and *Punch*

In the last two parts of this chapter all the German and the British cartoons are analyzed in detail according to the principles outlined above.

3.3 *Simplicissimus* cartoons

Cartoon 1   17.8.1914
Heading: *Der Hüter des Völkerrechts (The Guardian of International Law)*
Caption: „*Der Krieg ist ein Geschäft wie jedes andere!*" *("War is a business like any other!") Albion & Co* (sign over the shop)
Description: A shop owner with a pipe in his hand is standing behind the counter, on which human skulls are piled and from which blood is flowing.
Scenario 1: War is a (national) fight for honor, justice, freedom etc.
Scenario 2: War is a business activity such as selling goods in a grocery.
Explanation: Scenario 1 is a belief scenario, which the reader has to provide. The meaning of the pictorially given activity of 'selling bloody skulls' equals 'engaging in war activities for a profit, irrespective of the loss of lives'.

Type: Metonymic scene represents a communicative situation and interacts
             with the verbal part.
Invective: The British are abominable, because they are only interested in their
             profit. They are callous and cruel.

Simplicissimus cartoon 1

Cartoon 2   25.8.1914
Heading: *Der englische Geschäftskrieg (The English Business War)*
Caption: *„Wenn sich nur für jeden von uns einer fände, der per Procura sterben
              wollte!"* *("If only we could find somebody who would be willing to die
              for us.")*
Description: Three English officers are talking with each other.
Scenario 1:   Military officers are brave and are not afraid of dying for their country.
Scenario 2:   English officers want others to die for them.
Explanation: The two scenarios are contrasted.

Type:	Non-combatant military scene represents a communicative situation.
Invective:	The British (officers) are cowards.

Cartoon 3		8.9.1914
Heading:	*Englands Schmerz (England's Pain)*	
Caption:	*„Goddam! Jetzt wird mir meine Kundschaft nicht mehr glauben, daß die deutschen Stahlwaren schlecht sind!" ("Goddam! Now my customers will no longer believe me that German cutlery is poor quality!")*	
	Made in Germany (written on the sword)	
Description:	A lion with a British cap and a sword stuck in his behind is fleeing with his tail tucked between his legs. He looks distressed. A peddler is watching him with a surprised look on his face.	
Scenario 1:	A brave animal like a lion is fearless and does not flee when opposed by a stronger force.	
Scenario 2:	The British Lion is fleeing after having been pierced by a German sword.	
Scenario 3:	The British think that they are fearless and do not flee.	
Scenario 4:	The German weapons are stronger than theirs and therefore will make the British flee.	
Explanation:	The British Lion is a metonymy for the British army and the sword for the German one. The cartoon entails a cause-effect relation, i.e. the British Lion is fleeing because of the sword made of German steel is sticking in its behind. The British military should capitulate, because the German army is stronger than the British.	
Type:	Metonymic scene represents a communicative situation and interacts with the verbal part.	
Invective:	The British (try to) mislead the public, but their attempt is thwarted by their losses and the damage caused by the Germans. They are militarily inferior.	

Simplicissimus cartoon 3

Cartoon 4   15.9.1914
Heading: *Der Gentleman in der deutschen Gefangenschaft (The Gentleman as a German Prisoner of War)*
Caption: *„Diese Barbaren! Mich mit unseren Bundesgenossen zusammenzusperren!" ("These barbarians – locking me up with our allies!")*
Description: A captive English soldier and other prisoners of war of the Allies are sitting around a pot on top of a fire.
Scenario 1:   The British soldier and other prisoners of war have a sense of solidarity, because they are allies, have fought together and share the same fate.
Scenario 2:   The British soldier and other prisoners of war do not have a sense of solidarity in spite of the fact that they are allies, have fought together and share the same fate.
Explanation: The two scenarios are contrasted.
Type: Non-combatant military scene represents a communicative situation and interacts with the verbal part.
Invective: The British are callous; they are arrogant and look down on their allies.

Cartoon 5   22.9.1914
Heading: *Englands wilde verwegene Jagd (England's Wild and Audacious Chase)*
Caption: *„Come on, Tommy, das ist kein Sport für Engländer!" ("Come on, Tommy, this is no sport for Englishmen.")*
Description: An English and a German soldier are riding on horseback side by side. The German soldier is about to strike with his sword at the British soldier, who is trying to counter the blow. Next to the British soldier another comrade-in-arms is watching the exchange. In the background, there are four German soldiers to be seen.
Scenario 1:   In the given situation the British soldier acts clumsily, and his horse is panicking.
Scenario 2:   The German soldier is in control of the situation.
Explanation: The two scenarios are contrasted.
                Theodor Körner (1791-1813) wrote the poem *Lützows wilde Jagd (Lützow`s wild chase.)* whose stanzas end with the line: *Das war Lützows wilde, verwegene Jagd. (That was Lützow`s wild and audacious chase.)* Adolf Freiherr von Lützow lived from 1782 to 1834. He was a Prussian officer and a member of a volunteer corps, the Black Troops (or Black Rifles), in the War of Liberation against Napoleon I, which was known for its daring exploits. Körner was killed in battle.
                In the last stanza Körner emphasizes the fact that the fight is directed against hangmen and tyrants: *Die wilde Jagd und die deutsche Jagd / Auf Henkersblut und Tyrannen! (The wild chase and the German chase / after hengmen's blood and tyrants))*
                In alluding to this poem, the cartoonist intends to integrate a portion of its meaning into the cartoon. But it remains an open question to what extent the reader is able and/or willing to exploit the allusions. In many cases an allusion does not play a crucial role for the understanding of the current text. What it does is establish a tacit cooperation between the author and the reader because of the knowledge others do not possess. This solidarity may extend to the social or national group the author and the reader identify with.
                Fighting on horseback had no military significance at the western front because it was mainly trench warfare.
Type: War scene represents a communicative situation and interacts with the verbal part.
Invective: The British are militarily inferior to the Germans, e.g. the German soldiers are better riders than the British soldiers.

Cartoon 6   22.9.1914
Heading: *Das fromme England (Pious England)*
Caption: *„Es steht nirgends in der Bibel geschrieben, daß man keine Dum-Dum-*
                Geschosse¹ verwenden darf!" ("You will not find a ban on dum-dum
                bullets anywhere in the Bible.")
Description: An English military leader addresses four soldiers with a Bible in his
                left hand.
Scenario 1:   The British follow the rules of the Bible.
Scenario 2:   There are no rules in the Bible concerning modern weapons.
Explanation: It is naïve to disregard the historical background of the Bible. Another
                reading is that the British just present a silly pretext to be able to use
                such gruesome weapons.
Type: Non-combatant military scene represents a communicative situation.
Invective: The British are ignorant, because they are not aware of this discrepancy.
                They cannot be trusted, because they are Christian hypocrites.

Cartoon 7   22.9.1914
Heading: *Die Lügen-Zentrale (The Headquarters of Lies)*
Caption: *Da Englands Kabel noch intakt sind, ist es nach wie vor imstande,*
                seinen Hauptausfuhrartikel über die ganze Welt zu versenden. (Since
                England's cables are still intact, it is able to send her major export
                article all over the world.
Description: A toad with a British hat is sitting on the cliffs of Dover vomiting
                snakes. They move in all directions along the communication cable
                network.
Scenario 1:   News is sent out via the communication cable network.
Scenario 2:   Snakes are sent out via the communication cable network.
Explanation: The cartoon is a pictorial metaphor. The toad represents an English news
                agency. The snakes symbolize items of false news. The basic meaning is
                that England churns out masses of lies. The metaphorically conveyed
                semantic load is that these lies are nauseating like vomit and dangerous
                like snakes.² The cartoon is also a reflection of the German expression
                falsche Schlange (deceptive snake), which has no idiomatic equivalent
                in English. In addition, a snake is a Christian symbol of deception.
                Very soon after the beginning of the war, the British severed the
                German transatlantic cable.
Type: Metonymic scene interacts with the verbal part.
Invective: The British (try to) mislead the public; they are abominable liars and
                cannot be trusted.

Cartoon 8   13.10.1914
Heading: *Der Engländer und seine Weltkugel (The Englishman and his Globe)*
Caption: *„Oh verflucht. Blut ist doch schlüpfriger als Wasser!" ("Damn it. Blood*
                is more slippery than water, after all.")
Description: An English soldier is slipping down the globe. He tries to hold tight. He
                is losing his helmet. Europe and Africa can be seen. The diameter of the
                globe is about twice the size of the soldier.
Scenario 1:   An intelligent person expects that one cannot control one's movements
                on a wet sphere and will not be surprised. Control is even more difficult
                if the liquid is blood.
Scenario 2:   The Englishman is surprised that he cannot control his movements on
                the globe covered with blood.

---

¹ A soft-nosed bullet which expands upon contact causing a terrible wound.
  (http://www.spartacus.schoolnet.co.uk/FWWglossary.htm, 11/5/2001)
² Cf. the detailed analysis of this cartoon in chapter 2.3.

Scenario 3:   It is to be expected that controlling parts of the world by force will lead to difficulties.

Scenario 4:   England is surprised that there are difficulties in controlling its Empire.

Explanation: The cartoon entails a metaphor in which the tight grip of the figure on the globe represents control and the slipping, loss of control or difficulties. The hat and the dress of the figure are pictorial metonymies of British colonialism. The blood is a metonymy for the cruelty and callousness of a colonial power.

The fact that also Germany had colonies and colonial aspirations is ignored in this cartoon.

Type: Metonymic scene represents a communicative situation and interacts with the verbal part.

Invective: The British are ignorant and shortsighted.

Simplicissimus cartoon 8

Cartoon 9   13.10.1914

Heading: *Aus unserem Verbrecheralbum (From our Police Files)*

Caption: *Edward Grey, Brandstifter*   *Gavro Princip, Meuchelmörder*

                    (Edward Grey, Arsonist   *Gavro Princip, Assassin)*

Description: There are two drawings of Edward Grey and Gavro Princip each, showing them as criminals in a police file.

Scenario 1:   The British Minister of Foreign Affairs is an honorable man.

Scenario 2:   The British Minister of Foreign Affairs is a criminal.

Explanation: The context of showing Edward Grey like a criminal side by side with
the assassin Gavro Princip, whose murder triggered World War I, sheds
negative light on the Minister of Foreign Affairs.
The cartoon entails a quotation of a new type of text, i.e. a police file.
Type: Counterfactual scene interacts with the verbal part.
Invective: The British cannot be trusted, e.g. Edward Grey is a criminal.

Cartoon 10   13.10.1914
Heading: *England braucht Geld (England Needs Money)*
Caption: *Die englische Regierung hat die Besichtigung der französischen
Schlachtfelder an das Reisebüro Cook & Son verpachtet. (The English
government has given a license to the travel agency Cook & Son to
have sight-seeing tours on the French killing fields.)*
(On the cap of the guide:) *COOK & S(ON)*
(On the sash of the guide:) *COOK & SON*
Description: A guide is showing killing fields filled with dead soldiers and destroyed
weapons to a group of tourists.
Scenario 1: Killing fields with human corpses are a sad and deplorable sight and no
tourist attraction.
Scenario 2: For the British, killing fields with human corpses are tourist attractions.
Explanation: The two scenarios are contrasted.
Type: Counterfactual scene interacts with the verbal part.
Invective: The British are callous and incapable of human feelings.

Simplicissimus cartoon 11

Cartoon 11   27.10.1914
Heading: *Die Saat König Eduards geht auf. (King Edward's Seeds are Sprouting.)*
Left panel
Description: King Edward, wearing a top hat, is sowing a field like a farmer.
Scenario 1: A farmer sows his field in order to harvest corn etc. in order to sustain
human life.
Scenario 2: King Edward takes political steps in order to reach certain goals.
Explanation: The cartoon is a blend of agricultural and political 'sowing', which also

51

alludes to biblical rules such as *they sow the wind, and they reap the whirlwind* (Hosea 8: 7) or *a man reaps what he sows* (Galatians 6: 7).

Type: Metonymic scene interacts with the verbal part.

Description: Right panel Skulls of soldiers of different nationalities and other human bones 'grow' on the field. The different headgears indicate the different nationalities.

Scenario 1: Corn and vegetables grow on fields and are harvested to feed the people and sustain human life.

Scenario 2: King Edward`s harvest consists of the skulls and bones of killed soldiers.

Explanation: King Edward's harvest is the opposite of a life-sustaining natural harvest, i.e. his political steps are destructive and lethal and the outcome are killed soldiers.

Type: Metonymic scene interacts with the verbal part.

Invective: The British are callous. The political activities of King Edward are counterproductive and although this development is foreseeable, he does not care.

Cartoon 12   27.10.1914

Heading: *Von der Waterkant (From the Seashore)*

Caption: „*Die Engländer sünn as de Hering! Wenn man se up't Land smiet, möt se verrecken!*" *("The English are like herrings. If you throw them on land they perish.")*

Description: Two longshoremen on a quay are unloading a ship.

Scenario 1: The British have a superior marine force and a strong army.

Scenario 2: The British have a superior marine force but a very weak army.

Explanation: Although the marine and the army of a country are independent of each other, there is a general expectation that two military forces should be equivalent. It is regarded either as a flaw if a country is unable to achieve this or as a misjudgment of the military needs. Comparing the British to herrings also points to their inferiority.

Type: Everyday scene represents a communicative situation.

Invective: The British are militarily inferior, because they are not efficient enough to make their army as strong as their marine.

Cartoon 13   10.11.1914

Heading: *Britische Gerechtigkeit (British Justice)*

Caption: „*Was hat denn der Mann gemacht?*" „*Er hat den Laden seines deutschen Konkurrenten geplündert.*" „*Dann lassen Sie ihn laufen. Er hat doch nur nach dem englischen Staatsprinzip gehandelt!*" *("What did this man do?" "He looted the shop of his German competitor." "Then let him go. He only acted according to the guidelines of the English state.")*

Description: Two policemen on the left have arrested a soldier who is holding a clock. An army general on the right is stopping them.

Scenario 1: People who loot shops must be apprehended and punished.

Scenario 2: The British army general orders the policemen to let the looter go free.

Scenario 3: The principles and rules of a state apply to its citizens. Looting the shops of competitors is wrong for a state and its citizens.

Scenario 4: According to England's principles and rules, looting the shops of competitors is acceptable.

Explanation: An obvious wrong is justified by reference to the principles of a state. The cartoon has a complex structure of arguments. The example shows that British justice is a farce and the guidelines of the state corrupt. It follows that any demand on Germany is ill founded.

Type: Non-combatant military scene represents a communicative situation and interacts with the verbal part.

Invective: The British are abominable, because they behave like looters or thieves.

Cartoon 14   10.11.1914

First panel

Heading: *Die Spionenfurcht in London (The Fear of Spies in London)*

Caption: *„Ein deutscher Dachshund! Er hat mit seinem Schwanz dem Zeppelin ein Zeichen gegeben!" ("A German dachshund! It gave the zeppelin a sign with its tail.")*

Description: Throngs of people are watching a dachshund cross an open place. A boy is shouting something and pointing in its direction.

Scenario 1:   Dogs wag their tails for joy; a wagging tail is not a surreptitious sign.

Scenario 2:   This dachshund has communicated a sign to a German zeppelin by wagging its tail surreptitiously.

Type: Counterfactual scene represents a communicative situation and interacts with the verbal part.

Second panel

Caption: *„Verdammter deutscher Spion!" ("Damn German spy!")*

Description: The dachshund is lead away on a chain by three policemen. The discontented crowd maltreats it, curses and spits at it.

Scenario 3:   Dogs are unable to spy for a country.

Scenario 4:   This dachshund is suspected of being a German spy.

Type: Counterfactual scene represents a communicative situation and interacts with the verbal part.

Third panel

Caption: *„Feuer!!!" ("Fire!!!")*

Description: The blinded dachshund is being shot by a firing squad.

Scenario 5:   Dogs are not tried and sentenced to death for spying.

Scenario 6:   This dachshund is tried and shot for spying for Germany.

Explanation: The two scenarios are contrasted.

Type: Counterfactual scene represents a communicative situation.

Invective: The British are ignorant, naive and over exaggerating.

Cartoon 15   17.11.1914

Heading: *Englische Regel (English Rule)*

Caption: *Inder zurück! Nur beim Angriff habt ihr vorn zu laufen! (Indians back! You have to run in the front line only during an attack.)*

Description: English and non-English soldiers are fleeing. An Indian soldier is in front. The flight goes over some fallen soldiers.

Scenario 1:   The soldiers of the Allies should have equal chances of surviving.

Scenario 2:   The British want the Indian soldiers to fight and die for them; they do not want them to have the same chance of surviving.

Explanation: The front-runners of an attack are most likely to be killed, and the front-runners of a retreat or flight are most likely to be saved.

Type: War scene represents a communicative situation.

Invective: The British are callous, egotistic and racist.

Cartoon 16   17.11.1914

Heading: *Die Belgier in London (The Belgians in London)*

Caption: *„Wir haben doch gesagt, ihr sollt für uns sterben --- für uns zu leben braucht ihr nicht!" ("We asked you to die for us --- not to live for us.")*

Description: A well-dressed Englishman, wearing a top hat, is warding off poorly dressed people who follow him. In the background, there are (Belgian) men, women and children camping in the street.

Scenario 1:   The Belgians fight and die for the English.
Scenario 2:   The British do not care for the Belgians in need.
Explanation: The British want the Belgians to fight (and die) for them, they do not want to take any further responsibility for the Belgians, e.g. caring for their civilians who have fled to London. During the first months of the war about 200,000 Belgian refugees fled to Britain.
Type: Everyday scene represents a communicative situation and interacts with the verbal part.
Invective: The British are callous, because they violate the fairness principle (and the principle of equality).

Cartoon 17   1.12.1914
Heading: *Der Prince of Wales (The Prince of Wales)*
Caption: *„An was erkennt man denn, ob eine Schlacht gewonnen oder verloren ist, Mister French? Wer macht denn da den ‚umpire'?"* *("How does one know whether a battle is lost or won, Mr. French? Who is the umpire in such a case?")*
Description: General French is to be seen in the foreground on the left. Behind him in the center there is the Prince of Wales. In the background, a band wearing bearskin hats is playing.
Scenario 1:   A military leader should be able to give a straight answer to a simple question.
Scenario 2:   General French is unable to do so.
Explanation: Either General French does not even know the basics of war, or the British claim victories which do not exist. Sir John French was the Commander-in-Chief of the British Expeditionary Force (BEF). Some of his military decisions were controversial.
Type: Non-combatant military scene represents a communicative situation.
Invective: The British are ignorant; they have not achieved a clear-cut victory yet.

Cartoon 18   1.12.1914
Heading: *Ein Bild aus dem englischen Familienleben (A Picture from English Family Life)*
Caption: *Auch in England ist man im häuslichen Kreise emsig bestrebt, den Soldaten zu helfen. Die Damen wetteifern in der Herstellung von Dum-Dum-Geschossen. (Also in English homes everyone endeavors to help the soldiers as much as possible. The women compete with each other in producing dum-dum bullets.)*
Description: Eight women and a young girl are sitting around a table producing ammunition.
Scenario 1:   Normally women would produce something pleasant for the soldiers.
Scenario 2:   These women produce dangerous and crippling ammunition.
Explanation: The contrast is intensified by the fact that the women are shown in a private rather than a factory environment, which would have been closer to the truth.
Type: Everyday scene interacts with the verbal part.
Invective: The British are callous and cruel; these characteristics have even infiltrated into the family life.

Cartoon 19   8.12.1914
Heading: *Nach dem Untergang des 'Bulwark' (The Sinking of the 'Bulwark')*
Caption: *„Ein deutsches Unterseeboot in Sicht? Da bin ich neugierig, ob unser Schiff wieder von selber in die Luft fliegt!"* *("Any German submarines in sight? I'm curious to know if our ship explodes by itself again.")*
Description: A British admiral is leaning on the railing of a ship. Behind him there is a marine soldier.

Scenario 1:   In a previous incident the fact that a British ship had been torpedoed by a German submarine was presented to the public as an explosion on the ship without any external force.

Scenario 2:   The British admiral casts doubt on this explanation.

Explanation: It is a known fact that the military hesitates to acknowledge successes of the enemy and prefers to present different causes for a loss, even if they are utterly irrational and unlikely.

Type: Non-combatant military scene represents a communicative situation.

Invective: The British (try to) mislead the public; they will not succeed, because their attempts are blatantly illogical.

Cartoon 20   15.12.1914

Heading: *Parolenausgabe (The Issuing of a New Motto)*

Caption: *„Sorgen Sie dafür, daß die Soldiers der Royal Dum-Dum-Engeneers etwas vorarbeiten, damit auch im Felde das heilige Christmas nicht durch profane Arbeiten entweiht wird!" ("Take care that the soldiers of the Royal Dum-Dum Engineers work a bit in advance so that holy Christmas is not profaned on the battlefields.")*

Description: An English military leader addresses two soldiers who are taking notes. An elderly, senior military leader is watching the scene.

Scenario 1:   Christmas is a time of a deeply felt desire for peace.

Scenario 2:   The British intensify their war activities so that Christmas will be undisturbed by the war.

Explanation: The British do not have a genuine Christian desire for peace.

Type: Non-combatant military scene represents a communicative situation.

Invective: The British cannot be trusted, because they are bigoted, i.e. Christian hypocrites.

Cartoon 21   15.12.1914

Heading: *Der Richter von Falkmouth (The Judge from Falkmouth)*

Caption: *„Samuel Phillip, Sie waren im Irrtum, als Sie sich an einem englischen Mädchen vergingen. Dafür bestrafe ich Sie mit zehn Schilling. Wenn Sie das gleiche im Feindesland tun, werde ich Ihnen den Betrag vergüten." ("Samuel Phillip, you were mistaken when you raped an English girl. For this I fine you ten shillings. If you do the same in the country of the enemy, I'm going to reimburse this amount.")*

Description: In a courtroom the judge addresses the accused.

Scenario 1:   Rape is a crime against the dignity and integrity of women and must be punished.

Scenario 2:   Rape is not a crime when directed against the women of the enemy. In such a case it will even be rewarded.

Explanation: The two standards are contrasted. The fact that the judge calls the rape an error and that he does not punish it very severely is counter-intuitive, but does not constitute the main point of this cartoon.

Type: Everyday scene represents a communicative situation.

Invective: The British cannot be trusted, because their judges act according to partisan standards and against the principles of human rights. The British justice system is inconsistent and war mongering.

Cartoon 22   22.12.1914

Heading: *Cant*

Caption: *Die Engländer, welche man mit Unrecht als gemütsroh verschreit, legen am Weihnachtsabend nur Minen mit Christbäumchen aus. (On Christmas Eve, the English, who are unjustly reputed to be callous, lay out mines with little Christmas trees on them.)*

Description: Three people in a row boat place sea mines with little Christmas trees on them in the water. In the background, a row of floating mines with little Christmas trees can be seen.

Scenario 1: Mines are dangerous and lethal weapons.

Scenario 2: Mines with little Christmas trees on them are dangerous and lethal weapons.

Explanation: Decorating mines with little Christmas trees does not make them less dangerous or lethal. Therefore the cartoon must be regarded as cynical.

Type: Counterfactual scene interacts with the verbal part.

Invective: The British cannot be trusted, because they are bigoted, i.e. Christian hypocrites.

Simplicissimus cartoon 22

Cartoon 23   22.12.1914

Heading: *Weihnachten in England (Christmas in England)*

Caption: *Während früher kein Engländer mit einem Farbigen verkehrte, sind jetzt die dunkelhäutigen Waffenbrüder das tonangebende Element in der Londoner Gesellschaft geworden. Mancher von ihnen darf unter dem Mistelzweig einer blonden Miß den althergebrachten Weihnachtskuß geben. (In former times no Englishman associated with a colored person. Today the black brothers-in-arms have become the leading element in the society of London. Some of them are allowed to give a blonde miss the traditional Christmas kiss under the mistletoe.)*

Description: White English women are dancing with colored men under the mistletoe. In the center a very small man kisses a very tall woman.

Scenario 1:   In former times white people discriminated against colored people, who were represented in the upper echelons of London's society according to their ratio in the population.

Scenario 2:   At the present time colored people are not discriminated against, but they are over-represented in the upper echelons of London's society.

Explanation: In former times the British looked down on colored people and discriminated against them. This was not acceptable. Nowadays these colored people are over-represented in the upper echelons of London's society and therefore have become an important part of it, because the white British men are fighting in the war. This is also not acceptable.

Type: Everyday scene interacts with the verbal part.

Invective: The British cannot be trusted, because they are inconsistent in their treatment of their allies. They are too stupid to see a social development which is potentially detrimental for them.

Cartoon 24   22.12.1914

Heading: *Sir Eduards Neujahrsprogramm (Sir Edward's New Year's Program)*

Caption: *„Nichts von Frieden! England wird den Krieg fortsetzen, bis der letzte Franzose gefallen ist!" ("No peace! England will continue the war until the last Frenchman has been killed.")*

Description: Sir Edward Grey, the British Secretary of Foreign Affairs, is standing in front of a desk with several sheets of paper and an envelope on it. He is pointing in an authoritarian manner with the index of his left hand at one of the sheets. His index is drawn very long. He places his right hand on his waist, holding another piece of paper. He is staring at the reader.

Scenario 1: England will continue fighting until the last English soldier is killed.

Scenario 2: France will continue fighting until the last French soldier is killed.

Explanation: There is a blending of scenario 1 and 2. Normally a minister can only speak for his own country. The British Secretary of Foreign Affairs, Sir Edward Grey, arrogates to himself the right to speak for France.

Grey made the defense of France against Germany's aggression the central feature of British foreign policy, because he believed that he had to fulfill Britain's 'obligations to honor' by joining France in its war with Germany. He was the longest serving Secretary of Foreign Affairs in British history. He was removed from office in December 1916.

Type: Everyday scene represents a communicative situation.

Invective: The British are callous, because they sacrifice French soldiers. It is easy to take a pro-war decision when foreign soldiers are being killed.

Simplicissimus cartoon 26

Cartoon 25   22.12.1914

Heading: *Silvesterpunsch (Sylvester Punch)*

Caption: *„Scarborough und Hartlepool beschossen! In diesem Sinne auf eine weitere deutsch-englische Annäherung hurra, hurra, hurra!"* *("Scarborough and Hartlepool shelled! Let us drink to a further German-English approximation, hurrah, hurrah, hurrah!")*

Description: Four German officers are sitting around a table. A fifth officer is standing.

Scenario 1: People establish a closer social contact.

Scenario 2: The German navy is approaching British targets.

Explanation: Since the shelling of the two towns is stated in the first sentence, it is clear that not the normal meaning of *Annäherung* is used but a derived one, i.e. the negative meaning of an aggressive approach. Instead of an invective, there is an inference to be drawn, i.e. the wish of the German military to continue attacking Britain.

Type: War scene represents a communicative situation.

Invective: A positive relationship with England is ruled out without any explicit reason or invective.

Cartoon 26   22.12.1914

Heading: *Die Entwicklung des britischen Löwen (The Development of the British Lion)*

Caption:

Description: A proud looking lion with a British cap is changing into a (smaller) wild boar with two intermediate stages. Saliva is running from its mouth

Scenario 1: The symbol of England is a lion.

Scenario 2: The symbol of England has changed to a wild boar.

Explanation: England is in a process of deterioration.

Type: Metonymic scene interacts with the verbal part.

Invective: The British are abominable.

Cartoon 27   5.1.1915

Heading: *Where are your ships?*

Caption: *„Wo sind eure Schiffe?" ("Where are your Ships?")*

Description: On the turret of a surfaced submarine a sailor is searching the horizon with binoculars.

Scenario 1: The superior English marine is omnipresent and controls the oceans.

Scenario 2: The British marine is nowhere to be seen.

Explanation: If a marine force is genuinely superior, it will be omnipresent.

Type: War scene represents a communicative situation and interacts with the verbal part. (Voice from 'off-stage')

Invective: The British are militarily inferior, because their marine is cowardly.

Cartoon 28   19.1.1915

Heading: *John Bull beschreitet den Rechtsweg. (John Bull Goes to Court.)*

Caption: *„Ich will eine Klage gegen Mister Tirpitz!" – „Ja – aber der Krieg – " – „Nein, nein, das ist kein Krieg! Krieg ist, wenn auf dem Kontinent die Völker mit unseren bezahlten Leuten kämpfen. Aber das ist Landfriedensbruch! Ich will eine Klage gegen Mister Tirpitz!"* *("I want an indictment against Mr. Tirpitz." – "Yes, but the war –" "No, no, that's no war. War, that's when the nations on the Continent fight against our mercenaries. But this is breaching the peace. I want an indictment against Mr. Tirpitz.")*

Description: John Bull is addressing two judges pointing at damaged buildings in the background and three trails of smoke above the sea.

Scenario 1:   During war, damage will be inflicted on the warring factions.

Scenario 2:   During war, one of the factions involved will be exempt from any damage. The damage will only be inflicted on the allies.

Explanation: John Bull has a very naïve idea of what war means.

Type: Metonymic scene represents a communicative situation and interacts with the verbal part.

Invective: The British are ignorant and naïve, because they misjudge the consequences of the war.

Cartoon 29   19.1.1915

Heading: *Kitcheners neue Armeen (Kitchener's New Armies)*

Caption: *„Hier, Herr General, übergebe ich Ihnen Ihr neues Armeekorps. Es sind zwar nur zwölf Mann, aber jeder Engländer wiegt bekanntlich ein deutsches Regiment auf!" ("Here you are, General. I'm handing over a new army corps to you. I admit that they're only twelve men, but, as you know, every Englishman counterbalances one German regiment.")*

Description: Kitchener and an old army general are standing in front of a group of young men, of which nine are visible. Kitchener is pointing at them.

Scenario 1:   Normal expectation: one English regiment equals one German regiment.

Scenario 2:   Kitchener's assumption: one English soldier equals one German regiment.

Explanation: It is naïve to assume that one English soldier equals one German regiment.

Horatio Kitchener (1850-1916) initiated a recruitment campaign with the famous so-called Kitchener poster[1] designed by Alfred Leete in 1914. It shows Kitchener's head and his right hand with the index finger pointing at the reader and reads: *BRITONS* – [image of Kitchener] *WANTS YOU - JOIN YOUR COUNTRY'S ARMY – GOD SAVE THE KING*.

Adhering to the principle of British liberalism Kitchener insisted that military conscription was not required. The first Military Service Act was passed in January 1916. It called for the compulsory enlistment of unmarried men between the ages of 18 and 41. The second Military Service Act was introduced in May 1916. All men regardless of marital status between the ages of 18 and 41 had to enlist.

Type: Non-combatant military scene represents a communicative situation and interacts with the verbal part.

Invective: The British are ignorant and naïve, because they overrate themselves.

Cartoon 30   26.1.1915

Heading: *Der Engländer in der Hölle (The Englishman in Hell)*

Caption: *„Keine Zeppeline hier! Kein Kruppgeschütz! Keine Unterseeboote! Ich bin im Himmel!" ("No zeppelins, here! No Krupp guns! No submarines! I'm in heaven!")*

Description: An English soldier walks through a hell-like scenario accompanied by two devils and two fierce looking dogs, one of which is biting into his left calf. The devil behind him is breathing hot air on his neck. Several bats are hanging from the ceiling.

Scenario 1:   The soldier is obviously in hell, because of the two devils, the two fierce looking dogs and the bats.

Scenario 2:   The soldier feels like he is in heaven, because there are no zeppelins, no guns and no submarines.

---

[1] Cf.: http://www.spartacus.schoolnet.co.uk/FWWkitchener.htm (3/17/2002).

Explanation:	The German zeppelins, guns and submarines are so awe-inspiring that there is nothing English soldiers are more afraid of.
Type:	Counterfactual scene represents a communicative situation and interacts with the verbal part.
Invective:	The British are militarily inferior and therefore afraid of the Germans.

Simplicissimus cartoon 31

Cartoon 31	26.1.1915
Heading:	*Das Reuterdenkmal (The Reuter Memorial)*
Caption:	*In London hat sich bereits ein Komitee gebildet um dem genialen Erfinder der englisch-französisch-russischen Siege ein Denkmal zu setzen. (In London a committee has been formed to erect a monument for the ingenious inventor of the English-French-Russian victories.)*
Description:	In front of the Parliament buildings there is a memorial of Reuter who is sitting on a decorated horse. He is holding a pen, a sheet of paper and a telegraph pole like a knight would hold a lance.
Scenario 1:	A knight fights in a battle with a lance on horseback.
Scenario 2:	Reuter is fighting in the war (instead of just reporting).
Explanation:	1. The British, French and Russian victories are mere inventions of the news industry. Its most prominent representative is to be honored with a memorial.

2. Reuter uses lies and deception to fight in the war like a knight in a battle.

The mental spaces 'news reporter' and 'knight' are blended.

Type: Counterfactual scene represents a communicative situation and interacts with the verbal part.

Invective: The British (try to) mislead the public; they and their allies have used non-military and therefore unfair means in the war.

Cartoon 32   26.1.1915
Heading: *Englische Rekrutierung (English Recruitment)*
Caption: *„Laß Dich anwerben! Englands Sache steht ausgezeichnet!" „Dann braucht ihr mich ja nicht." „Nein, du hast mich missverstanden, England ist in größter Gefahr. Du mußt Dich sofort anwerben lassen!" „Nein, dann ist mir die Sache zu gefährlich." ("Let yourself be recruited. England's chances to win the war are excellent." "Well then you don't need me." "No, you've misunderstood me. England is in great danger. You have to let yourself be recruited immediately." "No, in that case this seems too dangerous for me.")*

Description: A tall recruiting officer walks up behind a bored looking working class man with a cap and a pipe.
Scenario 1: A recruiting officer presents the true facts and consistent and convincing arguments to the potential recruits.
Scenario 2: This recruiting officer presents facts, which he contradicts immediately when the potential recruit expresses his disinclination to join the army.
Explanation: The recruiting officer manipulates the facts according to his needs and is naïve enough to believe that the candidate will not notice this.
Type: Non-combatant military scenario represents a communicative situation.
Invective: The British (try to) mislead the public, e.g. their recruitment officers try to adapt the facts to their needs.

Cartoon 33   2.2.1915
Heading: *„Lord Kitchener Wants you!"*
Caption: *„Kommen Sie, Lord Kitchener braucht Rekruten!" ("Come on, Lord Kitchener needs recruits!")*
Description: A police constable with a torch surprises a burglar in a house *in flagranti.*
Scenario 1: A police constable arrests a burglar whom he catches immediately.
Scenario 2: This police constable ignores the fact that the man is burgling and invites him into the British army.
Explanation: The British are so keen on getting new soldiers into their army that they will accept even criminals.
The heading entails an allusion to the famous so-called Kitchener poster which reads: BRITONS – [image of Kitchener] *WANTS YOU - JOIN YOUR COUNTRY'S ARMY – GOD SAVE THE KING.*
Type: Everyday scene represents a communicative situation.
Invective: The British cannot be trusted.

Cartoon 34   9.2.1915
Heading: *Nach der Seeschlacht in der Nordsee (After the Naval Battle in the North Sea)*
Caption: *Das ist in England jetzt die Order:
Ein Seegefecht ist oft fatal,
Drum übernimmt der Herr Reporter
Die Meldung für den General!*

	(Since sea battles are dangerous
	There is a new tradition in England:
	The information is presented by reporters
	Rather than the military.)
Description:	Close-up on the guns of a war ship.
Scenario 1:	During a war, the generals inform the public about the latest developments.
Scenario 2:	After the battle in the North Sea, press reporters inform the public about the latest developments.
Explanation:	The British navy generals shun publicity, because they try to hide their defeat.
Type:	War scene interacts with the verbal part.
Invective:	The British (try to) mislead the public; they are militarily inferior and they are going to lose the war.

Cartoon 35		16.2.1915
Heading:	*Schonung für die alte Britannia (Forebearance for Old Britannia)*	
Caption of first panel:	*„Ich kann Ihnen eine große Freude machen. Ihre Flotte hat eine wonder – wondervolle Sieg errungen, und alle Ihre Schiffe sind unversehrt!"* *("I have good news for you. Your fleet has gained a wonderful victory and all your ships are intact.")*	
Type:	Metonymic scene represents a communicative situation.	
Caption of second panel:	*„Nur ein kleiner Torpedozerstörer und noch zwei kleine Zerstörer haben ein kleine Loch bekommen ---"* *("Only one small torpedo destroyer and two little destroyers have been hit and have a little hole.")*	
Type:	Metonymic scene represents a communicative situation.	
Caption of third panel:	*„Und eine kleine Schlachtkreuzer und noch eine kleine Schlachtkreuzer haben ein kleine Loch bekommen -"* *("And one small battle cruiser and another battle cruiser has a little hole now -")*	
Type:	Metonymic scene represents a communicative situation.	
Caption of fourth panel:	*„Ich wusste ja, dass das alte Biest nichts verträgt!! Den kaputen Schlachtkreuzer muß ich jetzt unterschlagen!"* *("I knew that the old hag couldn't take it. Now I have to suppress the fact that another battle cruiser was damaged.")*	
Type:	Metonymic scene represents a communicative situation.	
Description:	In the first two panels, Churchill feeds a frail old lady who is propped up with cushions in an armchair. In the last two panels, he feels the forehead and the pulse of the lady who has passed out after hearing the bad news.	
Scenario 1:	After a battle the public will be truthfully informed about good and bad news.	
Scenario 2:	After this battle in the North Sea the public is only partly informed about the bad news.	
Explanation:	The frail old lady, *Britannia*, to whom the news is spoon-fed like to a child, is a metonymy for the British public.	
Type:	Metonymic scene represents a communicative situation.	
Invective:	The British are militarily inferior; the British public is being ill informed about the relevant facts of the war by the officials.	

Cartoon 36		16.2.1915
Heading:	*U 21 auf der Jagd (U 21 – on the Hunt)*	
Caption:	*„Ja und was soll aus meiner Ladung werden? Siebenundzwanzig-tausend gefrorene Hammel!"* – *„Trösten Sie sich, das sind nicht die einzigen, die umsonst ihr Leben für England gelassen haben!"* *("What about my cargo? Twenty seven thousand frozen sheep." – "Take*	

comfort! They will not be the only ones who died pointlessly for England.")

Description:	A German marine officer from a submarine in the background is entering a ship from a small vessel in which three marine soldiers are sitting.
Scenario 1:	The twenty seven thousand sheep have lost their lives in vain, because the British will not consume the meat.
Scenario 2:	Many thousand English soldiers will have lost their lives in vain, because the war will not be won by England/the Allies.
Explanation:	The submarine has intercepted a merchant vessel. A cynical parallel is drawn between the slaughter of sheep for English consumption and the senseless killing of English soldiers.
	On 4th February 1915, Germany proclaimed the waters around Great Britain, including the whole English Channel, a war zone after February 18th.
Type:	War scene represents a communicative situation.
Invective:	The British are callous, because they let their soldiers die pointlessly.

Cartoon 37	16.2.1915
Heading:	*Letztes Mittel (Desperate Measures)*
Caption:	*Englische Sportsleute haben eine Seehundmeute auf Unterseeboote dressiert. (English sportsmen have trained a pack of seals to detect submarines.)*
Description:	A scuba diver under water is looking through binoculars into the distance. He has six seals on leashes with him. The seals are very playful and do not look interested in detecting German submarines.
Scenario 1:	There are efficient technical devices to detect submarines.
Scenario 2:	The British use seals in order to detect German submarines.
Explanation:	The British resort to absurd means of detecting German submarines. The technical devices of detecting submarines were still inefficient.
Type:	Counterfactual scene interacts with the verbal part.
Invective:	The British are militarily inferior, because the German submarines are superior to the British navy.

Cartoon 38	16.2.1915
Heading:	*Allgemeine Wehrpflicht in England (General Conscription in England)*
Caption:	*„Wart, John Bull, dein Fett wollen wir schon runterkriegen! Von jetzt ab musst du deine eigenen Kniee durchdrücken!" ("Just wait, John Bull, we will make you slim. From now on you will have to use your own legs.")*
Description:	John Bull is marching with a goose step in front of a drill sergeant. John Bull does not look particularly pleased.
Scenario 1:	England used to employ soldiers from other countries to fight for it.
Scenario 2:	Now England has to employ English soldiers to fight in the war.
Explanation:	The two scenarios are contrasted.
	John Bull is a metonymy for the British army.
Type:	Metonymic scene interacts with the verbal part.
Invective:	The British are callous, because they let other nations fight the war for them. Now it serves them right that they have to make a bigger military effort themselves.

Cartoon 39	23.2.1915
Heading:	*Ägir und Albion (Aegir and Albion)*
Caption:	*„Albion, fauler Kopp, überleg dir's nich so lange und komm rin!" ("Albion, you lazy bum, stop thinking and come in!")*
Description:	A human-like sea creature in the water with a trident is looking at

another human-like sea creature with a trident on the British coast, which looks rather concerned. In the background, there is a war ship with a German flag, and in the air above, there are four zeppelins.

Scenario 1: Great Britain accepts the German challenge and courageously sends its ships against the German fleet.

Scenario 2: Great Britain does not accept the German challenge and cowardly leaves its ships in the ports.

Explanation: The two scenarios are contrasted. The German and the British fleet are metonymically represented by the mythological figure Aegir on the one hand and a personification of the name for Britain, i.e. *Albion*, on the other. Aegir was the God of the ocean in Norse mythology. He would rise up from the waves, grasp ships and pull them down. He was both worshipped and feared by sailors. *Albion* is the earliest-known name for the islands of Britain. It was used by ancient Greek geographers from the 4th century BC.

Type: Metonymic scene represents a communicative situation.

Invective: The British are cowards, because they hesitate to engage their navy in a fight with the German navy.

Simplicissimus cartoon 40

Cartoon 40   16.2.1915

Heading: *Churchills Flaggenschwindel (Churchill's cheating with the flags)*

Caption: *„Mit diesem schäbigen Lappen traue ich mich wirklich nicht mehr hinaus." „Nur Mut, Frau Britannia, stehlen sie sich einfach was Besseres!" ("I don't dare go out in these tatters." - "Take courage, Mrs. Britannia. Just steel something better.")*

Description: There is a beach scenario with carts and a skinny, elderly woman, who wears a tattered dress with the patterns of the British flag. Above her head, the American and two other flags have been hung out to dry on a washing line. A man with a pipe in the background (Churchill?) is watching her.

Scenario 1: A ships flies the flag of the country it belongs to.

Scenario 2: British ships fly flags of other countries.

Explanation: The British cheat, because their ships fly flags of other countries and bring goods to Great Britain.

Type: Metonymic scenario represents a communicative situation. (Voice from 'off-stage').

Invective: The British cannot be trusted, because they are cheating with the flags of their ships.

Cartoon 41   2.3.1915

Heading: *The Splendid Isolation*

Description: John Bull is kneeling on a tiny island. Eleven submarines surround it, looking like sharks. He looks startled and frightened.

Scenario 1: A self-imposed isolation of a country can be splendid.

Scenario 2: The isolation forced on Great Britain is detrimental to it.

Explanation: The two scenarios are contrasted.

Type: Metonymic scene interacts with the verbal part.

Inference: The British are militarily inferior, because the German submarines, which surround Britain, are superior to the British navy.

Cartoon 42   2.3.1915

Heading: *John Bull beim Maskenverleiher (John Bull Renting a Mask)*

Caption: *„Welches Kostüm soll ich wählen, daß mich kein Mensch erkennt?" – „Gehn sie als Gentleman!" ("Which costume shall I choose so that nobody recognizes me?" – "Just dress up as a gentleman.")*

Description: A very fat John Bull is standing next to a shop owner in a shop for costumes.

Scenario 1: John Bull as he looks now who can easily be recognized.

Scenario 2: John Bull dressed as a gentleman who cannot be recognized.

Explanation: Dressing as a gentleman does not normally make a person unrecognizable.

Type: Metonymic scene represents a communicative situation.

Invective: The British are callous and cruel.

Cartoon 43   16.3.1915

Heading: *Auf Englischen Schiffen (On English Ships)*

Caption: *„Rettungsgürtel gibt's nicht! Sonst Schwimmen eure Leichen nachher wieder als Reklame für die deutschen Unterseeboote herum!" ("No lifebelts. Otherwise your corpses will be floating around as advertisements for the German submarines.")*

Description: On a ship, sailors are preparing to launch a lifeboat.

Scenario 1: After the sinking of the ship, the sailors have life belts and therefore German submarines can save them. This will be publicity for the Germans.

Scenario 2:   After the sinking of the ship, the sailors do not have life belts and therefore drown. German submarines cannot save them and thus there will be no publicity for the Germans.

Explanation: Surviving in the sea is not possible without a life belt. The British want to avoid a German success in public relations.

Type: War scene represents a communicative situation.

Invective: The British are callous, because they do not hesitate to sacrifice their own sailors.

Cartoon 44   23.3.1915

Heading: *Der britische Löwe (The British Lion)*

Caption under first and second panel: *„Zunächst ziehen wir mal den Schwanz ein. Die Mähne muß auch verschwinden. Und nun kostümieren wir uns. ("First we tuck the tail between the legs. The mane has to vanish, too. And finally, we dress up.)*

Caption under third, fourth and fifth panel: *Als Spanier, als Holländer oder als Norweger. Dann kennt uns kein Teufel von einem Deutschen. (As a Spaniard, as a Dutchman or as a Norwegian. Then no German devil will know us.)*

Caption under sixth panel: *Aber zu Hause sind wir wieder ganz Löwe!" (But at home we will be a perfect lion again.")*

Description: A lion is posing in front of a mirror. He changes into different national costumes.

Scenario 1:   A proud nation will not betray its identity.

Scenario 2:   Great Britain does.

Explanation: Ships with Spanish, Dutch and Norwegian flags bring goods to England.

Type: Metonymic scene interacts with the verbal part. (All six panels)

Invective: The British are cowards; therefore they have to cheat.

Cartoon 45   27.4.1915

Heading: *England und die U-Boote (England and the Submarines)*

Caption: *„Also bringen wir den Streit wie echte Kavaliere zum Ausgang!" ("Let's finish the quarrel like real gentlemen.")*

Description: Sir Edward Grey, the British Secretary of Foreign Affairs, is standing opposite a high military representative of the German Navy. Both are ready to start a fencing contest.
               Second panel

Caption: *„Schutzmann! Er hat mich verletzt! In das Gefängnis mit dem gemeinen Kerl!" ("Officer, he has injured me. Into the prison with this mean scoundrel!")*

Description: Blood is gushing from a wound in Grey's thigh. He is complaining to an English policeman, who is moving in the direction of the two opponents. Grey is pointing at the German on the right, who is holding his epée down.

Scenario 1:   The British Secretary of Foreign Affairs demands a fair fight.

Scenario 2:   When the British Secretary of Foreign Affairs is injured in a fair fight, he forgets his sense of fairness and calls the police.

Explanation: The two scenarios are contrasted.

Type: First panel: Metonymic scene represents a communicative situation and interacts with the verbal part.
               Second panel: Metonymic scene represents a communicative situation and interacts with the verbal part.

Invective: The British cannot be trusted, because they are bad losers.

Simplicissimus cartoon 45

Cartoon 46   4.5.1915
Heading: *Aus einer englischen Kulturgeschichte (From an English Cultural History)*
First panel
Caption: *Die sogenannten bayerischen Löwen, ein ganz besonders verwilderter Menschenschlag im Reiche der Barbaren. Unstät und flüchtig treiben sie sich im Hochgebirge herum. Dort sind sie der Schrecken der harmlos weidenden Gemsen und Rehe und der unschuldigen Vögelein in den Lüften, die von dieser Art Löwen gejagt und aufgefressen werden. (The so called Bavarian lions, an especially wild people in the realm of the barbarians. They roam the mountains like vagabonds and fugitives. They terrorize the harmless deer in the meadows and the innocent little birds in the air, which are hunted and eaten by this type of lion.)*
Description: In the foreground, two bearded men with Bavarian hats are holding rifles in their hands. In the background, another two are to be seen. One is shooting at a deer; the other one is climbing a hill.
Scenario 1:   The scenario of the verbal description.
Scenario 2:   The drawn scenario, which shows normal civilized hunters.
Explanation: The drawn scenario and the scenario of the verbal description are contrasted. Thus the verbal description is ridiculed as a nonsensical fairy tale depiction of Bavaria.
Type: Metonymic scene interacts with the verbal part.
Second panel
Caption: *Wie ganz anders ist es im alten Kulturland der englischen Kolonien. Kinder wachsen fröhlich mit den Tieren des Feldes auf; Männer und Jünglinge tanzen beim Absingen der englischen Nationalhymne Ringelreihen, und alles ist eitel Lust und Freude. Dieses heimatliche Idyll mussten nun die hoffnungsvollsten Jünglinge des Landes verlassen, um die guten Engländer im Kampfe gegen jene Barbaren zu unterstützen. (How different the cultured English colonies. Children grow up happily with the animals of the fields; men and youngsters dance in circles to the English national anthem, and everything is sheer bliss. In these days, the hopeful youngsters had to leave their country in order to support the fine Englishmen in their fight against those barbarians.)*
Description: In the foreground, there is a lion and two monkeys peacefully side by side. In the background, a man and a woman are standing in front of

straw huts. Another woman is pushing a pushchair with a child. Three people are dancing with their spears and their shields.

Scenario 3: The scenario of the verbal description.

Scenario 4: The drawn scenario is a replica of the verbal description.

Explanation: The scenario in the drawings of the second panel is partly inconsistent with reality, because the lion and the monkeys are resting peacefully side by side.

The last part in the description of the second panel is not given pictorially at all. But since the first two parts are inconsistent, by analogy, strong doubt is cast also on the third.

Type: Metonymic scene interacts with the verbal part.

Invective: The British (try to) mislead the public; but they will not succeed, because the way they inform the public about their soldiers from the colonies and about the Germans is absurd.

Cartoon 47   4.5.1915

Heading: *Lord Kitchener und Frankreichs Nachwuchs (Lord Kitchener and the Youth in France.)*

Caption: *„Nur Geduld, Kinder, ihr dürft alle noch für England kämpfen! So lange halten wir den Krieg schon hin." ("Just be patient, children, you will all be allowed to fight for England. For that purpose we will delay the war.")*

Description: Lord Kitchener in the uniform of a highly decorated general is surrounded by a large group of French youngsters, one of whom is about to present him with a bunch of flowers.

Scenario 1: It is neither desirable to prolong a war nor is it desirable to fight in a war for another nation.

Scenario 2: Lord Kitchener wants to prolong the war so that the youth of France will be able to fight (and die) in the war for England.

Explanation: The two scenarios are contrasted. Lord Kitchener formulates his statement like a promise, thereby flouting the felicity condition that a promise must be in the interest of the promisee.

The fact that Germany attacked Belgium and France and that England declared war on Germany only after that, is left unmentioned.

Type: Everyday scene represents a communicative situation.

Invective: The British are callous and egotistic.

Cartoon 48   11.5.1915

Heading: *Die haushälterische Britannia (Economical Britannia)*

Caption: *„Ich muß sie jede Woche abstauben, damit sie beim Friedensschluß noch wie neu sind!" („I have to dust them every week so that they will look like new, when peace comes.")*

Description: A housemaid is dusting a toy ship. Behind her in a harbor, there are many war ships lined up in a row.

Scenario 1: War ships are deployed in a war.

Scenario 2: The British leave their ships in the ports.

Explanation: The two scenarios are contrasted.

Type: Metonymic scene represents a communicative situation and interacts with the verbal part.

Invective: The British are militarily inferior and therefore afraid of the German fleet.

Simplicissimus cartoon 48

Cartoon 49   11.5.1915
Heading: *Englische Kriegskunst (The English Art of War)*
Caption: *William Tell Zurich (Schweiz)* - (written on the ship)
               Da auch in England die Künstler unter der Kriegszeit finanziell zu leiden haben, werden sie damit beschäftigt, die Schiffe mit neutralen Farben zu bemalen. (Since the artists in England are also suffering from the war, they are being employed to paint the ships in neutral colors.)
Description: A man with a ladder is painting the Swiss flag on a ship.
Scenario 1:   A painter decorates ships with colors.
Scenario 2:   This painter paints the Swiss flag on the ship in order to deceive the German marine forces.
Explanation: The term *neutral colors* is ambiguous.
Type: Everyday scene interacts with the verbal part.
Invective: The British cannot be trusted; they are militarily inferior and therefore have to cheat.

Cartoon 50	18.5.1915

Heading: *Wie Kitchener Beweise führt (Kitchener's Kind of Evidence)*

Caption: *„Der Mann behauptet, die Behandlung in Deutschland ist gut gewesen. Sie sehen, meine Herren, man hat den Ärmsten dort so gefoltert, dass er den Verstand verloren hat."* *("The man claims to have been treated well in Germany. You see, gentlemen, the poor man has been tortured so severely that he has lost his mind.")*

Description: Lord Kitchener is turning to two honoraries. On the left there is a soldier with his right arm in a bandage.

Scenario 1: There is no reason to doubt the statement of a soldier, who has been a prisoner of war, that he has been treated well.

Scenario 2: Kitchener claims that the soldier's statement that he has been treated well by the Germans must result from the fact that he has been tortured to insanity.

Explanation: The two scenarios are contrasted. Kitchener construes the absurd case that the soldier has been tortured without any evidence.

Type: Everyday scene represents a communicative situation.

Invective: The British cannot be trusted; they are prepared to forsake rational arguments in order to blame the Germans.

Cartoon 51	25.5.1915

Heading: *Lusitania*

Caption: *„Ist es nicht Wahnsinn, so viele Frauen und Kinder bei einem Munitionstransport mitzunehmen?" – „Im Gegenteil. Wenn dann das Schiff zum Teufel geht, ist wenigstens die ganze Welt auf Deutschland wütend!"* *("Isn't it crazy to have so many women and children on a ship with ammunition?" "On the contrary. When the ship goes to hell, the whole world will blame Germany.")*

Description: In the foreground on the deck of the *Lusitania*, two sailors are talking to each other. Women and children are boarding the ship with luggage in their hands. There are lifeboats in the background.

Scenario 1: The *Lusitania* has ammunition on board and therefore is a military target. Women and children are also on board and are thus in danger.

Scenario 2: The Germans sink the *Lusitania* as a non-military target. The women and children are killed.

Explanation: Civilians must not be aboard a military ship. The cartoonist states that the *Lusitania* was a military target and that the Allies hid this fact to give Germany a bad press. On 7 May 1915, the British liner *Lusitania* carrying almost 2.000 passengers, including US citizens but also 173 tons of ammunition was sunk by a German submarine.

Type: Everyday scene represents a communicative situation.

Invective: The British are callous and do not hesitate to sacrifice women and children. They themselves are to be blamed for the war atrocities they blame on the Germans.

Cartoon 52	25.5.1915

Heading: *Schiffe, die nachts sich begegnen (Ships which Meet at Night.)*

Description: Two British dogs say good bye to each other. When they meet again, they think they are enemies and fight till one of them is lying lifeless on the ground. Then, the other one notices that he has been fighting with his comrade.

Caption under first panel: *„Paß auf, Tommy, wenn es nachher ganz dunkel ist, werden wir den deutschen Hund kriegen!"* *(„Watch out, Tommy. When it is totally dark, we will get the German dog.")*

Type: Metonymic scene represents a communicative situation.

Caption under second panel:	*„Nur nichts sagen – gleich anpacken, wenn du ihn siehst!" ("Not a word– just grab him when you see him. ")*
Type:	Metonymic scene represents a communicative situation.
Caption under third panel:	*„Da – da kommt der Kerl!" ("Watch out – here comes the guy. ")*
Type:	Metonymic scene represents a communicative situation and interacts with the verbal part.
Caption under fourth panel:	*„Bautsch – bumm!" ("Bang – boom")*
Type:	Metonymic scene represents a communicative situation.
Caption under fifth panel:	*„Da – da liegt er! Wenn es nur bald hell wird, daß ich sehen kann, wie ich ihn zugerichtet habe." ("Look – there he is lying on the ground. If only it would be lighter soon, so that I can see what I did to him.")*
Type:	Metonymic scene represents a communicative situation and interacts with the verbal part.
Caption under sixth panel:	*„Ja, Tommy, Tommy, um Gottes willen – Tommy – du bist's?!" ("Oh, Tommy, Tommy, for heaven's sake – Tommy – it is you?!")*
Scenario 1:	Ships make sure that they do not exchange friendly fire.
Scenario 2:	A British ship, which takes another British ship for a German one, attacks it.
Explanation:	The heading indicates that the two dogs, which fight against each other inadvertently, symbolize British ships which exchange friendly fire. Whereas the darkness is responsible for the fact that the dogs do not recognize each other, the parallel to the ships has to be inferred by the reader: British ships flying false flags.
Type:	Metonymic scene represents a communicative situation and interacts with the verbal part.
Invective:	The British are ignorant and naïve. By cheating, they will only cause damage to themselves.

Cartoon 53	1.6.1915
Heading:	*Sie werden nicht alle - Englands Freunde (Not All of them will Become – England's Friends)*
Caption:	*„Wenn auch meine Freunde kaputt gehen, das macht nichts: ich kauf mir einfach neue!" ("Even if my friends hit the dust it doesn't matter: I'll simply buy myself some new ones.")*
Description:	In the foreground, a dead soldier of the Allies is lying on the ground. Behind him another is stooping down with a bleeding nose and a bandaged head. In the background, an Englishman with a pipe is reaching for his wallet in the back pocket of his pants. His left hand touches a globe.
Scenario 1:	Friends should care for one another and friends cannot be bought.
Scenario 2:	The British do not care for their friends and want to buy new ones when the old ones have died for them.
Explanation:	The two scenarios are contrasted.
Type:	Metonymic scene interacts with the verbal part.
Invective:	The British are callous and do not care whether their allies are killed. They are materialists.

Cartoon 54   1.6.1915

Heading:	*Pogrome in London (Pogroms in London)*
	Upper left panel
Caption:	*Sie hat die 'Lusitania' versenkt. (She has sunk the 'Lusitania'.)*
Description:	Five children surround a crying girl in an aggressive manner. Five adults watch this scene without interfering.
Scenario 1:	A child cannot be blamed for sinking a ship.
Scenario 2:	The other children blame this child for sinking the *Lusitania*.
Explanation:	The two scenarios are contrasted.
Type:	Everyday scene represents a communicative situation.
Invective A:	The British are ignorant and stupid, because they tolerate this irrational behavior.
	Upper right panel
Caption:	*Gib mir den Handwagen, Alte, ich kann meine Entrüstung über die Deutschen nicht mehr bemeistern. (Give me the wheelbarrow, old lady. I can't control my indignation towards the Germans.)*
Description:	A man who is pointing at two burglars entering a German shop through a broken window is addressing a woman with a wheelbarrow. A third burglar is leaving the shop with a sack full of loot on his shoulder. A policeman is passively watching the scene
Scenario 1:	Burglars break into shops and steal goods out of greed.
Scenario 2:	This man wants to steal goods from a German shop out of indignation towards the Germans.
Explanation:	The two scenarios are contrasted. The man uses a cheap excuse to steal goods from the German shop.
Type:	Everyday scene interacts with the verbal part.
Invective B:	The British cannot be trusted; they present silly pretexts in order to do damage to the Germans.
	Lower left panel
Caption:	*Englischer Kriegsbericht: In Ost-London wurden die Deutschen entscheidend geschlagen. Unübersehbare Beute blieb in unsern Händen ... (English war report: In East London the Germans were beaten decisively. On a grand scale, the spoils of war remain in our hands ...)*
Description:	Several adults and even two children with stolen goods are walking away from a shop with a broken window.
Scenario 1:	War reports refer to genuine events of the war.
Scenario 2:	This report refers to what is shown in the drawing.
Explanation:	The caption is recontextualized, i.e. it is not a war report but a description of the criminal behavior of British civilians.
Type:	Everyday scene interacts with the verbal part.
Invective C:	The British are cowards; they do damage to German civilians because they are unable to damage the German army.
	Lower right panel
Caption:	*Da sich bei den Londoner Pogromen ein bedauerlicher Dilettantismus einzuschleichen begann, verschrieb sich die englische Regierung einen Austausch-Kosaken zum Unterricht. (The English government has employed a Cossack exchange teacher, because the pogroms in London began to reveal a deplorable amount of amateurishness.)*
Description:	A Russian Cossack is showing an axe and other weapons to a large audience.
Scenario 1:	A civilian society will refrain from pogroms against minorities.
Scenario 2:	The British government invites a Russian Cossack to teach its population how to be cruel against a minority.
Explanation:	The two scenarios are contrasted. The statement *pogroms in London began to reveal a deplorable amount of amateurishness* can only be

72

interpreted as irony, because pogroms are spontaneous and not planned in advance.

Type: Everyday scene interacts with the verbal part.
Invective D: The British are callous and cruel.

Cartoon 55   22.7.1915
Heading: *Englische Diplomatenschule (English School of Diplomacy)*
Caption: *„Meine Herren, die besten Mittel zur Beseitigung lästiger Politiker und Potentaten gibt uns die Bakteriologie an die Hand. Sie sehen hier den Bazillus der Rippenfellentzündung. Seine Übertragung erfolgt am zweckmäßigsten vermittelst eines kräftigen Dolchstichs." ("Gentlemen, bacteriology provides us with the best measures for eliminating vexatious politicians and potentates. Here you see the pleurisy-bacillus. The most efficient way to pass on this disease is to stab someone with a dagger.")*
Description: A skinny looking man in a gown is showing a test tube to a group of elegantly dressed men, who are sitting in armchairs.
Scenario 1:   A politician is eliminated by vote.
Scenario 2:   English diplomats learn that an acceptable and easy way to get rid of a politician is to murder him.
Explanation: The two scenarios are contrasted. The style of the caption is scientific and cold. The drawing is slightly exaggerated.
Type: Everyday scene represents a communicative situation.
Invective: The British are callous and cruel. The British government is systematically teaching callous, cruel and illegal methods to their diplomats.

Simplicissimus cartoon 56

Cartoon 56   22.6.1915

Heading:	*Nur ein Säugling wurde getötet (Only one Baby was Killed)*
Caption:	*„Ein Zeppelin! Säuglinge an die Front!" ("A zeppelin! Babies to the front.")*
Description:	The scene is a view over the Thames with the Tower in the background. An English policeman with a helmet is shouting an order. Long poles are held out of buildings at the end of which there are babies.
Scenario 1:	A nation will take any precaution to protect children and babies from the dangers of war.
Scenario 2:	The British take special precaution to expose their children and babies to the dangers of war.
Explanation:	The British take outrageous measures so that the Germans can be blamed for war atrocities.
Type:	Counterfactual scene interacts with the verbal part.
Invective:	The British are callous, because they do not hesitate to sacrifice innocent babies. They are to be blamed for war atrocities.

Cartoon 57   22.6.1915

Heading:	*Eine Reutermeldung (A News Item from Reuter's)*
Caption:	*In München herrscht panikartige Furcht vor feindlichen Luftangriffen. Alle Keller sind überfüllt. (In Munich there is a panic caused by the fear of enemy air raids. All shelters are overcrowded.)*
Description:	People are sitting in a Munich 'Biergarten' enjoying themselves.
Scenario 1:	People are fleeing in panic and gather in overcrowded air shelters.
Scenario 2:	People are enjoying themselves in a relaxed way drinking beer.
Explanation:	The caption contradicts the drawn scene.
Type:	Everyday scene interacts with the verbal part.
Invective:	The British (try to) mislead the public; but they will not succeed because their lies, i.e. the lies of the British news agency Reuter, are blatantly false.

Cartoon 58   20.7.1915

Heading:	*Das englische Gold (The English Gold)*
Caption:	*„Der Hügel ist noch nicht hoch genug, Vittorio!" ("The hill isn't high enough yet, Vittorio!")*
Description:	A uniformed man with an epée is standing on a pile of corpses reaching for a bag with gold, which is dangling from a crane. John Bull operates the crane.
Scenario 1:	People long or reach for gold.
Scenario 2:	If the target, people long for, is higher than their normal reach, they use a support such as a stool to reach it.
Scenario 3:	John Bull puts the bag with gold higher than Vittorio's reach.
Scenario 4:	Vittorio needs more corpses in order to be able to reach it.
Explanation:	The four scenarios are contrasted. The British reward of an allied country depends on the number of soldiers it has killed.
Type:	Metonymic scene represents a communicative situation.
Invective:	The British are callous, because they exploit the Allies who die for the British gold.

Cartoon 59   7.9.1915

Heading:	*Englands Trost (England's Consolation)*
Caption:	*„Bis jetzt haben wir den Kürzeren gezogen; nun handelt es sich nur noch darum, ihn in die Länge zu ziehen." ("Until now we have been losing; now it is just a question of prolonging this 'fortunate' situation.")*

Description: English soldiers of a higher military rank are sitting round a table.
Scenario 1:   It is not desirable to prolong a military defeat.
Scenario 2:   Members of the British military prefer to prolong their defeat.
Explanation: The two scenarios are contrasted. The wordplay in the caption involves the concept of 'length' in two disparate domains, i.e. fortune and time.
Type: Non-combatant military scene represents a communicative situation.
Invective: The British are militarily inferior, because their military are unambitious and try to cover up their defeat.

Cartoon 60   28.9.1915
Heading: *In London nach einem Zeppelinbesuch (In London after a Visit by a Zeppelin)*
Caption: *„Schreiben Sie: Keinerlei Materialschaden. Drei Kinder tot." ("Write down: No material damage. Three children killed.")*
Description: A reporter is standing in the middle of demolished buildings writing on a pad. A policeman with just his head, chest and one arm sticking out of a sewage pipe points his finger at the pad, thereby dictating to a reporter what to write.
Scenario 1:   The material damage is huge.
Scenario 2:   There are no dead children to be seen.
Explanation: There is an obvious contrast between the demolished buildings in the background and what the policeman orders the reporter to write. The drawing is very distorted.
              Some readers may notice the pictorial metaphor: the policeman replaces the sewage of the pipe.
Type: Counterfactual scene represents a communicative situation.
Invective: The British (try to) mislead the public; therefore they cannot be trusted. Their officials are so desperate that they try to manipulate the reporters in Britain.

Simplicissimus cartoon 61

Cartoon 61   5.10.1915

Heading: *England und die deutschen Störche (England and the German Storks)*

Caption: *Da es England nicht gelungen ist, das deutsche Volk auszuhungern, versucht es jetzt, ihm seine Fortpflanzung zu unterbinden. (Because the plan of starving the Germans failed, the English now try to stop their reproduction.)*

Description: Two English soldiers are carrying a dead stork. In the background, two soldiers are aiming their canon at three storks flying above. One of them has been hit.

Scenario 1: An army tries to hit the enemy militarily.

Scenario 2: The British army tries to shoot storks.

Scenario 3: The Germans are responsible for their procreation themselves.

Scenario 4: Storks are responsible for German procreation.

Explanation: The first two and the second two scenarios are contrasted.

Type: Counterfactual scene interacts with the verbal part.

Invective: The British are ignorant and naive and they are cruel to animals.

Cartoon 62   23.10.1915

Heading: *Um die Wurscht (All or Nothing)*

Caption: *„Ja, meine Herren Verbündeten, jetzt werden Sie sich etwas besser anstrengen müssen - jetzt handelt sich's um meine Lebensinteressen!"*
("Well, Gentlemen of the Allies, now you will have to roll up your sleeves – now this is a case of my own vital interests.")

Description: A well-dressed Englishman sits in a comfortable armchair leaning back. He addresses three injured soldiers of the Allies.

Scenario 1: The British and their Allies should show a sense of solidarity.

Scenario 2: The British are not interested in their Allies, but only in how they can exploit them.

Explanation: The two scenarios are contrasted.

Type: Everyday scene represents a communicative situation.

Invective: The British are callous and selfish.

Cartoon 63   7.12.1915

Heading: *Der Totengräber[1] (The Gravedigger)*

Caption: *„Wenn jedes Jahr nur ein Volk für uns stirbt, können wir es noch vier Jahre aushalten." ("If one nation per year dies for us, we can last for another four years.")*
† 1914 BELGIEN (BELGIUM) (on the tombstone of the finished grave to the left) *SERBIEN (SERBIA) † 1915* (on the new grave to the right)

Description: A gravedigger wearing a military cap is standing in an open grave. His shovel is leaning against a corner of the grave. A second person who also is wearing a military cap is holding the cross for the grave in his left hand and a brush in his right.

Scenario 1: When a person dies, a grave is prepared for the corpse.

Scenario 2: When a nation is defeated a grave is prepared for it.

Scenario 3: The British and their Allies show a sense of solidarity.

Scenario 4: The British are not interested in their Allies, but only in how they can exploit them.

Explanation: The first and second two scenarios are contrasted. Calculating the loss of a friend or an ally in this way is callous.

Type: Metonymic scene represents a communicative situation.

Invective: The British are callous, because they sacrifice the soldiers of the Allies.

---

[1] On November, 5th, Nish, the Serbian war capital was captured by Bulgarians.

Cartoon 64   14.12.1915
Heading: *Englisches Gemüt (English Frame of Mind)*
Caption: *„John soll mir einen Korkzieher bringen!"- „John ist von einer*
                Granate zerrissen, Kapt'n." – „Well, dann bring mir das Stück mit dem
                Korkzieher!" ("Ask John to fetch me a corkscrew!" „John has been
                torn to pieces by a granade, Captain." – "Well, in that case, fetch me
                the piece with the corkscrew! ")
Description: The scenario is a fortified trench. An English corporal is shouting an
                order at a saluting soldier. In the background, a third soldier is
                watching.
Scenario 1:   The soldier, called John, is dead and cannot get the corkscrew.
Scenario 2:   The addressed soldier will get the piece of John's corpse with the
                corkscrew.
Explanation: Opening a bottle is more important for the corporal than the death of
                one of his soldiers and pious behavior towards the dead.
Type: War scene represents a communicative situation.
Invective: The British are callous, because they do not care whether their own
                soldiers are killed; in addition, they have no respect for the dead.

Cartoon 65   14.12.1915
Heading: *Jahresklasse 1917 (Class of (Draftees) 1917)*
Caption: *In Frankreich gärt es. Man möchte jetzt sogar schon wissen, in welches*
                englische Schlachthaus die Kälber geführt werden. (There is an
                upheaval in France. The people have the cheek to demand that they will
                be informed to which English slaughterhouse the calves are brought.)
Description: John Bull dressed like a butcher is standing in the midst of calves. He
                has a knife in his mouth and blood on his apron. The calves look at the
                reader with wide eyes.
Scenario 1:   A butcher leads calves to the slaughterhouse, where they are killed.
Scenario 2:   The British lead young French soldiers to the killing fields.
Scenario 3:   The French are responsible for their soldiers.
Scenario 4:   The British claim this responsibility for themselves.
Explanation: John Bull represents the British nation. He is the butcher who will
                slaughter the calves The calves, which are on their way to the
                slaughterhouse, represent French soldiers.
                The cartoon contains the invective that Great Britain is callous and
                selfish, thus blurring the historical fact that it was not Great Britain
                which initiated the killing of French soldiers on the battle fields for
                selfish reasons but that it sent an expeditionary military force to help
                Belgium and France, when they were attacked by Germany.
Type: Metonymic scene interacts with the verbal part.
Invective: The British are callous, because they take away the rights of the French.
                They thus prove to be undemocratic, egotistic and brutal bullies.

Cartoon 66   4.1.1916
Heading: *Marschall Frenchs Heimkehr (Marshall French Returns Home)*
Caption: *„Großpapa, was hast Du uns aus Berlin mitgebracht?" ("Grandpa,*
                what have you brought us from Berlin?")
Description: A highly decorated British Marshall stands in the midst of his four
                grandchildren. He looks puzzled.
Scenario 1:   The British army and Marshall French have occupied Berlin. Therefore,
                he brought his grandchildren presents from there.
Scenario 2:   The British army and Marshall French have not occupied Berlin.
                Therefore he has not brought his grandchildren any presents from there.
Explanation: The two scenarios (with the presupposition of the grandchildren in the
                first) are contrasted. Sir John French was the Commander-in-Chief of

the British Expeditionary Force (BEF). Some of his military decisions were controversial.

Type: Everyday scene represents a communicative situation.

Invective: The British (try to) mislead the public. But they will not succeed, because even children, who naively believe the false facts, will find out the truth eventually.

Cartoon 67   11.1.1916

Heading: *Überall zu spät (Everywhere too Late)*

Caption: *„Es liegt nicht an uns, die Zeit geht so schnell," sagte Lloyd George ("It's not our fault. Time is passing so fast," said Lloyd George)*

Description: Lloyd George is riding on a snail whipping it forward with a stick.

Scenario 1: People manage their time consciously and are not ruled by it.

Scenario 2: Lloyd George is ruled by time.

Explanation: The two scenarios are contrasted. Lloyd-George's excuse is obviously silly.

Type: Counterfactual scene interacts with the verbal part.

Invective: The British are ignorant and naïve, e.g. Lloyd George is looking for pretexts, which are not convincing.

Cartoon 68   18.1.1916

Heading: *Die Wehrpflicht in England (Compulsory Military Service in England)*

Caption: *„Also so sieht die Bekämpfung des Militarismus aus?" ("So, fighting militarism looks like this?")*

Description: John Bull's arms and legs are fettered; he is held by a man, who looks like a Roman soldier, on a pulley. His bottom almost touches the point of a huge spiked helmet.

Scenario 1: Fighting militarism presupposes being in control.

Scenario 2: John Bull is not in control at all.

Explanation: The two scenarios are contrasted. The point of the cartoon, that the introduction of compulsory military service will not achieve anything, is made pictorially. In addition, there is a face value contradiction, i.e. that militaristic means are adopted to fight militarism.

Type: Metonymic scene interacts with the verbal part.

Invective: The British are militarily inferior; the introduction of compulsory military service will not achieve anything.

Cartoon 69   18.1.1916

Heading: *Englische Klubgenossen 1915 und 1916 (English Club Members in 1915 and 1916)*

Caption under first panel: *„Na, alter Junge, habt ihr in Flandern guten Sport gehabt?" ("Well then, old boy, did you enjoy sports in Flanders?")*

Description: An English general is standing in front of three elegantly dressed men who are relaxing in armchairs.

Caption under second panel: *„Rührt euch, Leute!" ("Stand easy!")*

Description: An English general is standing in front of the same three men, who are now wearing uniform, standing at attention.

Scenario 1: The relationship between the general and the three club members is very relaxed.

Scenario 2: The relationship between the general and the three club members is very formal.

Explanation: The two scenarios are contrasted.

Type: Non-combatant military scene represents a communicative situation.

Invective:	Life is deteriorating in Britain, e.g. the comfortable life of the British aristocracy is ending.

Cartoon 70   1.2.1916
Heading: *Die Unverheirateten in England (Unmarried Men in England)*
Caption: *„Mein Bauch hat mich mehr gekostet als drei Frauen. Es wäre recht und billig, ihn mir wenigstens für eine anzurechnen." ("My belly cost me more than three wives. It would only be fair to regard it as the equivalent of at least one wife.")*
Description: A military official observes a group of nine undressed and undressing men who are waiting for a military examination. The man in the center, who is only wearing trousers, has a huge belly.
Scenario 1:   Being married makes men exempt from compulsory military service in England. How much money a husband spends on his wife is irrelevant.
Scenario 2:   This man wants that the money he has spent on his belly counts as a reason to exempt him from compulsory military service.
Explanation: The two scenarios are contrasted. The first Military Service Act was passed in January 1916. It called for the compulsory enlistment of unmarried men between the ages of 18 and 41.
Type: Non-combatant military scene represents a communicative situation.
Invective: The British are ignorant and naïve.

Cartoon 71   8.2.1916
Heading: *Die verschärfte Blockade (The Tightened Blockade)*
Caption: *„Freund Hunger, du hast dich in Indien und Irland so gut bewährt, jetzt hilf uns auch gegen Deutschland!" – „Bedaure, ich fresse nur englische Untertanen." ("Hunger, old friend, you proved yourself in India and Ireland, now help us to fight against Germany, too." – "I'm sorry but I only eat English citizens.")*
Description: John Bull is standing above the cliffs of Dover. He is touching the skeleton of a tall animal wearing rags. He is pointing in the direction of the Continent. The skeleton is holding an empty basket.
Scenario 1:   In India and Ireland famines have killed many people. John Bull wishes that in Germany many people would starve similarly.
Scenario 2:   The personified *Hunger* predicts that only in England people will starve.
Explanation: The evil wishes of the British are based on wrong analogies.
Type: Metonymic scene represents a communicative situation and interacts with the verbal part.
Invective: The British are ignorant and naïve; they are abominable, because they are evil.

Cartoon 72   15.2.1916
Heading: *Englische Kriegstrauungen (English War Marriage Ceremonies)*
Caption: *„Ich brauche jetzt nicht mehr einzurücken, aber mir scheint, meine Frau rückt aus." ("Now I don't have to go to the army, but it seems that my wife is a deserter.")*
Description: A man in an armchair is observing his wife talking to a member of the military in the background.
Scenario 1:   The husband finds military service so unattractive that he has married in order to avoid it.
Scenario 2:   His wife finds this member of the military so attractive that she leaves her husband.
Explanation: The two scenarios are contrasted.
Type: Everyday scene interacts with the verbal part.

Invective:	Life is deteriorating in Britain. The British are cowards, e.g. the husband wants to avoid military service, but his plans have a counter-productive effect.

Cartoon 73   22.2.1916

Heading:	*Der Greis auf den Orkney Inseln (The Senile Old Man on the Orkneys)*
Caption:	„*Mister Neptun, die Deutschen sind im Atlantic!" – „Ja, ja die Jugend!"* ("*Mr. Neptune the Germans are in the Atlantic!" – "Oh well, these youngsters!"*)
Description:	An aged, devil-like 'merman' with a beard and a trident is lying on a rock surrounded by the sea. A mermaid has swum to the rock and is addressing the 'merman'.
Scenario 1:	The British with their superior marine force are very keen on information about the movement of the enemy.
Scenario 2:	The 'merman' takes no notice of this item of news.
Explanation:	The two scenarios are contrasted. The 'merman' is a metonymy for the British navy.
Type:	Metonymic scene represents a communicative situation.
Invective:	The British are militarily inferior, because their navy is old, weak and tired of fighting against the Germans.

Cartoon 74   29.2.1916

Heading:	*Schutz gegen U-Boote (Protection against Submarines)*
Caption:	„*Wo kommt denn auf einmal der Drahtzaun her?"* – „*Das ist das Gitter hinter dem sich der Beherrscher des Weltmeeres verstecken muss."* ("*Where, in the world, has this fence come from?" – "These are the bars behind which the ruler of the seas has to hide."*)
Description:	A sea creature is looking at a fence in the water behind which an elderly looking mermaid is sitting, resting her head in her hand. In the background, a sunken ship is lying on the bottom of the sea.
Scenario 1:	The ruler of the seas does not fear any other force.
Scenario 2:	The British have established a naïve defensive measure against possible attacks, because part of their fleet has been sunk.
Explanation:	The two scenarios are contrasted.
Type:	Metonymic scene represents a communicative situation and interacts with the verbal part.
Invective:	The British are militarily inferior, i.e. Britain is not the ruler of the seas.

Cartoon 75   7.3.1916

Heading:	*Die Strafe des Einkreisers (The Punishment of the King)*
Caption:	*Eduard VII muss die Seelen der gefallenen Engländer über den Styx rudern. (Edward VII has to ferry the souls of the fallen English soldiers across the Styx.)*
Description:	In the middle of the drawing Edward VII dressed in a Greek tunic is using a pole to drive a boat full of soldiers across a lake. In the foreground, a large group of injured and dejected looking soldiers are in the water; some of them are longingly reaching out their arms toward the boat.
Scenario 1:	Edward VII is the king of England.
Scenario 2:	King Edward VII is transformed into Charon of the Underworld.
Explanation:	The two scenarios are contrasted. In Greek mythology, it was the duty of Charon, the son of Erebus and Nyx (Night), to ferry over the Rivers Styx and Acheron those souls of the deceased who had received the rites of burial. In payment he received the coin that was placed in the mouth of the corpse.

Type:	Metonymic scene interacts with the verbal part.
Invective:	The British are responsible for (the continuation of) the war. Therefore the king of England is responsible for the deaths of many English soldiers.

Cartoon 76   21.3.1916

Heading:	*London in Erwartung der Zeppelingefahr (London Preparing for the Threat of the Zeppelins)*
Caption:	*SCHONEN! HIER WONEN* [sic] *GUTE LEUTE (SPARE THIS HOUSE! GOOD PEOPLE LIVE HERE)* (written on the roof of a house)
Description:	People try to protect their houses from zeppelin attacks by writing on the roofs and placing a baby cart on one of them.
Scenario 1:	People try to protect themselves from zeppelin attacks by resorting to air raid shelters and fortifying their houses.
Scenario 2:	People try to protect their houses by appealing to the compassion of the zeppelin pilots.
Explanation:	The two scenarios are contrasted.
Type:	Everyday scene interacts with the verbal part.
Invective:	The British are ignorant and naïve.

Simplicissimus cartoon 76

Cartoon 77   28.3.1916

Heading:	*Der britische Löwe und Wilson-Androklus (The British Lion and Wilson-Androclus)*
Caption:	
Description:	The American President, Wilson, attends to a crying British Lion with a cap and the point of a spiked helmet stuck in his paw.

81

Scenario 1:	Androclus was spared by a lion, which recognized him as the man who had removed a thorn stuck in his paw some time before.
Scenario 2:	Wilson is about to remove the point of a spiked helmet from the paw of the British Lion.
Explanation:	America is about to help England in the war against Germany. The parallel between Androclus and the lion does not include the gratefulness of the injured lion.
Type:	Metonymic scene interacts with the verbal part.
Invective:	The British are militarily inferior. Therefore they have to seek help from the USA.

Cartoon 78   18.4.1916
Heading: *Golf–Horizont (Golf Horizon)*
Caption: *„Dieser Mister Brown ist ein sehr gebildeter Mann. Er hat seinen Shakespeare im Kopf wie nur irgend ein Deutscher." ("This Mister Brown is a very well educated man. He knows his Shakespeare just like any German.")*

Description:	In the foreground, two women are playing golf on a course with several other players.
Scenario 1:	The British should know Shakespeare better than members of other nations.
Scenario 2:	The Germans know Shakespeare better than the British.
Explanation:	The two scenarios are contrasted.
Type:	Everyday scene represents a communicative situation.
Invective:	The British are ignorant, because the Germans know Shakespeare better than they.

Cartoon 79   25.4.1916
Heading: *Aus gepreßter Seele (From a Dejected Soul)*
Caption: *„Oh, mein Gott, wie konntest Du es zulassen, daß diese Barbaren und nicht wir Engländer die Zeppeline erfunden haben!" ("Oh my God, how could you allow these barbarians to invent zeppelins and not us.")*

Description:	A British priest is standing in the middle of destroyed buildings with his left arm raised, addressing an elderly man, who looks at him in surprise.
Scenario 1:	God allowed the Germans to invent zeppelins and use them in the war for military, i.e. cruel purposes.
Scenario 2:	If God had allowed the British to invent zeppelins, they would also have used them in the war for military, i.e. cruel purposes.
Explanation:	God should only be asked to help in a peace process and not for help in achieving cruel purposes.
Type:	Everyday scene represents a communicative situation.
Invective:	The British cannot be trusted, because they are Christian hypocrites.

Cartoon 80   2.5.1916
Heading: *Englische Eintracht (English Concord)*
Caption: *„Laßt Euren Streit, ihr verheirateten und unverheirateten Gentlemen! Einigen wir uns brüderlich und opfern wir zunächst die sechzehnjährigen Franzosen." ("Stop fighting, you married and unmarried gentlemen. Let us settle our differences in a brotherly manner by sacrificing the sixteen year old French youngsters first.")*

Description: A priest is standing between two men with both his hands raised in a gesture to stop. The two men are wearing boxing gloves. The one on the right is holding up a small baby.

Scenario 1:	In spite of the intervention of the priest, the two men start a fight in order to decide which group will be drafted.
Scenario 2:	Due to the intervention of the priest, the two groups adopt a peaceful way of deciding who will be drafted.
Explanation:	It takes an intervention of the church to avoid discord between the different factions eligible for compulsory military service in England. The first Military Service Act was passed in January 1916. It called for the compulsory enlistment of single men and childless widowers between the ages of 18 and 41. The second Military Service Act was introduced in May 1916. All men regardless of marital status between the ages of 18 and 41 had to enlist. By 1918 compulsory service had been extended to include all men aged 18 to 51. More than 2.3 million conscripts were enlisted before the end of the war.[1]
Type:	Metonymic scene represents a communicative situation.
Invective:	Life is deteriorating in Britain, e.g. there is social discord in England.

Cartoon 81	16.5.1916
Heading:	*Englische Sorgen (English Sorrows)*
Caption:	*„Wie lange soll der Krieg mit Deutschland eigentlich noch dauern? Irland haben wir in 700 Jahren nicht durch Hunger bezwingen können." ("How long is this war against Germany supposed to last? We have not been able to starve Ireland in 700 years.")*
Description:	Lloyd George is sitting with braced arms. A general is standing beside him.
Scenario 1:	In the last 700 years the British were not able to force Ireland to surrender by blockading it.
Scenario 2:	In the last two years the British have not been able to force Germany to surrender by blockading it.
Explanation:	A parallel is drawn between the two scenarios, evoking the prediction that England will never be able to force Germany to surrender.
Type:	Everyday scene represents a communicative situation.
Invective:	The British are militarily inferior, i.e. they are too weak to win the war.

Cartoon 82	20.6.1916
Heading:	*Heimkehr vom Skagerrak (Returning Home from Skaggerak)*
Caption:	*„Mir scheint, den Dreizack habe ich an der dänischen Küste verloren." ("Looks like I lost the trident near the Danish coast.")*
Description:	A human-like sea creature with an British hat and a British flag round his waist is standing in the dark water looking at the reader. Behind him there is a dark sky.
Scenario 1:	If a sea power loses its force, it will remember where it happened and make an effort to reconstruct it.
Scenario 2:	The representative of the British navy does not exactly remember where a part of his fleet was lost.
Explanation:	The two scenarios are contrasted. The British have been defeated and are too dejected to try to restock their fleet.
Type:	Metonymic scene represents a communicative situation and interacts with the verbal part.
Invective:	The British are militarily inferior, e.g. they have been beaten at the sea battle of Jutland.

---

[1] Cf. http://www.spartacus.schoolnet.co.uk/FWWglossary (6/18/2001).

Cartoon 83   20.6.1916

Heading: *Mister Greys Erklärung dafür (Mister Grey's Explanation)*

Caption: *„Englands Bestreben, immer und überall das europäische Gleichgewicht herzustellen, ist unverkennbar. Die ewigen Niederlagen zu Lande mußten endlich einmal durch eine Niederlage zur See aufgehoben werden." ("England's endeavors to create a universal European balance of power is obvious. Losing land battles all the time had to be counterbalanced by a lost sea battle.")*

Description: A chaotic scene of overturned and sinking ships and explosions.

Scenario 1:   It is illogical to claim that a military defeat on land is compensated by a military defeat at sea.

Scenario 2:   The British minister of foreign affairs believes that a military defeat on land is compensated by a military defeat at sea.

Explanation: The two scenarios are contrasted.

Type: War scene interacts with the verbal part.

Invective: The British are ignorant and stupid, e.g. the British minister of foreign affairs is illogical.

Simplicissimus cartoon 84

Cartoon 84   20.6.1916

Heading: *In einem Londoner Restaurant (In a London Restaurant)*

Caption: *„John Bull-Kopf in Skagerrak-Tunke!" ("John Bull's head in Skaggerak gravy!")*

Description: A giant waiter rushes into a dining hall with John Bull's large cooked head on a serving tray. The guests are shocked. Some of them throw their arms in the air and cause chairs and tables to fall over.

Scenario 1:   A normal waiter walks calmly into a dining hall with enjoyable food on a serving tray. The guests wait for their food, then eat and enjoy it quietly.

Scenario 2:   A giant waiter rushes into a dining hall with John Bull's large cooked head on a serving tray. The guests are shocked. Some of them throw their arms in the air and cause chairs and tables to fall over.

Explanation:	The two scenarios are contrasted.
	The population is shocked by the fact that England lost several war ships in the sea battle of Jutland.
Type:	Metonymic scene represents a communicative situation and interacts with the verbal part.
Invective:	The British are militarily inferior.

Cartoon 85   4.7.1916

Heading:	*In englischen Häfen (In English Harbors)*
Caption:	*„Bei unserer Siegesfeier waren nur drei Mann anwesend, die anderen waren in den Docks mit Flicken beschäftigt." ("Our victory celebration was attended by three men only. The others were busy repairing our ships in the docks.")*
Description:	John Bull is talking to another man. Behind them, workers are repairing two huge war ships with major damages.
Scenario 1:	After a sea battle all the sailors will take part at the victory celebration.
Scenario 2:	After the sea battle of Jutland only three English sailors took part at the victory celebration. The others were busy repairing the severe damage to their ships caused by the Germans.
Explanation:	The two scenarios are contrasted.
Type:	War scene represents a communicative situation and interacts with the verbal part.
Invective:	The British are militarily inferior, i.e. their claim that they have won the sea battle of Jutland is false.

Cartoon 86   4.7.1916

Heading:	*Für das britische Museum (For the British Museum)*
Caption:	*„Rufen Sie noch einen letzten Abschiedsgruß an England in das Grammophon hinein! Sie sind der letzte Franzose." ("Say a final farewell to England into the gramophone. You are the last Frenchman.")*
Description:	A French soldier is sitting on the ground with his head down. An Englishman with a checkered suit is standing behind him holding a gramophone in front of his mouth.
Scenario 1:	If a man is dying for another country, that country owes him gratitude and respect.
Scenario 2:	The Englishman tries to exploit the death of the last Frenchman for cynical reasons.
Explanation:	The two scenarios are contrasted.
Type:	Everyday scene represents a communicative situation.
Invective:	The British are callous and cynical.

Cartoon 87   8.8.1916

Heading:	*Die Nationalspende (The National Donation)*
Caption:	*Alle Frauen Englands stricken an einem großen Netz, mit dem der Atlantic gegen Handles-U-Boote abgesperrt werden soll. (All English women are knitting a big net to block the Atlantic against commercial submarines.)*
Description:	Women sitting in a long row are knitting a net.
Scenario 1:	It is not possible to produce a net which would stop submarines.
Scenario 2:	All English women are knitting such a net.
Explanation:	The two scenarios are contrasted.
Type:	Everyday scene interacts with the verbal part.
Invective:	The British (women) are ignorant and naïve, because they believe that they can block submarines with a fishing net.

Cartoon 88   22.8.1916
Heading: *Der englische Neptun im Reuter-Büro (The English Neptune in the Reuter Office)*
Caption: *„Ich möchte die Herren ersuchen, auch weiterhin meine Unfälle mit der bewährten Diskretion zu behandeln." ("I want to ask you gentlemen to kindly treat my future accidents with the same discretion that has proved so useful in the past.")*
Description: The very tall English Neptune with a distorted trident and a bandaged leg is standing in front of an office desk talking to two Reuter reporters. Through a door at the back, a sinking ship is to be seen.
Scenario 1:   The British stick to the truth and admit their losses.
Scenario 2:   The British try to manipulate the press and thereby cover up their losses.
Explanation: The two scenarios are contrasted.
Type: Metonymic scene represents a communicative situation.
Invective: The British mislead the public by manipulating the press.

Cartoon 89   5.9.1916
Heading: *An den Ufern des Ganges (On the Banks of the Ganges)*
Caption: *„Dummer Kerl warum meldest du dich nicht als Freiwilliger? Hier stirbst du elend Hungers - und deine Brüder sterben in Frankreich den schönsten Heldentod." ("You fool! Why don't you volunteer as a soldier? Here you are starving pitifully – and your brothers are dying a great heroic death in France.")*
Description: An Englishman wearing a sun helmet is sitting in a deckchair in front of an emaciated Indian with a turban who is sitting on the floor. There is a second emaciated Indian also sitting on the floor.
Scenario 1:   The emaciated Indian is dying of hunger.
Scenario 2:   The emaciated Indian is killed in fighting for England on the battlefield in France.
Explanation: The Englishman suggests that the way a person dies does not make a difference.
Type: Everyday scene represents a communicative situation.
Invective: The British are callous, because they do not care whether the Indians die of hunger or are all killed in battle. They just try to exploit them.

Cartoon 90   5.9.1916
Heading: *Der Reuter-Kuli (The Reuter-Slave)*
Caption under   *„Das mit dem Handels-U-Boot 'Deutschland' ist ein Bluff, über den*
first panel: *wir nur mitleidig lächeln können. Ganz Deutschland beweint seine von England zertrümmerte Flotte." ("The story of the commercial submarine 'Deutschland' is a bluff, which amuses us mildly. Germany is mourning the fact that its entire fleet has been destroyed by the English navy."*
Description: A reporter is sitting behind his desk. He is writing something with his pen and is smoking a cigarette.
Type: Everyday scene represents a communicative situation.
Caption under   *„Wa - a - as? Die verfluchte 'Deutschland' noch immer nicht*
second panel: *erwischt?" ("Wha - a - at? The cursed 'Deutschland' not yet sunk?")*
Description: He is not writing any more, but has picked up the phone.
Type: Everyday scene represents a communicative situation.
Caption under   *„Na, und wenn schon. Viel wichtiger ist das völlige Versagen der U-*
third panel: *Boote. Die Erdrosselung Deutschlands geht programmgemäß vor sich – " ("So what? Much more important is the fact that the submarines have failed completely. The throttling of Germany is proceeding according to plan – ")*

Description:	He is writing something with his pen.
Type:	Everyday scene represents a communicative situation.
Caption under fourth panel:	*„Sind Sie wahnsinnig oder ich? Wieviel Tonnen haben die Deutschen versenkt? In einer Woche? Unmöglich! Schluß!" ("Are you mad? How many tons did the Germans sink? In a single week? Impossible! No more!")*
Description:	He has picked up the phone again and is now standing behind his desk leaning over it. He is shouting into the receiver.
Type:	Everyday scene represents a communicative situation.
Caption under fifth panel:	*„Vier Kriegsschiffe haben sie uns torpediert? Die 'Deutschland' wohlbehalten zurück? Der Schlag soll sie treffen! - -" ("They torpedoed four warships of our fleet? The 'Deutschland' returned safely? To hell with them! - -")*
Description:	He has sat down again, still shouting with eyes wide open, his left hand behind his ear.
Type:	Everyday scene represents a communicative situation.
Caption under sixth panel:	*„Der Teufel hol' alle Siegesberichte! Stellen Sie das Telefon ab!" ("To hell with all the victory reports! Turn off the phone.")*
Description:	He has got up again, shouting even more intensely, his eyes even wider open, holding the receiver right in front of his face.
Scenario 1:	A reporter states the facts in a war objectively and without any emotional involvement.
Scenario 2:	This Reuter reporter rejects the facts, which cause him to become furious.
Explanation:	The two scenarios are contrasted.
Type:	Everyday scene represents a communicative situation.
Invective:	The British mislead the public by manipulating the press. But they will not succeed, because they cannot ignore the facts.

Cartoon 91	12.9.1916
Heading:	*„Krieg an Deutschland" ("War on Germany")*
Caption:	*„Endlich hat er seine Lektion gelernt. Jetzt kann er wieder was zu fressen kriegen." ("Finally he has learned his lesson. Now he can get something to eat again.")*
Description:	Elegantly dressed John Bull, who is holding a cane in his hand, gives a piece of food to a parrot.
Scenario 1:	The parrot is punished for not being verbally abusive towards Germany.
Scenario 2:	The parrot is rewarded for being verbally abusive towards Germany.
Explanation:	The two scenarios are contrasted.
Type:	Metonymic scene represents a communicative situation.
Invective:	The British hate the Germans.

Cartoon 92	12.9.1916
Heading:	*Nach der neuen großen Offensive (After the Great New Offensive)*
Caption:	*„Wieder ein Kilometer Raumgewinn ... vielleicht erleben unsere Enkel doch noch, daß die Deutschen hinaus geworfen werden." ("Another kilometer of gained territory ... perhaps our grandchildren will see the day when the Germans will be kicked out.")*
Description:	Two English generals are standing in a spacious trench. Behind them are two soldiers.
Scenario 1:	Generals make efficient plans to win a war in the shortest possible time.
Scenario 2:	The British generals accept the fact that the war will last for two generations.
Explanation:	The two scenarios are contrasted.

Type:	War scene represents a communicative situation.
Invective:	The British are militarily inferior. Therefore they have no chance of driving the Germans out of France.

Cartoon 93		31.10.1916
Heading:	*Deutsche Mode im Eismeer (German Fashion in the Arctic Sea)*	
Caption:	„*Was hast denn du da an?*" – „*Das ist ein Periskop – das trägt man jetzt.*" *("What are you wearing?" – "That's a periscope – it's the latest fashion.")*	
Description:	Two whales are swimming in the sea. One of them is swimming upside down with a periscope on its belly.	
Scenario 1:	Whales do not have a sense of fashion.	
Scenario 2:	These whales have adopted a sense of fashion derived from the German submarines.	
Explanation:	The two scenarios are contrasted.	
Type:	Metonymic scene represents a communicative situation and interacts with the verbal part.	
Invective:	The British are militarily inferior. This is proved by the fact that the German submarines can move freely and are ubiquitous.	

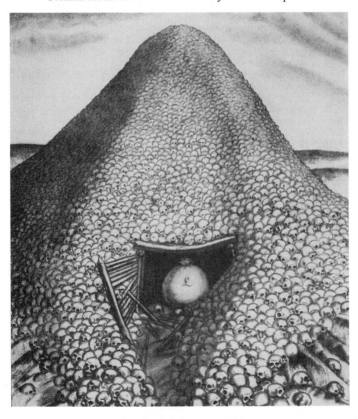

Simplicissimus cartoon 94

Cartoon 94	7.11.1916

Heading: *Der britische Unterstand (The British Shelter)*
Caption:
Description: At the front of a hill of skulls, there is an entrance to a shelter, behind which a large sack is to be seen with the symbol of Pound Sterling on it.
Scenario 1: A shelter is made of earth, mud or clay. It contains people and weapons.
Scenario 2: This British shelter is made of skulls. It just contains a large sack of money.
Explanation: The two scenarios are contrasted.
Type: Metonymic scene interacts with the verbal part.
Invective: The British are abominable, because monetary interests are the major driving force for them in this war.

Cartoon 95	21.11.1916

Heading: *Die Jagd auf U-Deutschland (Hunting German commercial subs)*
Caption: *Seit es unbestreitbar feststeht, daß die deutschen Handelstauchboote unbewaffnet sind, ist die verwegene britische Flotte zu ihrer Vernichtung ausgelaufen. (Since it is an indisputable fact that the German commercial submarines are unarmed the audacious British fleet has left port to destroy them.)*
Description: In the foreground, a duck has its head in the water of the sea, not far from the shore. In the background, there are four war ships moving towards the open sea.
Scenario 1: The commanders of a strong fleet will not be afraid to face any opponent.
Scenario 2: The commanders of the British fleet are afraid and dare only face an opponent, who is unarmed.
Explanation: The two scenarios are contrasted.
Type: War scene interacts with the verbal part.
Invective: The British are cowards.

Cartoon 96	12.12.1916

Heading: *Der Beherrscher der Meere (The Lord of the Seas)*
Caption: *„Merken Sie sich ein für allemal! Wenn Deutsche zu Besuch kommen, bin ich nicht zu Hause." ("Remember once and for all: When Germans call, I'm not at home.")*
Description: An elderly Neptune is lying in bed turning towards a female servant at the door. A bottle and a trident are in front of the bed and under the bed is a bedpan. On the wall over the bed is a painting with sailing ships.
Scenario 1: The commanders of a strong fleet will not be afraid and face any opponent.
Scenario 2: The commander of the British fleet is afraid of the Germans.
Explanation: The two scenarios are contrasted.
Type: Metonymic scene represents a communicative situation.
Invective: The British are cowards.

Cartoon 97	12.12.1916

Heading: *Christmas Carol*
Caption: *Den englischen Friedensabwehrkanonen ist es glücklich gelungen, den Weihnachtsengel wieder zu vertreiben. (Fortunately, the English anti-peace cannons have succeeded in driving away the Christmas Angel.)*
Description: An angel is hovering over the dark nightly silhouette of Tower Bridge

in London. The Thames and its embankment are also visible. The angel has a halo and is holding a small Christmas tree with burning candles. A searchlight illuminates her; five small smoke clouds indicate explosive projectiles directed at her.

Scenario 1: The Christmas Angel of Peace will be awaited quietly and peacefully.

Scenario 2: The British put a spotlight on the Christmas Angel of Peace and shoot at it.

Explanation: The two scenarios are contrasted. On 12 December 1916, Germany and its allies proposed peace.

Type: Metonymic scene interacts with the verbal part.

Invective: The British are responsible for (the continuation of) the war. They are cruel and war mongering.

Cartoon 98   2.1.1917

Heading: *Zur englischen Schlachtbank (To the English Shambles)*

Caption: *„Nur nicht schwach werden im letzten Augenblick!" ("Just don't show any weakness at the last moment?")*

Description: John Bull, dressed like an executioner, drags the fettered French Marianne by the hair up the stairs to the guillotine.

Scenario 1: An executioner leads convicts to the guillotine and kills them.

Scenario 2: England leads the French youth to the killing fields.

Scenario 3: The French government is responsible for their youth.

Scenario 4: England ignores this responsibility (and these rights).

Explanation: The first and the second two scenarios are contrasted. John Bull represents the British. Marianne, who is forced by John Bull to walk up the stairs to the guillotine, represents France and its soldiers. The guillotine represents the killing fields of the war. John Bull's comment is sarcastic.

Type: Metonymic scene represents a communicative situation and interacts with the verbal part.

Invective: The British are callous, because they take away the rights of the French government. They are undemocratic, egotistic and brutal bullies. They just follow their own interests and have no sympathy for the feelings of the French.

Cartoon 99   9.1.1917

Heading: *Lloyd Georges Entdeckung (Lloyd George's Discovery)*

Caption: *„Anfangs hatten wir gemeint, der Krieg sei ein gutes Geschäft ... jetzt merken wir erst, daß wir ihn aus Haß führen." ("At first we thought that war yields a profit ... now we realize that we wage war because of hatred.")*

Scenario 1: Business interests cause the British to wage war.

Scenario 2: Hate causes the British to wage war.

Explanation: There is a naive frankness in expressing this sudden awareness, i.e. in changing the belief scenario.

Type: Everyday scene represents a communicative situation.

Invective: The British are ignorant and naïve. They hate the Germans.

Cartoon 100   9.1.1917

Heading: *Lloyd George und die Friedenslawine (Lloyd George and the Avalanche of Peace)*

Caption: *Wenn der Friede ins Rollen kommt ... (When peace starts rolling ...)*

Description of first panel: Lloyd George is standing at the foot of a snowy hill on the top of which an avalanche is forming. He looks rather disconcerted.

Type: Metonymic scene interacts with the verbal part.

Description of second panel:	The avalanche is half way down the hill. Lloyd George is screaming and throwing his arms in the air, falling backward.
Type:	Metonymic scene interacts with the verbal part.
Description of third panel:	The avalanche has buried Lloyd George. Only his legs, which are pointing upward, are showing.
Scenario 1:	Lloyd George believes that he takes the decisions.
Scenario 2:	There are influences which are stronger than Lloyd George.
Explanation:	The forces of peace are so strong that Lloyd George will not be able to halt them.
Type:	Metonymic scene interacts with the verbal part.
Invective:	The British are responsible for (the continuation of) the war. Peace will be achieved in spite of the British Prime Minister.

Cartoon 101   16.1.1917

Upper panel
Heading:	*Winter 1916 (The Winter of 1916)*
Caption:	*Der Mann, der die Beendigung des Kriegs in London zu empfehlen wagte. (The man who dared to suggest an end to the war in London.)*
Description:	A man with his head and left eye bandaged is lying in a hospital bed. Bottles of medicine are on a table at the side of the bed.
Scenario 1:	A man who suggests an end to the war will be praised and welcome.
Scenario 2:	This man who suggested an end to the war at the end of 1916 was badly beaten up.
Explanation:	The two scenarios are contrasted.
Type:	Everyday scene interacts with the verbal part.
Invective:	The British are responsible for (the continuation of) the war.

Lower panel
Heading:	*Frühjahr 1917 (The Spring of 1917)*
Caption:	*Der Mann der die Fortsetzung des Kriegs in London zu empfehlen wagte. (The man who dared to suggest that the war should continue in London.)*
Description:	A man with his head and both eyes bandaged is lying in a hospital bed. Bottles of medicine are on a table at the side of the bed.
Scenario 1:	A man who suggests an end to the war will be praised and welcome.
Scenario 2:	This man who suggested an end to the war in the spring of 1917 was badly beaten up, suffering even more.
Explanation:	The two scenarios are contrasted.
Type:	Everyday scene interacts with the verbal part.
Invective:	The British are responsible for (the continuation of) the war.

Cartoon 102   16.1.1917
Heading:	*Lloyd George als Historiker (Lloyd George as a Historian)*
Caption:	*„Meine Herren Neutralen beachten Sie die überwältigende Ähnlichkeit des Deutschen mit dem Räuber und Mordbrenner Napoleon, der uns armen Engländern auch schon ans Leben wollte!"* *("Gentlemen of the Neutral Powers, please observe the overwhelming resemblance between this German exemplar and the thief and murderer Napoleon who, in the past, had intended to kill us poor Englishmen.")*
Description:	Lloyd George is pointing at the figure of Napoleon and the German 'Michael'. Napoleon is small and looks discontented and gloomy; the German 'Michael' is tall, he is smoking a pipe and looks contented and peaceful.
Scenario 1:	The two figures show no resemblance at all.

91

Scenario 2:	Lloyd George sees a close resemblance between Napoleon and the German 'Michael'.
Explanation:	Lloyd George's statement and the visible facts are contrasted.
Type:	Everyday scene represents a communicative situation and interacts with the verbal part.
Invective:	The British are ignorant and naïve, e.g. Lloyd George' s sense of judgment is totally disturbed.

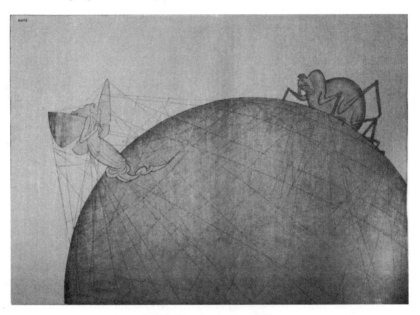

Simplicissimus cartoon 103

Cartoon 103   23.1.1917

Heading: *Der Friedensengel und die Reuterspinne (The Angel of Peace and the Reuter Spider)*

Caption: *Hoffentlich zerreißt der Frühlingsturm das Lügennetz. (Hopefully the spring storm will tear apart this web of lies.)*

Description: A spider with a British hat, symbolizing the news agency Reuter, is about to attack its victim, the Peace Angel, who is caught in the cobwebs. The web spans the whole of the globe.

Scenario 1:   People long and hope for peace.

Scenario 2:   The British news agency Reuter is destroying the hope for peace by producing false news.

Explanation: Spiders are of a sly, ravenous and unrelenting nature. They catch, poison and eat their victims. The news agency Reuter is like a spider attacking its victim, the Angel of Peace, which represents people's hope for peace. The influence of the news agency is worldwide and detrimental.

The cartoon represents a narrative scenario with clear cut roles: the villain is the spider representing the British news agency Reuter, the victim is the Angel of Peace, which summarizes the hopes of all people of good will, and the hero is a natural force, i.e. the spring storm. Thus the achievement of peace is conceptualized metaphorically as an event brought about by a non-human agent.[1]

Type: Metonymic scene interacts with the verbal part.

Invective: The British mislead the public They are responsible for (the continuation of) the war, because they are untruthful.

Cartoon 104   30.1.1917

Heading: *Sorgen in der Hölle (Sorrows in Hell)*

Caption: *„Sei unbesorgt, lieber Kitchener, solange die Entente noch nicht alle Gemeinheiten ausgeführt hat, die der Teufel ersinnen kann, wird sie keinen Frieden machen." ("Don't worry, dear Kitchener, as long as the Entente has not committed all the atrocities the devil can think of it won't make peace.")*

Description: A devil sitting on a chair is holding a small, naked baby over an open flame. In the background, there are two naked men - Edward VII and Kitchener. In the left hand corner of the cartoon, the back of a human head is to be seen. The left ear is being tortured in a vice.

Scenario 1: Politicians hope that a war will be over as soon as possible. They do anything they can to achieve this.

Scenario 2: Kitchener hopes that the war will last as long as possible. He does everything he can to achieve this.

Explanation: The two scenarios are contrasted.

Type: Metonymic scene represents a communicative situation.

Invective: The British are callous and cruel, e.g. the British minister of war is not interested in making peace.

Cartoon 105   30.1.1917

Heading: *Lloyd Georges Traum (Lloyd George's Dream)*

Caption: *Sorgen, Sorgen, Verantwortung (Sorrows, sorrows, responsibility)* (written on the sacks carried by the angels)

Description: In the foreground, Lloyd George is sleeping in a meadow. Behind him there is a ladder from the sky to the ground. On it there are four angels. The bottom angel places a sack with *Verantwortung (responsibility)* written on it into a bag next to Lloyd George. The two at the top each carry a bag with *Sorgen (sorrows)* written on it.

Scenario 1: Lloyd George is unaffected by sorrows and a sense of responsibility for the ongoing war.

Scenario 2: Sorrows and a sense of responsibility cause him to have nightmares.

Explanation: The two scenarios are contrasted.

Type: Metonymic scene interacts with the verbal part.

Invective: Life is deteriorating in Britain, e.g. the war is beginning to worry Lloyd George even in his sleep. The British are responsible for (the continuation of) the war, because they are untruthful.

Cartoon 106   6.2.1917

Heading: *Rule Britannia*

Caption: *Im nördlichen Eismeer hat eines unserer U-Boote ein englisches Schiff torpediert, das noch aus dem Anfang des vorigen Jahrhunderts stammte. Nelsons Flotte lebt also noch! (In the northern Arctic Sea one of our submarines has torpedoed an English ship dating from the beginning of the last century. Nelson's fleet is still alive, after all.)*

Description: There is a surfaced submarine on the calm sea with its spotlight pointing against the horizon. Within the boundary of the light, the white silhouette of a sailing ship is standing out against the dark sky.

---

[1] Cf. Hawkins (2001).

Scenario 1:	The British fleet consists of modern and efficient war ships.
Scenario 2:	The British fleet has outdated ships from the previous century.
Explanation:	The two scenarios are contrasted. The old British ships are easy prey for the German submarines.
Type:	Metonymic scene interacts with the verbal part.
Invective:	The British are militarily inferior, because their fleet is old and therefore inferior to the German submarines.

Cartoon 107	13.2.1917
Heading:	*„ Wir wollen die Deutschen wie die Ratten aus ihren Löchern jagen."* "We Want to Chase the Germans out of their Holes like Rats."
Caption:	*„ O verflucht – so hatten wir es nicht gemeint ... jetzt können wir in unsere Löcher kriechen!"* ("Oh, damn it – that is not what we meant ... now we are the ones to crawl into our holes.")
Description:	An English sea admiral is standing in a small row boat. In his left hand he is holding a rattrap, his right hand is touching his chin. About thirty rats are swimming toward the boat. In the background, the white cliffs of Dover are to be seen.
Scenario 1:	The British fleet will chase the German ships and submarines like rats, so that they will have to hide.
Scenario 2:	The German ships and submarines are chasing the British fleet, so that they have to hide.
Explanation:	The two scenarios are contrasted.
Type:	Everyday scene represents a communicative situation and interacts with the verbal part.
Invective:	The British are militarily inferior. Therefore their arrogance is ill-founded.

Cartoon 108	27.2.1917
Heading:	*Englische Pessimisten (English Pessimists)*
Caption:	*„ Und unsere Dreadnoughts?"* – *„Die werden eingeweckt, bis die deutschen Kanonen unser U-Bootsabwehr-Komitee aufwecken!"* ("And what about our dreadnoughts?" – "They'll be preserved until the Germans wake up our Anti-Submarine-Committee.")
Description:	An English general and an admiral are talking to each other. In the background, there is a large ship.
Scenario 1:	In a war all military sections are equally on alert.
Scenario 2:	The German canons have to awaken the committee of submarine defense.
Explanation:	Dreadnoughts are war ships. There is a word play on the verbs *einwecken* ('to preserve') and *aufwecken* ('to wake up').
Type:	War scene represents a communicative situation.
Invective:	The British are militarily inferior. This is proved by the fact that they, themselves, are skeptical about the very lax attitude of the British military with regard to the German submarine threat.

Cartoon 109	27.2.1917
Heading:	*Wasserkur (Hydropathic Treatment)*
Caption:	*„ Gib Achtung, John Bull – in der Stellung verlierst Du noch die Kriegshitze!"* ("Watch out, John Bull – in this position you might lose your hot martial fighting spirit.")
Description:	A German sailor with a relaxed smile on his face is pushing the head of John Bull under water grabbing him by the scruff of his neck and twisting his right arm. John Bull's face is distorted. In his left arm he is holding a dagger. In the background, there is a huge explosion on a sinking ship.

Scenario 1:	The British marine feels superior to the German one and thus is highly motivated to fight in the war.
Scenario 2:	The German marine is putting pressure on the British fleet, which, thus, is losing its motivation to fight in the war.
Explanation:	The two scenarios are contrasted. There is a verbal-pictorial antonymy between the term *Kriegshitze (hot martial fighting spirit)* and the cool sea water.
Type:	Metonymic scene represents a communicative situation and interacts with the verbal part.
Invective:	The British are militarily inferior. Therefore they should not overestimate themselves.

Cartoon 110 6.3.1917
Heading:	*Britannia auf dem Trockenen (Britannia Stranded)*
Caption:	*Die besten Köpfe Englands denken Tag und Nacht darüber nach, wie sie den Fisch wieder ins Wasser kriegen. (Day and night the best brains of England think about getting the fish back into the water.)*
Description:	A whale is lying on an island, which has the shape of the British island. Around the coast of the island, men are standing and thinking.
Scenario 1:	The British fleet is active.
Scenario 2:	The British fleet is idle.
Explanation:	The two scenarios are contrasted. A whale metonymically represents the British fleet.
Type:	Metonymic scene interacts with the verbal part.
Invective:	The British are militarily inferior. This is proved by the fact that they hesitate to let their fleet leave port.

Cartoon 111 6.3.1917
Upper left panel
Heading:	*Organisation der Landwirtschaft in England (The Organization of Agriculture in England)*
Caption:	*Die Fuchsjagd 1917 ist einigermaßen durch die Ernte behindert. (In 1917 harvesting has encumbered fox hunting considerably)*
Description:	Riders on horseback are riding through cornfields.
Scenario 1:	Harvesting is the foundation of and a prerequisite for human livelihood.
Scenario 2:	Fox hunting is a recreational activity.
Explanation:	In an ironical way, the verbal description turns the priorities upside
Type:	down ironically.
	Everyday scene interacts with the verbal part.
Invective:	The British are ignorant and stupid, because they combine things which should be kept apart, e.g. harvesting and fox hunting.

Upper right panel
Caption:	*Für das große Mäh-Matsch zwischen Mr. Brown und Mr. Smith, welches am 15. Juni stattfinden soll, stehen die Wetten 10:1. (For the great mowing competition between Mr. Brown and Mr. Smith, which is to take place on June 15th, the bets are ten to one.)* *Joe Radly* (written on the box and on the blackboard)
Description:	A very small man with a bag round his neck and a blackboard beside him is standing on a box waiting for a punter to bet on a horse.
Scenario 1:	Harvesting is the foundation of and a prerequisite for human livelihood.
Scenario 2:	Competing and betting are recreational activities.
Explanation:	In an ironical way, the verbal description turns the priorities upside down.
Type:	Everyday scene interacts with the verbal part.

Invective:	The British are ignorant and stupid, because they combine things which should be kept apart, e.g. harvesting and betting.

Lower left panel

Caption:	*Die Kartoffeln werden mittels Golfspiel gewonnen. (The potatoes are harvested by playing golf.)*
Description:	Two men are playing golf on a potatoe field.
Scenario 1:	Harvesting potatoes is hard work.
Scenario 2:	Playing golf is a recreational activity.
Explanation:	The two scenarios are contrasted. Using golf clubs to harvest potatoes is inefficient.
Type:	Everyday scene interacts with the verbal part.
Invective:	The British are ignorant and stupid, because they combine things, which should be kept apart, e.g. harvesting and playing golf.

Lower right panel

Caption:	*Die Bohnenzucht in Sheffield und Glasgow gedeiht vorzüglich; die Wärme der Fabrikschlote zeitigt überwältigende Resultate. (In Sheffield and Glasgow the beans are growing excellently; the heat of the factory chimneys provides superb results.)*
Description:	Beans are growing around tall industial chimneys.
Scenario 1:	Growing beans is an agricultural activity.
Scenario 2:	Chimneys are used in industrial production.
Explanation:	Industrial and agricultural production methods are merged.
Type:	Everyday scene interacts with the verbal part.
Invective:	The British are ignorant and stupid, because they combine things, which should be kept apart, e.g. industry and agriculture.

Cartoon 112	13.3.1917
Heading:	*Englische Angststatistik (English Statistics of Fear)*
Caption:	*„Ich muß euer Schiff notieren ... es ist das zweihunderteinund-siebzigste, das in dieser Woche die Küste angelaufen hat!" ("I have to book your ship ... it's the two hundred and seventy first that has approached the coast this week.")*
Description:	An English policeman is standing on a beach. He is holding a pen and a notebook in his hands. In front of him there is a boy with a small toy sailing boat on a string. Another child next to him has a toy boat under its arm.
Scenario 1:	German troops or spies reaching the British coast by boat are dangerous.
Scenario 2:	Children playing with toy boats on the beach are not dangerous.
Explanation:	Fear and cowardice leads the policeman to misjudge the situation.
Type:	Everyday scene represents a communicative situation.
Invective:	The British are cowards. This is proved by the fact that they are afraid of a German invasion and of German spies.

Cartoon 113	20.3.1917
Heading:	*Englische Neuorientierung (New English Orientation)*
Caption:	*Lloyd George hat die Engländer nicht umsonst eingeladen, sich Tag und Nacht dem neuen Geschäft der Landwirtschaft hinzugeben. (Not in vain has Lloyd George invited the Englishmen to work in the new field of agriculture day and night.)*

Upper panel

Description:	A racehorse with a plow behind it and a jockey on its back is galloping over a field.
Scenario 1:	The plowing scenario.
Scenario 2:	The racing scenario.
Explanation:	There is a blending of the plowing and the racing scenario.

Type:	Counterfactual scene interacts with the verbal part.
Invective:	The British are ignorant and stupid, because their sense of efficiency is deplorable.
	Lower panel
Description:	In the darkness of the night a woman with a burning candle is walking behind a harrow, which is drawn by two horses.
Scenario 1:	Harrowing is done during daylight hours.
Scenario 2:	This woman is harrowing at night.
Explanation:	The two scenarios are contrasted.
Type:	Metonymic scene interacts with the verbal part.
Invective:	The British are ignorant and stupid, because they are agrarian dilettante.

Cartoon 114	10.4.1917
Heading:	*Der Weltbefreier (The Liberator of the World)*
Caption:	
Description:	A giant octopus with a British flag is holding the globe in its tentacles. A German knight is about to chop off its tentacles with a sword.
Scenario 1:	Great Britain is about to rule the whole world.
Scenario 2:	Germany is succeeding in breaking that rule.
Explanation:	The two scenarios are contrasted.
Type:	Metonymic scene interacts with the verbal part.
Invective:	The British are responsible for (the continuation of) the war, because they are tyrannous colonialists. They will be stopped by German valor.

Cartoon 115	17.4.1917
Heading:	*Ums Heiligste (The Fight for what is Most Sacred)*
Caption:	*„Ihn kann ich nicht mehr retten - aber vielleicht das Geld!"* *("I cannot save him – but maybe the money.")*
Description:	John Bull is sitting on the wreckage of a ship, which is about to sink in the rough sea. With his left arm he is clinging to a piece of the mast and with his right arm he is holding up a bag with money (pounds). The American president, Woodrow Wilson is stepping into the water his right arm ready to take the money.
Scenario 1:	Allies make any effort to help each other under any circumstances and are not only interested in each other's money.
Scenario 2:	Wilson and the U.S. do not make a special effort to help the British and are only interested in British money.
Explanation:	The two scenarios are contrasted. Wilson remained neutral until April, 6th 1917, when he declared war on Germany. This tipped the scales in favor of the Allies.
Type:	Metonymic scene interacts with the verbal part.
Invective:	The British are abominable, because money is the only thing they care about.

Cartoon 116	17.4.1917
Heading:	*Die Deutschen im Atlantic (The Germans in the Atlantic)*
Caption:	*„Die Deutschen lassen ihre Seeadler fliegen – wir haben sie im Käfig!"* *("The Germans let their eagles fly – ours remain in the cage.")*
Description:	In the foreground, the British Lion and John Bull with a pipe and a stick are standing on a cliff in the middle of the sea. In the background, a white-tailed eagle with a fish in its claws is flying over the water.
Scenario 1:	The German fleet is moving freely through the seas.
Scenario 2:	The British fleet is restrained to the ports.
Explanation:	The two scenarios are contrasted. The flying of the German eagles has

a metaphorical meaning. Just as white-tailed eagles fly freely over the sea and catch their prey, the German ships and submarines move freely through the Atlantic and destroy vessels of the enemy.

Type: Metonymic scene represents a communicative situation and interacts with the verbal part.

Invective: The British are militarily inferior, because their fleet is inferior to the German one.

Cartoon 117   17.4.1917

Heading: *John Bull, Tod und Teufel, (John Bull, Death and the Devil)*

Caption: *über das Wohl der Menschheit beratend. (discussing the welfare of mankind.)*

Description: John Bull, drawn with tusks, is sitting in a circle with personified *Death* and the devil. The globe of the earth is in the middle. The hand of *Death* is touching it.

Scenario 1: The world as it is now.

Scenario 2: The world ruled by John Bull, *Death* and the devil.

Explanation: John Bull is cooperating with personified *Death* and the devil. Therefore, the future of the world can only be very gloomy.

Type: Metonymic scene interacts with the verbal part.

Invective: The British are abominable, because they are negative, destructive and evil. They follow their interests without any scruples.

Simplicissimus cartoon 117

Cartoon 118   1.5.1917

Heading: *Deutschen-Progrom (Pogromes against the Germans)*

Caption: *„Wir lassen in Amerika alle deutschen Geldschränke aufbrechen. Wenn wir keine Verschwörungsakten finden, finden wir wenigstens Geld." ("We're having all German safes forced open in America. If we do not find any conspirational material, at least we find some money.")*

Description:	In the background, two black safecrackers are at work. In the foreground, a civilian is watching them and a British soldier is standing on guard.
Scenario 1:	Searching for spies is done as efficiently as possible and without any monetary interests.
Scenario 2:	The British just pretend to be searching for German spies in America.
Explanation:	What the British really want is to get at the money of the Germans.
Type:	Everyday scene represents a communicative situation and interacts with the verbal part.
Invective:	The British are abominable, because they are perfidious and deceitful capitalists.

Cartoon 119   8.5.1917
Heading: *Der große 'Durchbruch' (The Great 'Breakthrough')*
Caption: *Dulce et decorum est, pro Britannia mori! (It is sweet and honorable to die for Great Britain!)*
Description: A skeleton with an English soldier's cap is pushing two young French soldiers forward through barbed wire. Their faces are filled with fear.
Scenario 1:   In a war soldiers die for their own county.
Scenario 2:   The British send French soldiers to die on the killing fields of the war.
Explanation: The British act like *Death* personified as a person who selects his victims and leads them to death. They are responsible for the demise of French soldiers.
Type: Metonymic scene interacts with the verbal part.
Invective: The British are callous and cruel, because they do not hesitate to sacrifice French soldiers.

Cartoon 120   8.5.1917
Heading: *Im englischen Kriegslaboratorium (In English War Laboratories)*
Caption: *„Jetzt werden wir mit den deutschen U-Booten fertig – ich habe ein unsichtbares Schiff erfunden!" „Hören Sie auf – wir haben schon eine ganze unsichtbare Flotte!" ("Now we can beat the German submarines – I have invented an invisible ship." "Be quiet – our whole fleet has become invisible.")*
Description: Three scientists are working in a laboratory, filled with all kinds of apparatus.
Scenario 1:   There are no invisible ships.
Scenario 2:   One of the scientists claims that he has invented an invisible ship.
Scenario 3:   The British fleet is invisible because of some invention.
Scenario 4:   The British fleet is invisible, because it has been chased and reduced by the Germans.
Explanation: The first two and the second two scenarios are contrasted.
Type: Everyday scene represents a communicative situation.
Invective: The British are militarily inferior, because their fleet is inferior to the German one.

Cartoon 121   8.5.1917
Heading: *Das Ende der Tanks (The Demise of the Tanks)*
Caption: *„Reuters Erfindungen haben sich besser bewährt!" ("Reuter's inventions were more efficient.")*
Description: In the center of the cartoon, there is a completely devastated tank. One soldier is creeping out of the rubble. Another one is standing in front of the tank.
Scenario 1:   Tanks have been invented as efficient weapons in the war.
Scenario 2:   The British tanks are proving ineffective.
Scenario 3:   News agency should inform and not mislead the public.

Scenario 4:	The inventions of the news agency Reuter have been efficient in misleading the public.
Explanation:	The first two and the second two scenarios are contrasted. On 15 September 1916, tanks were used by the British forces in combat for the first time, at Flers-Courcelette (the Somme).
Type:	War scene represents a communicative situation and interacts with the verbal part.
Invective:	The British are militarily inferior, because their tanks prove to be ineffective.

Cartoon 122   15.5.1917
Heading:	*Wer andern eine Grube gräbt (What Goes around, Comes around.)*
Caption:	*„Wie kann man auf die verbrecherische Idee kommen, ein Volk auszuhungern?" ("How can anybody have such a criminal idea to starve an entire nation.")*
Description:	A skeleton in tatters is sticking a bill on a column. A disconcerted and pompously dressed John Bull is watching it.
Scenario 1:	England tries to starve Germany.
Scenario 2:	Germany tries to starve England.
Explanation:	John Bull fails to understand the principle 'an eye for an eye'.
Type:	Metonymic scene represents a communicative situation and interacts with the verbal part.
Invective:	The British are ignorant, naive and shortsighted.

Cartoon 123   22.5.1917
Heading:	*Die Sorge des Landesvaters (The Worries of the Father of the Country)*
Caption:	*„Lloyd George, wir stehen vor einer ernsten Krise. Haben Sie auch genug Korn in Reserve für meinen Whisky?" ("Lloyd George, we are facing a serious crisis. Do we have enough barley in store for my whisky?")*
Description:	King George VII is sitting on the armrest of his royal armchair with a glass that is partially filled next to him. Lloyd George is standing beside the armchair.
Scenario 1:	A king should not be an alcoholic.
Scenario 2:	This king is an alcoholic.
Explanation:	The two scenarios are contrasted.
Type:	Everyday scene represents a communicative situation.
Invective:	The British are militarily inferior, because they have a king who is more interested in whiskey than anything else.

Cartoon 124   22.5.1917
Heading:	*Britische Rote-Kreuz-Munition (British Red Cross Ammunition)*
Caption:	*„Was? Mit dem Lazarettschiff bist Du in die Luft geflogen?" – „Ja, unsere Medikamente sind explodiert." ("What? Your hospital-ship was blown up?" – "Yes, our medical supplies exploded.")*
Description:	In a heavenly scenario, a deceased sailor meets St. Peter, who is accompanied by two small angels at the door of heaven.
Scenario 1:	On a hospital ship there is only medicine, which cannot explode.
Scenario 2:	On this hospital ship there was not medicine but ammunition, which exploded.
Explanation:	The two scenarios are contrasted. The reader has to infer what happened through the unacceptable collocation of *our medical supplies* and *exploded*.
Type:	Counterfactual scene represents a communicative situation.

Invective:	The British (try to) mislead the public, e.g. they try to cover up the fact that they transport ammunition on hospital ships.

Cartoon 125   22.5.1917
Heading: *Pharao John Bulls Traum (The Dream of Pharao John Bull)*
Caption: *Und die mageren Kähne fraßen die fetten Kähne, und die mageren Ähren machten John Bull nicht mehr fett. (And the lean boats ate the fat boats, and the lean ears stopped fattening John Bull.)*
Description: An emaciated John Bull is sitting on a tiny island with steep cliffs. He is pushing corn ears into his mouth. Around the island, there are surfaced submarines among commercial ships, which are sinking.
Scenario 1:   In the biblical story seven years of affluence are followed by seven years of starvation.
Scenario 2:   The years of affluence in Great Britain are followed by years of starvation.
Explanation: This cartoon entails an allusion to the biblical story of Joseph's dream, in which the lean cows ate the fat ones. Here the German submarines equal the lean cows. They sink the well-filled commercial ships, i.e. the fat cows, which bring goods to Britain. The years of affluence are followed by years of starvation, which John Bull is experiencing now. During the first years of the blockade, one quarter of the commercial ships bound for England were sunk by German submarines. Later these ships moved in convoys and were protected by war ships and could not be intercepted as easily as before.
Type: Metonymic scene interacts with the verbal part.
Invective: The British are militarily inferior. This is proved by the fact that the German blockade is so efficient, that the British are starving. Therefore they will be defeated.

Cartoon 126   5.6.1917
Heading: *Das Ärgste (The Worst)*
Caption: *„Da hoaßt's allaweil: Gott strafe England ... Koa Dünnbier müssen s' do net trink'n!" ("They keep sayin': God punish England ... no diluted beer they don't have to drink!")*
Description: Two well-fed Bavarian men are sitting in a *Biergarten*.
Scenario 1:   The British are still enjoying proper beer.
Scenario 2:   If the curse 'may God punish England' were really effective, the British would be drinking diluted beer as well.
Explanation: For Bavarian men the most severe punishment is to have to drink diluted beer, i.e. to go without proper beer. They do not have their priorities straight.
Type: Everyday scene represents a communicative situation.
Invective: This is self-irony rather than an invective against the British.

Cartoon 127   12.6.1917
Heading: *Englische Landwirtschaft (English Agriculture)*
Caption: *„Verflucht! Das Handwerk scheint mir doch nicht recht zu liegen." ("Damn it! It seems to me that this craft is not my cup of tea.")*
Description: An old sea creature with a British flag on his trousers is standing on a meadow with hay. He is using his trident as a hayfork and is wiping the sweat from his forehead. In the background, there is a horse in front of a carriage full of hay.
Scenario 1:   Everyone knows that a sea creature will find it hard to do agricultural work.
Scenario 2:   The British as a commercial people with a large fleet find it hard to do agricultural work.

Explanation: The two scenarios are contrasted.
Type: Metonymic scene represents a communicative situation and interacts with the verbal part.
Invective: The British are ignorant and stupid because this was to be expected.

Simplicissimus cartoon 127

Cartoon 128   12.6.1917
Heading: *Lloyd George*
Caption: *„Sie wollen uns verschlingen --- das verstieße gegen jedes Naturgesetz!"* *("They want to devour us --- this would violate the laws of nature, indeed!")*
Description: Lloyd George is standing in front of a large map of the world.
Scenario 1: The geographical area of the Middle Powers is a tiny fraction of that of the Entente.
Scenario 2: In nature larger animals devour smaller ones.
Explanation: Lloyd George is giving a counterfactual description.
Type: Everyday scene represents a communicative situation.
Invective: The British (try to) mislead the public, e.g. Lloyd George tells an obvious lie. They are ignorant and naïve to assume that the public will believe such lies.

Cartoon 129   19.6.1917
Heading: *Der britische Seelöwe (The British Sea Lion)*
Caption: *„Goddam – jetzt habe ich mich ganz durchgelegen!"* *("Goddam – now I've developed bedsores.")*

Description:	A sea lion with a British cap is looking at its behind, which is sore. In the background, there is a dune with gulls and the sea.
Scenario 1:	Everyone knows that inactive fleets will rust and deteriorate.
Scenario 2:	The British are surprised that their fleet is rusting and deteriorating.
Explanation:	The two scenarios are contrasted. The sea lion symbolizes the idle British fleet.
Type:	Metonymic scene represents a communicative situation and interacts with the verbal part.
Invective:	The British are ignorant and stupid not to expect this.

Cartoon 130   26.6.1917

Heading:	*Flandern (Flanders)*
Caption:	*Der britische Löwe will sich zum letzten Sprung erheben – aber die deutschen Torpedos sitzen ihm zu schwer im Rücken. (The British Lion wants to prepare his last jump – but the German torpedos are too heavy on his back.)*
Description:	In the foreground, there is the British Lion with two torpedoes in his back. Blood is streaming from the wounds, and he is also vomiting blood. In the background, there is a tall brick wall with spikes on it, and from a pole behind it a German flag is flying.
Scenario 1:	England wants to attack the German defense lines in Flanders.
Scenario 2:	The attacks by the German submarines have been too severe, i.e. they have taken away too much military energy to allow this.
Explanation:	A saying has been translated pictorially.
Type:	Metonymic scene interacts with the verbal part.
Invective:	The British are militarily inferior. This is proved by the fact that the German submarine blockade is very efficient. Therefore Britain will be defeated.

Cartoon 131   3.7.1917

Heading:	*Siegesfanfaren (Fanfares of Victory)*
Caption:	*„So sicher die Sonne morgen aufgeht, so sicher ist mir der Sieg – vorausgesetzt, daß mir jemand aus der Tunke hilft." (" My victory is as certain as the sun rises tomorrow – provided someone helps me out of the stew.")*
Description:	John Bull is sitting in a giant sauce dish, which is placed on a steep white cliff. In the background, there is a light house
Scenario 1:	The sun rises every morning without any condition.
Scenario 2:	England can only win the war if some other country helps it.
Scenario 3:	People like to help other people who are pleasant.
Scenario 4:	John Bull's aggressive facial expression and his gesture do not render it likely that anybody will volunteer to help him.
Explanation:	The first two and the second two scenarios are contrasted.
Type:	Metonymic scene represents a communicative situation.
Invective:	The British are ignorant and stupid. In addition they are arrogant.

Cartoon 132   7.8.1917

Heading:	*Lloyd George*
Caption:	(Written on slips of paper:) *NO DOUBT WE SHALL WANT MORE MEN; THE HUN (three times); IF THE PRUSSIAN TRIUMPHS IT WILL BE BUT THE BEGINNING OF WAR; ENGLAND HAS GONE INTO THE WAR FOR LIBERTY; WE WANT TO PRODUCE AS MUCH SHELL ...; A BIG LOAN WILL HELP TO SAVE EUROPE; THE EMBANKMENT BUILT AGAINST BARBARISM; ENGLAND THE PROTECTOR OF SMALL NATIONS; I FEEL NOW*

CONFIDENT THAT VICTORY IS ASSURED; WE HAVE WITH THE SILVER BULLETS; THE GERMAN POTATO-BREAD SPIRIT; THE TRIUMPH OF PRUSSIA WOULD SWEEP; THE SPIRIT OF POTSDAM; BORROW TO LEND; THE GERMAN MILITARISM; THE EIGHT AGAINST PRUSSIANISM.
Die Munition für dieses Schnellfeuergeschütz wird immer schnell zu beschaffen sein – sie liegt auf der Straße. (It will always be easy to come by the ammunition for this automatic weapon – it is lying in the street.)

Description: There is a large machine with an output device, which consists of Lloyd George's head with his mouth wide open.
Scenario 1: A politician will make intelligent statements which he has thought about deeply.
Scenario 2: Lloyd George churns out slogans from the street without further reflection.
Explanation: The two scenarios are contrasted. There is a blending of a human being, an automatic weapon and a printing machine, which is based on the conceptual metaphor 'WORDS ARE WEAPONS'.
Type: Metonymic scene represents a communicative situation and interacts with the verbal part.
Invective: The British (try to) mislead the public, e.g. Lloyd George churns out masses of meaningless slogans. The British are ignorant and stupid enough to follow him and his government.

Cartoon 133 14.8.1917
Heading: *Ihre Antwort (Their Answer)*
Caption: „*Wir reichen Euch die Hand zum Frieden.*" – „*Erst Hände hoch! Dann Frieden!*" (*"We give you our hands for peace." – "Hands up first! Then peace!"*)
Description: A German soldier is reaching out his hand to a British and a French soldier. The British soldier is looking very indignantly, and the French soldier is pointing the index finger of his right hand at his forehead.
Scenario 1: In a stalemate everybody, including the opponent, will appreciate a move towards peace.
Scenario 2: The British and the French demand surrender by the Germans before any move toward peace.
Explanation: The two scenarios are contrasted.
Type: Everyday scene represents a communicative situation.
Invective: The British cannot be trusted, because they are not genuinely interested in peace, but only in disparaging Germany. The same applies to the French.

Cartoon 134 14.8.1917
Heading: *Wenn der Feind bei uns herrschte (If the Enemy Ruled)*
Caption: *(Daily Chronicle): Die arbeitenden Klassen Deutschlands werden in Zukunft für fremde Regierungen zu arbeiten haben. Verschiedene Gruppen des deutschen Volkes müssen zu Strafe ohne Entgelt Sklavenarbeiten leisten. (The working classes in Germany will have to work for foreign governments. As their punishment several sections of the German population must work as slaves without pay.)*
(Senator Charles Humbert, 'Pariser Journal'): Deutschlands Bergwerke, seine Fabriken, seine Werften werden uns umsonst Schienen, Lokomotiven, Waggons, Maschinen, Schiffe liefern müssen. Als Sklaven werden wir die Rassen von Sklaven behandeln, die davon träumen, die Welt tyrannisch zu beherrschen. (Germany's mines, its factories, its shipyards will have to produce railways, rolling stock,

machines, ships for us free of charge. We will treat as slaves the race of slaves which dreamed of ruling the world as tyrants.)

	First panel
Description:	A farm hand on the left is plowing a field with two oxen. A supervisor with a helmet like that of an English policeman is holding him by the scruff of his neck. Another farm hand is cutting corn with a scythe. Another such supervisor holding a truncheon is standing next to him.
Scenario 1:	As free citizens, the Germans work without oppression from the British.
Scenario 2:	The British oppress the Germans.
Explanation:	The two scenarios are contrasted.
Type:	Counterfactual scene interacts with the verbal part.
	Second panel
Description:	On the right an English policeman is driving a dejected couple with a small child away from their house. On the left a second policeman is leading a cow away.
Scenario 1:	As free citizens, the Germans live in their homes and own their property.
Scenario 2:	The British drive the Germans out of their homes and take away their property.
Explanation:	The two scenarios are contrasted.
Type:	Counterfactual scene interacts with the verbal part.
	Third panel
Description:	On the right, four men are kneeling in front of an elevated armchair or throne, on which an arrogant man is sitting. In the background, a mother with four small children is kneeling down with a baby in her arms. On the left an English policeman is pulling the ear of a kneeling man and takes a big sack of money from him.
Scenario 1:	As free citizens, the Germans live comfortably and can keep their money for themselves.
Scenario 2:	The British subdue the Germans and let them starve; they also take away their money.
Explanation:	The two scenarios are contrasted.
Type:	Counterfactual scene interacts with the verbal part.
	Fourth panel
Description:	In a factory scenario a man with a top hat and a truncheon is holding several hard working men on a leash.
Scenario 1:	As free citizens, the Germans are respected and receive adequate wages for their work.
Scenario 2:	The British do not respect the Germans and take away their wages.
Explanation:	The two scenarios are contrasted.
Type:	Counterfactual scene interacts with the verbal part.
Invective:	The British are callous and cruel. In addition they are domineering and inhumane.

Cartoon 135	28.8.1917
Heading:	*In Flandern (In Flanders)*
Caption:	*Ein englischer Gentleman setzt sich nie mit einem Farbigen an einen Tisch – aber er legt sich mit ihm in ein Grab. (An English gentleman never sits at the table with a colored person – but he lies in the same grave as he.)*
Description:	It is a nighttime scene. The translucent silhouettes of a white English soldier and a black soldier embracing each other are to be seen. They are sitting next to the wooden cross of a graveyard with an English helmet and a raven on it. In the background, there are more crosses,

and on the hilly horizon some crippled trees are standing against the light of a waning moon.

Scenario 1: An English gentleman does not share the table with a colored person.

Scenario 2: An English gentleman shares his grave with a colored person.

Explanation: The inconsistency of the Englishman's behavior is stated in the caption.

Type: Counterfactual scene interacts with the verbal part.

Invective: The British are callous and cruel. In addition they are arrogant racists.

Simplicissimus cartoon 136

Cartoon 136   4.9.1917

Heading: *Aus der Rede des Lloyd Guck in die Luft (From the Speech of Lloyd Head-in-the-air)*

Caption: *„ - - - Passen Sie auf, daß Sie nicht schielen! Richten Sie beide Augen auf den Sieg und lassen Sie kein Auge rechts oder links schweifen! So wollen wir es haben!" (" - - - Make sure you look straight ahead! Focus on the victory and keep your eyes peeled. That's what we like to see.")*

Description: Lloyd George is sitting on the shoulders of John Bull. He is wielding a sword with a wreath of laurels. John Bull is carrying a sack with money and is stepping over the wall of a quay with his gaze turned upward like *Hans Guck in die Luft (Johnny Head-in-the-air)*. In the water three submarines drawn like fish of prey with open mouths and sharp teeth are awaiting the two.

Scenario 1: In Hoffmann's story *Hans Guck in die Luft (Johnny Head-in-the-air)* a boy falls into the water, because he does not watch his step.

Scenario 2: John Bull and Lloyd George are about to fall into the water and become prey of the German 'submarine-fish' because they do not follow Lloyd George's own advice.

Explanation: There is a blending of the *Johnny Head-in-the-air* story space and the political space with some changes added: whereas the three fish in the story are small and just watch the accident which is about to happen

	the three submarine-fish are about to attack. Also the sword with the wreath held by Lloyd George and the sack with money carried by John Bull are added items. The caption contradicts the drawn scenario.
Type:	Metonymic scene interacts with the verbal part.
Invective:	The British are ignorant and stupid, because they do not follow their own advice.

Cartoon 137   11.9.1917

Heading:	*Lloyd George*
Caption under first panel:	*„ Wir haben den Endsieg in der Tasche ("The final victory is ours)*
Type:	Metonymic scene interacts with the verbal part.
Caption under second panel:	*vorausgesetzt natürlich, (provided, of course,)*
Type:	Metonymic scene interacts with the verbal part.
Caption under third panel:	*daß die Tasche kein Loch hat." (the pocket has no hole.")*
Description:	In the first panel, a fully inflated rubber turkey with Lloyd George's head is to be seen, which is reduced to half its size in the second and again to half that size in the last panel.
Scenario 1:	Normally a condition is not attached to a strong conviction.
Scenario 2:	Lloyd George's conviction is void, because the drawing demonstrates that the condition applies.
Explanation:	The inflated rubber turkey with Lloyd George's head is losing air, i.e. it has a hole. The condition which is stated verbally is refuted pictorially. There is a blending of a human being and a turkey.
Type:	Metonymic scene interacts with the verbal part.
Invective:	The British are ignorant and stupid. In addition they are arrogant.

Cartoon 138   18.9.1917

Heading:	*Divisionen des Todes in Flandern (Doomed Regiments in Flanders)*
Caption:	*„Ich muß noch einmal ausrechnen, wieviel schweigende Engländer auf jedes laute Wort des redenden Lloyd George kommen, womit er seine Feinde zerschmettert." ("I have to calculate the ratio of the number of silenced Englishmen and of the loud-mouth words by Lloyd George again; this orator smashes his enemies with words.")*
Description:	Personified *Death* as a skeleton is sitting on top of a destroyed tank. Many dead soldiers are lying on the battlefield.
Scenario 1:	Words do not crush people, weapons do.
Scenario 2:	Lloyd George has very many words and also very many dead soldiers.
Explanation:	There is a word play on *silenced Englishmen* and *loud-mouth words* spoken by Lloyd George. *Death* does not know whether the number of killed British soldiers exceeds the number of loud-mouth words which Lloyd George has uttered in his speeches. This means that the British Prime Minister just talks while more and more of his soldiers are killed.
Type:	Metonymic scene represents a communicative situation.
Invective:	The British are militarily inferior.

Cartoon 139   25.9.1917

Heading:	*Im demokratischen England (In Democratic England)*
Caption:	*„Es soll Länder geben, wo unsereins auf solchen Wiesen grasen darf. Hier gehören sie zum Golfspielen." ("They say there are countries*

where cows like us are allowed to graze the meadows. Here they are reserved to the golf players.")

Description: A cow and her calf are behind a fence, looking over it and watching golf players on a meadow.

Scenario 1: Meadows are used for the grazing of cattle.

Scenario 2: In England meadows are used to play golf on.

Explanation: The two scenarios are contrasted.

Type: Counterfactual scene represents a communicative situation.

Invective: The British are abominable, because they pervert the use of meadows.

Cartoon 140   16.10.1917

Heading: *Freiheit, die Ich meine (The Freedom, I Mean)*

Caption under first panel: *„Dieser Krieg bringt unbedingt die Freiheit und das Selbstbestimmungsrecht der Völker!" ("Undoubtedly, this war will guarantee freedom and provide the nations with their sovereign rights.")*

Description: Some indigenous people carry John Bull in a sedan chair with a canopy. A row of armed African and other indigenous people are saluting him.

Type: Everyday scene represents a communicative situation and interacts with the verbal part.

Caption under second panel: *„Aber das bezog sich doch nur auf die Deutschen!" ("But I was only referring to the Germans!")* (says John Bull)

Description: The indigenous people have disappeared leaving the weapons lying around. John Bull is still sitting in his sedan chair, which has been put on the ground.

Scenario 1: John Bull wants freedom and autonomy for all people. This means that foreign people will not go on fighting a war for the Germans.

Scenario 2: John Bull wants freedom and autonomy for all people. He still wants foreign people to fight for the British.

Explanation: The two scenarios are contrasted. It is an intellectual underachievement to expect a general principle to apply in the way one prefers.

Type: Everyday scene represents a communicative situation and interacts with the verbal part.

Invective: The British are callous and arrogant, because they look down on indigenous people; they are also ignorant and short sighted, because they fail to see that also the indigenous people want their freedom and their sovereign rights.

Cartoon 141   16.10.1917

Heading: *Im englischen Parlament (In the English Parliament)*

Caption: *„Es ist ein Zeichen dieses despotischen und despotisch regierten Landes, daß es den wahren Kulturvölkern seine verrückten Institutionen aufzwingt, Gentlemen! Wir haben hundertsechzig Jahre nach Preußen die Volksschule einführen müssen, wir haben hundert Jahre nach Preußen die Wehrpflicht einführen müssen. Wir werden fünfzig Jahre nach Preußen die Arbeiterversicherung haben. Nieder mit dem despotischen Preußen!" ("A symbol of this despotic and despotically-governed country is that it forces its crazy institutions on the truly civilized nations, gentlemen! One hundred and sixty years after Prussia we had to introduce elementary schools. One hundred years after Prussia we had to introduce the military draft. Fifty years after Prussia we will have introduced unemployment insurance. Down with despotic Prussia!")*

Description: A politician is standing in the Parliament raising his right hand. Behind him another politician is to be seen.

Scenario 1: Prussia has introduced advantageous institutions such as schools, an army and social security. It has not forced these institutions on England; instead England has adopted them in its own interests.

Scenario 2: This politician claims that Prussia has imposed these institutions on England and in addition that these institutions are disadvantageous.

Explanation: The British are so biased against Germany that they fail to see the advantages of Prussian social inventions.

Type: Everyday scene represents a communicative situation.

Invective: The British are ignorant and shortsighted, because they fail to see the progressive nature and the advantages of those Prussian inventions. They cannot be trusted, because they are liars.

Cartoon 142   30.10.1917

Heading: *See-Jägerlatein (Spinning a Yarn)*

Caption: *„- - - Und wie ich mitten auf hoher See bin und gerade den Seelefanten aufs Korn nehmen will - - was soll ich euch sagen - - - da seh ich auf einmal wirklich und wahrhaftig die ganze große englische Flotte angedampft kommen!" ("- - - And as I am at high seas and just as I am getting ready to take aim at the sea elephant - - what should I tell you - - - I suddenly see the whole entire English fleet come storming towards me, truly and surely I did? ")*

Description: In an underwater scenario three sea creatures are sitting around a box used as a table. A fourth female sea creature is standing in the background. One of the sitting sea creatures is talking, the other three are bursting out laughing.

Scenario 1: Talking about a large English fleet is realistic and serious.

Scenario 2: Talking about a large English fleet is unrealistic and hilarious.

Explanation: The two scenarios are contrasted.

Type: Counterfactual scene represents a communicative situation.

Invective: The British are militarily inferior. This is proved by the fact that they avoid an open battle with the German fleet.

Cartoon 143   4.12.1917

Heading: *Der Mannschaftsersatz in England (Recruitment in England)*

Caption: *„Nach Ihnen!" ("After you!")*

Description: A small naked man and a big one are sitting on a bench in front of a military inspection officer.

Scenario 1: It is polite to wait for someone when it is to his advantage.

Scenario 2: It is no advantage to see a military inspection officer first.

Explanation: The two scenarios are contrasted.

Type: Everyday scene represents a communicative situation.

Invective: The British are cowards.

Cartoon 144   4.12.1917

Heading: *Die Tuchknappheit in London Westend (Cloth is Scarce in London's Westend)*

Caption: *Carrying on. Praktische Versuche im sparsamen Kleiderverbrauch. (Carrying on. Practical attempts to be economical in saving cloth.)*
Upper panel

Description: On the left hand side a tailor is showing a piece of cloth behind a counter. He looks normally dressed. On the right hand side he is seen from the side, and it becomes obvious that his upper garment only covers his front side.
Lower panel

Description: On the left hand side an elegant man is seen from the front looking normally dressed. On the right hand side he is seen from the side. He has taken off his coat and is only wearing underwear underneath.

Scenario 1:	The first impression is that of normal clothing.
Scenario 2:	The second impression allows the reader to see the makeshift arrangement.
Explanation:	The two scenarios are contrasted. The British have a naive way of coping with wartime restrictions. They want to uphold the impression of gentlemanliness at all costs.
Type:	Everyday scene represents a communicative situation.
Invective:	The British are militarily inferior.

Cartoon 145   4.12.1917

Heading:	*Die Kartoffelnot in England (The Potato Famine in England)*
Caption:	*„Bitte weitergehen, Frau! Sie können hier nicht sitzen." – „Aber ich bin doch nur der Schwanz einer Kartoffel-Polonäse!" ("Please move on, woman. You cannot sit here." – "But I'm just the end of the line of a potato-polonaise.")*
Description:	At the corner of a building, a policeman is addressing a sitting woman. Around the corner - and not visible to the policeman - the back of another woman is to be seen.
Scenario 1:	The policeman thinks that the woman is sitting there without any reason.
Scenario 2:	The woman builds the end of a line of people waiting to buy potatoes.
Scenario 3:	Several people waiting to buy potatoes form *a line*.
Scenario 4:	This line is called *a polonaise*.
Explanation:	The first and second two scenarios are contrasted.
Type:	Everyday scene represents a communicative situation and interacts with the verbal part.
Invective:	The British are ignorant and naïve, e.g. the British policemen fail to see wartime reality. The British custom of waiting in line is a weird way of behavior.

Cartoon 146   4.12.1917

Heading:	*Englisches Kriegsbrot (English War Bread)*
Caption:	*Panik im Cafe. Ein Gast hat ein zweites Kriegsbrot bestellt, weil es so ausgezeichnet schmeckt. (Panic in a cafe. A guest has ordered a second helping of war bread, because it tastes so good.)*
Description:	In a restaurant a waitress is lying on her back on the floor in front of the table of a guest, who looks a little disconcerted. On the left another guest has jumped up in indignation.
Scenario 1:	Ordering a second helping in a restaurant is normal.
Scenario 2:	Ordering a second helping in a restaurant during this war is a scandal.
Explanation:	The two scenarios are contrasted.
Type:	Everyday scene interacts with the verbal part.
Invective:	The British are ignorant and naïve because they fail to see wartime reality.

Cartoon 147   11.12.1917

Heading:	*Lloyd George der Redestratege (Lloyd George, the Speech Strategist)* First panel
Caption:	*In Paris: „Aber was würden wir sagen, wenn wir 50 Kilometer über die feindlichen Linien hinaus vorgedrungen wären, wenn wir 250,000 Gefangene gemacht und dem Feinde 200 seiner besten Geschütze weggenommen hätten?!" (In Paris: "But what would you say if we had gained 50 kilometers of territory from the enemy's defense lines, taken 250,000 prisoners and stolen 200 of the enemy's best guns?!")*

Description: Lloyd George looks weary. He is resting both hands on a table.
Type: Everyday scene represents a communicative situation.
Second panel
Caption: *„Nieder mit Lloyd George! Er spricht die Wahrheit! Er spricht wie ein Deutscher!" ("Down with Lloyd George! He is telling the truth! He talks like a German!")*
Description: He has pushed his hands into his pockets. Behind him a crowd of indignant men is protesting, wielding sticks.
Type: Everyday scene represents a communicative situation.
Third panel
Caption: *In London: „Jetzt habe ich keine Furcht mehr vor den U-Booten. Ich unterstütze jeden Plan, der uns auf dem Meer weiter hilft zu einem wirklichen Sieg, einem überwältigenden Sieg, der der Welt Frieden und Wohlfahrt bringen wird." (In London: "Now I am not afraid of the submarines any more. I support every plan that helps us gain a true victory, an overwhelming victory at sea, which will bring the world peace and prosperity.")*
Description: He is raising both arms, shouting something with closed eyes.
Type: Everyday scene represents a communicative situation.
Fourth panel
Caption: *„Hoch, Lloyd George! Er spricht wieder wie ein echter Engländer!" ("Long live Lloyd George! He talks like a real Englishman.")*
Description: He is posing pride. The crowd of men is applauding him.
Scenario 1:   When Lloyd George makes realistic statements in Paris, people protest.
Scenario 2:   When Lloyd George makes unrealistic statements in London, people applaud.
Explanation: The two scenarios are contrasted. People want to hear what they want to believe and Lloyd George acts accordingly.
Type: Everyday scene represents a communicative situation.
Invective: The British (try to) mislead the public, e.g. Lloyd George adapts his speeches to what people want to hear and not to reality.

Cartoon 148   18.12.1917
Heading: *Cant*
Caption: *„Ein schrecklicher Krieg, Reverend!" – „Yes, grauenvoll – in den Schützengräben wird am Sonntag gearbeitet!" ("A terrible war, Reverend!" – "Yes, horrible – they are working in the trenches on Sundays.")*
Description: An elegantly dressed woman is talking to a priest. In the background, there is an elegantly dressed gentleman.
Scenario 1:   Priests find war abominable, because people get killed and wounded.
Scenario 2:   The British priest finds war abominable, because the soldiers fight also on Sundays.
Explanation: The two scenarios are contrasted.
Type: Everyday scene represents a communicative situation.
Invective: The British cannot be trusted. Their priests are callous and bigoted Christians.

Cartoon 149   25.12.1917
Heading: *Der Friedensengel und John Bull oder: der Kuß unter dem Mistelzweig (The Angel of Peace and John Bull or: Kissing under the Mistletoe)*
Caption: *„Vielleicht nach dem nächsten Cambrai ---- ?!" ("Perhaps after the next Cambrai ---- ?!")*
Description: The Angel of Peace is trying to kiss John Bull who is sitting in an armchair under the mistletoe. He is raising his arms in defense.
Scenario 1:   The British agree to end the war now.

Scenario 2:	The British only agree to peace after another defeat like the one in Cambrai.
Explanation:	The two scenarios are contrasted.
Type:	Metonymic scene represents a communicative situation and interacts with the verbal part.
Invective:	The British are responsible for (the continuation of) the war; they are shortsighted warmongers.

Cartoon 150   1.1.1918

Heading:	*Englische Bilanz (English Death Count)*
Caption:	*oder John Bulls Alpdrücken (or John Bull's nightmares)* (Title of the book:) *Hauptbuch 1917 (General military ledger of 1917)*
Description:	John Bull is sleeping in his bed. He has a sorrowful expression on his face. A huge military ledger is lying on his belly. Blood is ouzing out from the bottom of the book.
Scenario 1:	John Bull is sleeping peacefully.
Scenario 2:	John Bull is having nightmares because of the wartime losses.
Explanation:	The two scenarios are contrasted. The moral obligation emanating from the heavy British losses is emphasized.
Type:	Metonymic scene interacts with the verbal part.
Invective:	The British are responsible for (the continuation of) the war. They are callous and irresponsible, because in spite of the wartime losses, they do not seek peace.

Cartoon 151   1.1.1918

Heading:	*Sein oder Nichtsein (To be or not to be)*
Caption:	*„Je mehr sie wagen, desto weniger wiege ich!" ("The more they risk, the less I weigh.")*
Description:	John Bull is standing on a scale on a small rock in the middle of the sea with his hat in his hand. The rock is surrounded by seven submarines, which look like aggressive fish.
Scenario 1:	The British suffer from the war, because they do not make peace.
Scenario 2:	If they gave in or made peace, their food supplies would return to normal.
Explanation:	The German submarine blockade has a detrimental effect on British food supplies.
Type:	Metonymic scene represents a communicative situation and interacts with the verbal part.
Invective:	The British are militarily inferior.

Cartoon 152   8.1.1918

Heading:	*Silvester-Bleigießen (Pouring Molten Lead into a Bowl of Water on New Year's Eve)* Upper panel
Caption:	*„Sieg! Ein herrlich wundervoll schöner amerikanischer Truppentransportdampfer!" ("Victory! A lovely, wonderful, nice American troop carrier!")*
Description:	An exuberant Lloyd George is showing two rejoicing allies a piece of lead in the form of a submarine which he has taken from a bowl on a table.
Type:	Metonymic scene represents a communicative situation and interacts with the verbal part. Lower panel with the verbal part. Lower panel
Caption:	*„ --- eigentlich noch etwas schöner wäre er, wenn er nicht den*

häßlichen periskopähnlichen Auswuchs hätte." (" --- actually, it would be even nicer if it did not have this ugly periscope-like deformity.")

Description: A disappointed Lloyd George is showing two dejected looking allies the same piece of lead.

Scenario 1:   The piece of lead has the form of an American war ship.

Scenario 2:   The piece of lead has the form of a German submarine.

Explanation: The two scenarios are contrasted. There is a German tradition of pouring molten lead into a bowl of water on New Year's Eve. The shape of the solidified lead is interpreted with regard to what might happen to the pourer in the New Year.

Type: Metonymic scene represents a communicative situation and interacts with the verbal part.

Invective: The British are militarily inferior. They and their allies are prone to wishful thinking.

Simplicissimus cartoon 152

Cartoon 153   29.1.1918

Heading: *Realpolitiker und Ideologe (A Realpolitiker and Ideologist)*

Caption: *„Ich würde Ihnen für Ihre Verdienste gern eine Professur in Oxford verschaffen, aber Sie nützen uns mehr, wenn Sie in Deutschland bleiben." ("Because of your merits, I would love to get you a professorship in Oxford, but you are more useful to us, if you stay in Germany.")*

Description: Lloyd George is putting a wreath of honor around a man with a sheep's head on his shoulders.

Scenario 1:   German professors serve Germany to the best of their abilities and are appreciated for this.

Scenario 2:   Lloyd George appreciates German professors, because they serve the interests of Great Britain.

Explanation: The two scenarios are contrasted. The cartoon alludes to the fact that some German intellectuals assessed the war efforts of Germany very critically.

Type: Metonymic scene represents a communicative situation and interacts with the verbal part.

Invective: The British are abominable, because they exploit German professors. German professors are ignorant and stupid.

Cartoon 154   5.2.1918

Heading: *Lloyd Geroge macht Schule (Lloyd George Becomes Fashionable)*

Caption: *„Ich habe das Selbstbestimmungsrecht des Portemonnaies* *proklamiert!" ("I have proclaimed the right of self-determination of the wallet.")*

Description:	A British policeman apprehends a thief, who is about to steal a man's wallet.
Scenario 1:	The right of self-determination belongs to people.
Scenario 2:	There is no 'right of self-determination of the wallet'.
Explanation:	The thief uses 'the right of self-determination of the wallet' as a pretext to steal from people. This is a blending of the political and the criminal domain.
Type:	Everyday scene represents a communicative situation.
Invective:	The British are abominable, because they manipulate other nations to their disadvantage.

Cartoon 155   12.3.1918

Heading:	*Lloyd Georges Reden (Lloyd Georges Speeches)*
Caption:	*oder das wackelnde Fundament (or the shaky foundation)*
Description:	Lloyd George is trying to keep his balance standing on a pile of 15 books. In the background, there are five sinking ships.
Scenario 1:	Lloyd George is standing on firm ground.
Scenario 2:	Lloyd George is standing on shaky ground.
Explanation:	Lloyd George's speeches are contrary to the reality of the war and therefore mean shaky ground.
Type:	Metonymic scene interacts with the verbal part.
Invective:	The British (try to) mislead the public, e.g. Lloyd George deludes people with his speeches.

Cartoon 156   14.5.1918

Heading:	*Zeebrügge oder ein neues Mittel gegen den U-Boot-Krieg (Zeebrugge or a New Measure against the Submarines)*
Caption:	*„Wir wollen den Deutschen zuvorkommen – wir versenken unsere Schiffe selbst!" ("We want to beat the Germans to it – we sink our ships ourselves.")*
Description:	Two sailors are holding a sea creature by the arms and legs overboard. They are about to drop it into the sea. It has a stone tied to its neck. In the background, a British officer is watching the scene.
Scenario 1:	The British marine musters all its strength to fight against the Germans.
Scenario 2:	The British marine give up the fight against the Germans and sink their own ships.
Explanation:	The two scenarios are contrasted. On 22nd April 1918, the British planned to put a blockade across the entrance of the harbor of Zeebrugge where several German submarines were stationed. They wanted to stop them from getting in and out. They sent three blockships into the canal, which were ordered to sink themselves. Only two of them succeeded in doing so at the planned location. The third was sunk by the Germans before it reached its destination. But the entrance was not sufficiently blocked so that the plan failed.
Type:	Metonymic scene represents a communicative situation and interacts with the verbal part.
Invective:	The British are militarily inferior to the German submarines.

Cartoon 157   28.5.1918

Heading:	*Englische Gerücht-Offensive (The English Rumor Offensive)*
Caption:	*Die Soldaten werden weniger – die Lügen mehr. (The soldiers decrease – the lies increase.)*
Description:	A man with a British hat standing at the seafront is releasing a large

number of bats from a box. The bats fly over the sea towards the reader.

Scenario 1:	John Bull releases a large number of bats.
Scenario 2:	The British (authorities) produce a large number of lies.
Explanation:	There is a blending of releasing bats and spreading lies. For many people bats are aggressive and bloodthirsty creatures. British (authorities) have to produce a large number of lies in order to compensate for the loss of soldiers.
Type:	Metonymic scene interacts with the verbal part.
Invective:	The British (try to) mislead the public. The British (authorities) spread lies. They are militarily inferior.

Cartoon 158   28.5.1918

Heading:	*Die neuen englischen Dum-Dum-Geschosse (The New English Dum-dum Projectiles)*
Caption:	*,,Wir stopfen Blätter aus der Bibel in unsere Geschosse - So verbreiten wir das Wort Gottes unter den Barbaren." ("We stuff pages from the Bible into our projectiles – That's how we spread the word of God among the barbarians.")*
Description:	An English priest is standing in the middle of a group of women clasping his hands. They look critical.
Scenario 1:	Spreading the gospel by preaching saves the souls of the converts.
Scenario 2:	Shooting potential converts with bullets which contain texts from the gospel kills them.
Explanation:	Salvation cannot be achieved by killing someone.
Type:	Everyday scene represents a communicative situation.
Invective:	The British cannot be trusted, because they are Christian hypocrites.

Cartoon 159   2.7.1918

Heading:	*Der Lohn der Iren (The Reward for the Irish)*
Caption:	*England hat den Irländern, die sich freiwillig melden, ein Stück Land versprochen (England has promised Irishmen who enlist voluntarily a piece of land.)*
Description:	A gravedigger wearing a military cap is sitting next to an open grave in the middle of a very large graveyard. He is smoking a pipe. Every graveyard has a cross on it.
Scenario 1:	An Irish soldier fighting for England will receive a piece of land, e.g. a field, as a reward.
Scenario 2:	An Irish soldier fighting for England will receive a piece of land, i.e. a grave, as a reward.
Explanation:	The phrase *ein Stück Land* is ambiguous, meaning either a patch of land or a grave. The crosses around the open grave indicate that it is a very large graveyard. Thus the meaning is disambiguated pictorially.
Type:	Everyday scene interacts with the verbal part.
Invective:	The British are callous; they mislead and exploit the soldiers of the Allies.

Cartoon 160   9.7.1918

Heading:	*Bundesgenossen unter sich oder der englische Schutzmann in Paris (Allies amongst themselves or the English Police Officer in Paris)*
Caption:	*,,Sie dürfen vor den Deutschen nicht davonlaufen!" – ,,Ah so, das darf nur der englische Frontsoldat?" ("You must not run away from the Germans!" – "I see, only the English soldier on the front line is allowed to do so?")*
Description:	The drawing is crude. In a town an English policeman is trying to stop

115

	fearful French civilian pedestrians who are fleeing from an explosion in the background. They are carrying luggage in both hands.
Scenario 1:	An official tries to stop French civilians fleeing from a military attack.
Scenario 2:	No one tries to stop English soldiers fleeing from an attack.
Explanation:	English officials try to apply rules of bravery to the civilian population in France, which they do not apply to their own soldiers.
Type:	Everyday scene represents a communicative situation.
Invective:	The British are cowards; their rules are partial and egotistic.

Cartoon 161	15.10.1918
Heading:	*Englischer Siegestaumel (English Flush of Victory)*
Caption:	„*Küsse mich Jumbo – die Kultur triumphiert!*" *("Kiss me Jumbo – culture triumphs.")*
Description:	A Scottish soldier with a kilt and a pipe is dancing with a black warrior with a spear and a shield.
Scenario 1:	A civilized way of celebrating a victory means that the cultures stay separate.
Scenario 2:	The British celebrate a victory by mixing cultures.
Explanation:	There is an underlying ethnic discrimination against blacks.
Type:	Everyday scene represents a communicative situation and interacts with the verbal part.
Invective:	The British are abominable, because they have no culture.

Cartoon 162	22.10.1918
Heading:	*Der deutsche Gent (The German Gentleman)*
	First panel
Caption:	„*Na, und wenn Sie schon kämen, dann würde man endlich mal Gelegenheit haben, mit einem echten Engländer Football zu spielen.*" *("So what if they came; then we would finally have the chance to play football with a genuine Englishman.")*
Description:	Two German gentlemen are sitting next to each other in armchairs.
Type:	Everyday scene represents a communicative situation.
	Second panel
Caption:	„*Oder der echte Engländer mit ihm?*" *("Or the genuine Englishman with him?")*
Description:	An English soldier with a pipe is kicking one of the Germans in the back. The other has an insurgent look on his face.
Scenario 1:	There is solidarity between Germans with regard to their attitudes of superiority towards Englishmen.
Scenario 2:	The second speaker undermines this solidarity and casts doubt on the feelings of superiority.
Explanation:	The two scenarios are contrasted. The arrogance of the self-satisfied German is undermined by what happens in the second panel.
Type:	Everyday scene represents a communicative situation.
Invective:	The cartoon contains German self-irony but no invective against the British.

Cartoon 163	22.10.1918
Heading:	*Cambrai*
Caption:	„*Kein Stein darf auf dem anderen bleiben – das gibt prächtiges Hetzmaterial gegen den deutschen Frieden!*" *("No stone must remain untouched – this will be great propaganda material against the German peace.")*
Description:	A giant John Bull is having an angry fit on the small town of Cambrai on which he is trampling with the intention of destroying it.
Scenario 1:	The party that causes the destruction of a town must be blamed.

Scenario 2:	The British who have caused the destruction of Cambrai want the Germans to be blamed for it.
Explanation:	The two scenarios are contrasted. The British caused some damage to Cambrai when they attacked the German military in the town. The cartoon renders the impression that the attack was directed against the French town itself in order to achieve a negative propaganda effect against the Germans.
	Cambrai became famous because the first great tank battle took place there. But the tanks and the armored vehicles did not play a decisive role in the war.
Type:	Metonymic scene represents a communicative situation and interacts with the verbal part.
Invective:	The British mislead the public by using propaganda tricks. They are warmongers and thus responsible for (the continuation of) the war.

Simplicissimus cartoon 163

3.4 *Punch* cartoons

Cartoon 1	19.8.1914
Heading:	*A Quick Change of Front.*
Description:	A single panel with the heading at the bottom has been vertically divided into two equal sections, in which the same shop is shown in a 'before-and-after' presentation. On the left it has German goods and on the right it has English goods.
	Left part
Caption:	*JOHANN SCHMIDT* (name of shop); *SAUERKRAUT* (over the

entrance door); *FRANKFURT SAUSAGES - WESTPHALIAN HAM – HOCK - STRASSBURG PIE - LIMBURGER CHEESE - VIENNA BREAD* (on the goods); *DELIKATESSEN* (on the shop window).

Description: The shopkeeper with a dachshund at his feet is standing in the door smoking a German pipe.

Type: Everyday scene interacts with the verbal part.

Right part

Caption: *JOHN SMITH* (name of shop); *PICKLES* (over the entrance door); *CAMBRIDGE SAUSAGES - YORK HAM - GINGER BEER - LEMONADE - MELTON MOWBRYA PIE - STILTON CHEESE - FARMHOUSE BREAD* (on the goods); *ENGLISH DELICACIES* (on the shop window).

Description: The shopkeeper with a small beagle at his feet is standing in the door smoking a cigarette.

Scenario 1: Individuals retain their identities irrespective of outer circumstances.

Scenario 2: This shopkeeper changes his identity because the Germans have become war enemies of the British.

Explanation: The two scenarios are contrasted. - In 1915 shops of German shop owners were looted and wrecked in London and other places. This occurred particularly after the sinking of the *Lusitania* and after air raids by the Germans.

Type: Everyday scene interacts with the verbal part.

Invective: The Germans are abominable, e.g. the German shopkeeper has a weak and fickle character.

Punch cartoon 1

Cartoon 2   19.8.1914

Heading: *"It's an Ill Wind ..."*

Caption: *Old cock grouse: "I see they've all gone shooting eagles."*
WAR SPECIAL (newspaper heading)

Description: Five grouse are sitting in the grass. The largest bird wears glasses and is reading a newspaper.

Scenario 1:	Grouse cannot communicate about how they are hunted, e.g. by reading newspapers.
Scenario 2:	These grouse do and they are happy that their potential hunters are busy fighting the Germans.
Explanation:	There is a pun on the expression *shooting eagles*, which here is not taken literally but in its figurative meaning. The eagle symbolizes Germany and its people. Therefore in this context 'eagles' refers to German soldiers fighting against the British. This pun is used pejoratively, i.e. fighting against German soldiers is conceptualized as a one-sided activity like hunting birds.
Type:	Metonymic scene represents a communicative situation and interacts with the verbal part.
Invective:	The Germans are militarily inferior. Therefore even a grouse can look down on them.

Cartoon 3	26.8.1914
Heading:	
Caption:	*TO PARIS AS THE CROW FLIES 150 MILES* (on signpost)
	German bird: "I see it doesn't say anything about eagles."
Description:	An eagle with a lowered head and raised wings and a spiked helmet is sitting on a signpost looking at the sign.
Scenario 1:	Eagles cannot read.
Scenario 2:	This eagle can read.
Scenario 3:	The meaning of the phrase *as the crow flies* is independent of the type of bird.
Scenario 4:	This German Eagle does not understand the correct meaning of the phrase.
Explanation:	The German Eagle with a spiked helmet represents the German military. The first two and the second two scenarios are contrasted.
	There is a background assumption that it is not the business of Germans to be in Paris or France.
Type:	Metonymic scene represents a communicative situation and interacts with the verbal part.
Invective:	The Germans are ignorant and stupid, because they do not understand the figurative meaning of an expression.

Cartoon 4	26.8.1914
Heading:	*The Triumph of 'Culture'.*
Caption:	
Description:	A German soldier with a German flag in his left hand and a smoking revolver in his right is standing over a dead family (husband, wife and a small girl).
Scenario 1:	A triumph of culture is an achievement to the advantage of mankind.
Scenario 2:	What has been achieved here is murder of civilians.
Explanation:	The phrase is used ironically.
Type:	War scene interacts with the verbal part.
Invective:	The Germans are callous and cruel, because they commit war atrocities.

Cartoon 5	2.9. 1914
Heading:	
Caption:	*WARNING* ... (sign on a wall)
	("Special constables who can speak German are particularly required." - Daily paper.)
	Special constable (having cornered his man): "Sprechen Sie Deutsch?"
	Suspect: "Nein! Nein!"
Description:	A prototypical stout German is lying with his back on the ground

raising his arms. A sportsman-like young man, i.e. a special constable, is sitting on top of him holding him by the neck and wielding a truncheon. In the background another special constable is running towards the scene of the arrest.

Scenario 1: If someone who pretends not to be German is asked whether he can speak German, he will not understand the question and thus cannot answer 'Nein! Nein!' in German.

Scenario 2: This German spy understands the German question and answers it in German.

Scenario 3: A spy should be able to assess such situations and act accordingly.

Scenario 4: This German spy does not.

Explanation: This German spy gives away his national identity because of his silliness. There was a mania about (German) spies in Britain which was "egged on by crude journalism like 'The Kaiser's Eyes' in the Daily Express for 29 September 1914."[1]

Type: Everyday scene represents a communicative situation and interacts with the verbal part.

Invective: The Germans are ignorant and stupid, e.g. this German spy acts in a particularly unintelligent way.

Cartoon 6   2.9. 1914

Heading:

Caption: *Ethel (in apprehensive whisper which easily reaches her German governess, to whom she is deeply attached): "Mother, shall we have to kill Fräulein?"*

Description: In a spacious dining room, a young mother is sitting around the table with her two young children, a son and a daughter. The girl is leaning over toward her mother. In the background the German governess is preparing some plates.

Scenario 1: Children do not normally conceptualize killing a member of the household.

Scenario 2: This girl does.

Scenario 3: If England is at war with Germany, it does not mean that English people are at war with Germans who work for them in England.

Scenario 4: This girl holds this assumption.

Explanation: The first two and the second two scenarios are contrasted.

Type: Everyday scene represents a communicative situation and interacts with the verbal part.

Invective: neutral

Cartoon 7   2.9. 1914

Heading: *For Neutral Consumption.*
Left part

Caption: *German diplomacy* (written on the piglet)

Description: A stout German official with small round glasses and a moustache is pushing a squeaking piglet into a mincing-machine.

Type: Metonymic scene interacts with the verbal part.
Right part

Caption:

Description: Uncle Sam looks with disgust at the sausages the spout of the machine is churning out. He has raised his right arm and with his left hand is clutching his mouth.

Scenario 1: Political diplomacy should be smooth and acceptable.

Scenario 2: German diplomacy is murderous and disgusting.

---

[1] Wilson (1986: 160).

120

Explanation:	The Americans find the result of German diplomacy disgusting.
Type:	Metonymic scene interacts with the verbal part.
Invective:	The Germans are abominable; their diplomacy is murderous and disgusting.

Cartoon 8   2.9. 1914

Heading:

Caption: *Ex-Teuton (to landlady): "Ach! Madame, eet is all right! I vos Engleesh now! I have to-day mein papers of nationalization to your home office sent off. Dere vos several oaths by half-a-dozen peoples to be svorn. It vos a tremendous affairs!"*

Description: A stout German man with eyeglasses is standing in front of a stiff English landlady. He has raised his right arm and in his left is holding a top hat and an umbrella.

Scenario 1: A naturalized Englishman will speak English in a near-native way.

Scenario 2: This German speaks English with an extreme German accent and many grammatical mistakes. He is not aware of this.

Explanation: The two scenarios are contrasted.

Type: Everyday scene represents a communicative situation and interacts with the verbal part.

Invective: The Germans are ignorant and stupid.

Cartoon 9   16.9. 1914

Heading:

Caption: *Teutonic Barber: "Shafe, sir?"*
Customer: "Ye-es – that is, no! – I think I'll try a hair-cut."
The Evening ... GERMANS ON THE R... (on a newspaper)

Description: A stout German barber with a moustache like the one of the German Kaiser is setting his razor. He is staring in an unfriendly way at a bald customer, who is sitting in the chair in front of him clutching the backrest.

Scenario 1: A customer will state his wishes overtly.

Scenario 2: This customer uses a pretext to cover up his fear.

Scenario 3: A bald man cannot get a haircut.

Scenario 4: This bald man wants a haircut.

Explanation: The first two and the second two scenarios are contrasted. It is obvious that the customer changed his mind because he does not trust the German barber. 'Shafe' represents the pronunciation of 'shave' by the German barber.

Type: Everyday scene represents a communicative situation and interacts with the verbal part.

Invective: Germans cannot be trusted.

Cartoon 10   23.9. 1914

Heading:

Caption: *The Wolff: "Good morning, my dear Little Red Riding Hood. Wouldn't you like me to tell you one of my pretty tales?"*
Little Miss Holland: "Thanks; but I'm not Little Red Riding Hood, and don't want any of your fairy stories."
WOLFF BUREAU (written on the wolf)

Description: A wolf is standing next to a little girl in a Dutch national costume. She is carrying a basket with food and a bottle of wine.

Scenario 1: Wolff is a German publisher, whose roll is to inform the public.

Scenario 2: Wolff takes the place of the near-namesake, wolf, in the counterfactual fairy tale scenario where his role is to cheat and then devour Little Red Riding Hood.

Scenario 3:   In the fairy tale the little girl is cheated and devoured by the wolf.

Scenario 4:   This little girl rejects her supposed identity and thus also the course of events of the fairy tale.

Explanation: Theodor Wolff, the publisher of the *Berliner Tageblatt*, is blended into the fairy tale as well as Holland in the role of Little Red Riding Hood. Wolff cannot cheat the public about Germany's attack on Holland.

Type: Metonymic scene represents a communicative situation and interacts with the verbal part.

Invective: The Germans try to mislead the public, e.g. the German press is fraudulent.

Punch cartoon 10

Cartoon 11   30.9. 1914

Heading:

Caption: *Youthful patriot: "Oh, Mummy, you must speak to baby: he's most awfully naughty. He won't let nurse take his vest off, and (in an awe-struck voice) he keeps on screaming and telling that he likes the Germans! Anybody might hear him."*

Description: A child is standing near its mother pointing in the direction of a toddler, who is standing next to its nurse.

Scenario 1:   No one will take political statements of a baby seriously.

Scenario 2:   The little sister takes the political statement of the baby seriously.

Explanation: The two scenarios are contrasted.

Type: Everyday scene represents a communicative situation and interacts with the verbal part.

Invective: Neutral.

Cartoon 12   7.10. 1914

Heading:

Caption: *Unreported casualty to the football of the 85th infantry regiment of the enemy.*

Description: Seven German soldiers are playing soccer in a very stiff manner. One of them has punctured the ball while heading it with the point of his spiked helmet.

Scenario 1:	For Englishmen, playing soccer is a sportsman-like activity
Scenario 2:	For Germans, playing soccer is a militaristic activity.
Scenario 3:	Intelligent people foresee the disadvantages their inadequate military equipment may have in playing soccer and act accordingly.
Scenario 4:	The German soldiers are too stupid to foresee the disadvantages of their inadequate military equipment.
Explanation:	The two scenarios are contrasted.
Type:	Non-combatant military scene represents a communicative situation.
Invective:	The Germans are militarists. In addition, they are ignorant and stupid.

Cartoon 13   21.10. 1914

Heading:	*Facts from the Front.*
Caption:	*We learn (from German sources) that the professors of a celebrated Prussian university have conferred the honorary degree of doctor upon a distinguished general on his departure for the front.*
Description:	Five elderly men are standing next to a big and tall general, who has raised his saber. One of the men is attaching an armlet with a (red) cross to his left arm.
Scenario 1:	Professors confer the honorary degree of doctor upon a person for extraordinary scientific results or achievements in the arts.
Scenario 2:	German professors confer the honorary degree of doctor upon a person for military achievements and activities.
Explanation:	The two scenarios are contrasted. The armlet with the red cross can be taken as an allusion to the fact that at the front there will be many casualties which need to be attended to by a medical doctor.
Type:	Non-combatant military scene interacts with the verbal part.
Invective:	The Germans are militarists.

Cartoon 14   21.10. 1914

Heading:	*Why Have we no Supermen like the Germans?*
	Upper left panel
Caption:	*How they might brighten Regent Street.*
Description:	Two German soldiers are goose-stepping on the sidewalk of a street, scaring an old man and a little girl away.
Scenario 1:	English soldiers walk on the of a street in a relaxed manner without scaring anybody.
Scenario 2:	German soldiers retain their militaristic behavior, scaring people.
Explanation:	The two scenarios are contrasted. Through the heading a contrast is established between the German soldiers in the cartoon and English soldiers or Englishmen in general. Since the behavior of the German soldiers is rude, the caption is read to be ironic.
Type:	Non-combatant military scene interacts with the verbal part.
	Upper right panel
Caption:	*How they might wake up our restaurants.*
Description:	Two German soldiers are at a table in a restaurant. One is sitting and shouting, the other is standing, pulling the ear of the waiter.
Scenario 1:	British soldiers behave in a relaxed and unaggressive manner in a restaurant.
Scenario 2:	German soldiers retain their militaristic behavior anywhere, shouting and being aggressive.
Explanation:	The two scenarios are contrasted. Since their behavior is rude, the caption is read to be ironic.
Type:	Non-combatant military scene interacts with the verbal part.
	Lower left panel
Caption:	*And honour us with their gallantry.*
Description:	The two German soldiers are staring and grinning at a woman, who has

123

stepped off the sidewalk in an evading movement. One of the soldiers is blowing the smoke of his cigar into her face.

Scenario 1:	British soldiers make charming and polite advances to English women.
Scenario 2:	These two German soldiers make a rude advance to this English woman.
Explanation:	The two scenarios are contrasted. Since their behavior is rude, the caption is read to be ironic.
Type:	Non-combatant military scene interacts with the verbal part.

Lower right panel

Caption:	*And, best of all, how amusing to see them meet a super-superman.*
Description:	The two German soldiers salute a passing general in a very submissive manner.
Scenario 1:	British soldiers behave in a self-assertive way.
Scenario 2:	These two German soldiers behave in a submissive way and look like little boys, who have been caught doing something naughty.
Explanation:	The two scenarios are contrasted. It is typical of militarist that they show extreme submissiveness to superiors.
Type:	Non-combatant military scene interacts with the verbal part.
Invective:	The Germans are militarists.

Cartoon 15   21.10. 1914

Heading:	*Facts from the Front.*
Caption:	*Storm of righteous indignation. At the enemy's headquarters on their being shown a 'barbarous and disgusting engine of war' in use by the allies. (The Germans have taken a strong objection to the French 75 m/m gun.)*
Description:	In the center a man in a uniform is showing a short sword to several members of the German military. A general to his right is touching it, falling backward as if about to faint. A stand with a map and binoculars has fallen to the ground.
Scenario 1:	In times of war the opponents expect that the other side will develop the most efficient lethal weapons possible.
Scenario 2:	The members of the German military do not expect this.
Explanation:	The two scenarios are contrasted. There is a metonymic relationship involved: the sword and its sharpness stand for the French 75 m/m gun and its efficiency.
Type:	Counterfactual scene interacts with the verbal part.
Invective:	The Germans are ignorant and naïve.

Cartoon 16   21.10. 1914

Heading:	
Caption:	*"Pfutsch! Dey vas just a few tings vat I use to frighden der cats from mein garten!"*
Description:	A man with a moustache pointing upward, small round glasses and short hair is standing in the middle of many rifles and revolvers. Two policemen are investigating this suspicious find.
Scenario 1:	Any noise will do to frighten cats from a garden.
Scenario 2:	This man uses rifles and revolvers to frighten cats from his garden.
Scenario 3:	When committing subversive actions, one must find plausible excuses and explanations to convince policemen.
Scenario 4:	The explanation of this man is absolutely unconvincing.
Explanation:	The first two and the second two scenarios are contrasted.
Type:	Everyday scene represents a communicative situation and interacts with the verbal part.
Invective:	The Germans are ignorant and naïve, e.g. this German is stupid enough to underrate British policemen.

Cartoon 17   4.11. 1914

Heading:	*Forewarned.*
Caption:	*Zeppelin (as 'the fat boy'): "I wants to make your flesh creep." John Bull: "Right-o!"*
	ZEPPELIN (written on the zeppelin)
Description:	John Bull with a top hat and a walking stick is standing in a garden looking up at a zeppelin. It has a face with a gaping mouth and two stretched-out arms.
Scenario 1:	An attacking zeppelin will frighten people.
Scenario 2:	John Bull is not frightened in the least.
Explanation:	The two scenarios are contrasted. A 'fat boy' is a school bully who tries to try to frighten other pupils, but after a short time these pupils will call the fat boy's bluff.
Type:	Metonymic scene represents a communicative situation and interacts with the verbal part.
Invective:	The Germans are ignorant and naïve, because they expect that an ineffective weapon such as the zeppelin will frighten the British.

Cartoon 18   4.11. 1914

Heading:	*Facts from the Front.*
Caption:	*Tactical use, by the enemy, of the more resilient units of the landstorm for negotiating Belgian dykes.*
Description:	German soldiers are running towards a very fat soldier lying in front of a canal; they step on him like on a springboard and are thus catapulted over the canal landing in a safety net, which is held by other soldiers.
Scenario 1:	The military have efficient means of crossing a canal, e.g. movable bridges.
Scenario 2:	The Germans use their adipose soldiers as spring boards to cross a canal.
Explanation:	The two scenarios are contrasted. *Landstorm* is a calque of the German term *Landsturm* which referred to the last category of four types of military service in Germany: active, reserve, *Landwehr* and *Landsturm*. Members of the *Landwehr* and the *Landsturm* consisted of soldiers who were too old for the active service and the reserve.
Type:	Counterfactual scene interacts with the verbal part.
Invective:	The Germans are ignorant and stupid, because they adopt inadequate means of military problem solving.

Cartoon 19   4.11. 1914

Heading:	*Latest Device of the Enemy.*
Caption:	*Learning to sing 'It's a long; long way to Tipperary' for the purpose of deceiving the allies.*
	IT'S A LONG, LONG WAY TO TIPPERARY IT'S ... LONG W... T... IT'S L... WAY T... (written on a placard on the wall).
Description:	In the center, several German soldiers are singing, marching in a goose step. On the left a German is acting as their conductor.
Scenario 1:	In order to deceive an enemy in war, one must adopt subtle means such as choosing an appropriate dress and behavior.
Scenario 2:	These German soldiers are singing a song in English.
Explanation:	The soldiers look and act like Germans, and the fact that they are singing an English song will not deceive anybody.
Type:	War scene interacts with the verbal part.
Invective:	The Germans are ignorant and naïve, because they adopt inadequate means of deceiving their enemy.

Punch cartoon 20

Cartoon 20   11.11. 1914
Heading: *How to Bring up a Hun.*
Caption: *The Teutonic substitute for milk*
                BLOOD AND IRON TONIC (written on the bottle)
Description: A very stern looking German soldier with a spiked helmet and a red
                cross armlet is feeding a toddler 'blood and iron tonic' with a giant
                spoon. The child also wears a spiked helmet and is chained to its
                highchair.
Scenario 1:   Toddlers are brought up with milk in a loving and caring way.
Scenario 2:   German toddlers are brought up with 'blood and iron tonic' in a
                militaristic way.
Explanation: The two scenarios are contrasted. It is small wonder that the Germans
                are militaristic given the way they are brought up.
Type: Counterfactual scene interacts with the verbal part.
Invective: The Germans are militarists. In addition they are cruel to their children.

Cartoon 21   11.11. 1914
Heading:
Caption: *A Prussian court-painter earning an Iron Cross by painting pictures in*
                praise of the fatherland for neutral consumption.
                (Subtitles of the paintings:) *WILHELM THE PEACEMAKER -*
                UHLAN'S KINDNESS TO BELGIAN PEASANT - THE ANGELUS -
                GERMAN SOLDIER'S REVERENCE AT A FRENCH CATHEDRAL -
                GERMAN SOLDIER CARRYING PARCELS FOR BRITISH PRISONER
                - GERMAN HELPING A WOUNDED BRITISH SOLDIER – GE... TEA
                TO ENEMIES - GERMAN SOLDIERS ROMPING WITH BELGIAN
                CHILDREN - GERMAN FEEDING STARVING BELGIANS
Description: In the center a very fat man with a moustache, a pipe and small round
                glasses is painting a picture. On the wall in the background, there are
                another eight paintings with the above subtitles.
Scenario 1:   The German Kaiser is a warmonger. German soldiers behave cruelly to
                civilians and soldiers of the enemy.

Scenario 2:	The German Kaiser is peace loving. German soldiers behave in a kind and helpful way to civilians and soldiers of the enemy.
Explanation:	The two scenarios are contrasted.
Type:	Everyday scene interacts with the verbal part.
Invective:	The Germans try to mislead the public, but they present themselves in such a blatantly false manner that no one can be deceived.

Cartoon 22   9.12. 1914
Heading:
Caption: *Owing to the outcry against high-placed aliens a wealthy German tries to look as little high-placed as possible.*
Description: A stout man with a small round monocle and a moustache is walking on the sidewalk with a walking stick. He is wearing an expensive-looking coat with fur on the sleeves and the collar, but a tattered top hat and torn trousers. A British policeman has half-turned and looks at him, leaning forward.
Scenario 1:   Looking as little high-placed as possible means wearing inexpensive clothes.
Scenario 2:   This German is wearing a tattered top hat and torn trousers but a very expensive coat.
Explanation: The two scenarios are contrasted.
Type: Everyday scene interacts with the verbal part.
Invective: The Germans are ignorant and stupid, because they are unable to assess adequately how German they look.

Cartoon 23   9.12. 1914
Heading: *The Master Word.*
Description: In seven similarly drawn scenes a man is insulting another man who is sitting on a chair in front of him reading a newspaper.
                   First panel
Caption: *No Gentleman* (in a speech bubble)
Type: Everyday scene represents a communicative situation.
                   Second panel
Caption: *Cad* (in a speech bubble)
Type: Everyday scene represents a communicative situation.
                   Third panel
Caption: *Poltroon* (in a speech bubble)
Type: Everyday scene represents a communicative situation.
                   Fourth panel
Caption: *Bounder* (in a speech bubble)
Type: Everyday scene represents a communicative situation.
                   Fifth panel
Caption: *Brute* (in a speech bubble)
Type: Everyday scene represents a communicative situation.
                   Sixth panel
Caption: *Swine* (in a speech bubble)
Type: Everyday scene represents a communicative situation.
                   Seventh panel
Caption: *German* (in a speech bubble)
Type: Everyday scene represents a communicative situation.
Description: The insulter is walking away. The insultee has dropped his paper and looks around in disgust.
                   Eighth panel
Description: The insultee is smashing his chair on the insulter, who then falls backwards.

Scenario 1:	The insultee is so calm that he is not stirred by the different English insults.
Scenario 2:	*German* is such a great insult that even a very calm person blows his top.
Explanation:	The two scenarios are contrasted.
Type:	Everyday scene represents a communicative situation. (Six times)
Invective:	The Germans are abominable. Therefore, to call someone a 'German' is the most severe insult.

Cartoon 24	9.12. 1914
Heading:	*The Zeppelin Menace.*
Caption:	*A smart London cellar in wartime. Pictured by a Berlin artist.*
Description:	In a rough cellar vault two elegantly dressed couples are having dinner. They look shocked when their butler brings in a dead rat on a tray.
Scenario 1:	According to the Berlin artist, the British are so afraid of the German zeppelins that they hide in cellars, and the supply lines are so badly affected that even the gentry has to eat rats.
Scenario 2:	In fact, the British are not at all afraid of the German zeppelins and their supply lines are hardly affected.
Explanation:	The two scenarios are contrasted. The Germans are victims of their own wishful thinking. The German artists are willing collaborators of the German propaganda machine.
Type:	War scene interacts with the verbal part.
Invective:	The Germans try to mislead the public.

Cartoon 25	
Heading:	
Caption:	*"Run avay, you leedle poys; don't come here shpying about!"*
Description:	On a cliff near the sea, a man in a trench coat with small round glasses and a moustache is releasing pigeons from a basket, which fly away over the sea. Two youngsters are watching him startled.
Scenario 1:	A spy should be able to cover up his activity and also speak English proficiently.
Scenario 2:	This German spy is caught red handed by the boys. His poor English betrays his identity and so does his use of the expression 'spy about'.
Explanation:	The two scenarios are contrasted. This German spy gives away his identity because of his silliness.
Type:	Everyday scene represents a communicative situation and interacts with the verbal part.
Invective:	The Germans are ignorant and stupid, e.g. this German spy betrays himself in a very naïve manner.

Cartoon 26	16.12.1914
Heading:	*Unrecorded Events in the History of the War.*
Caption:	*German soldiers being roused to enthusiasm by the 'hymn of hate.'*
Description:	German soldiers walk past a gramophone in an orderly manner. When they have heard the 'hymn of hate', they start firing their rifles. A general watches the procedure.
Scenario 1:	Soldiers fight enthusiastically for (the defense of) their country.
Scenario 2:	German soldiers have to be pattern-drilled to develop enthusiasm for (the defense of) their country.
Explanation:	The two scenarios are contrasted. The German soldiers are treated like guinea pigs.
Type:	Counterfactual scene interacts with the verbal part.
Invective:	The Germans hate the British.

Punch cartoon 26

Cartoon 27	23.12.1914
Heading:	*Language-Kultur.*
Caption:	*Voice from the darkness: "Doand shood! Doand shood! Ve vos de Viltshires."*
Description:	English soldiers are sitting in a trench with their rifles ready. In the background there is a field with barbed wire.
Scenario 1:	The German soldier speaks English so well that the English soldiers could be misled, which could be fatal for them.
Scenario 2:	This German soldier imitates English so poorly that the English soldiers do not fall for the trick.
Explanation:	The two scenarios are contrasted.
Type:	Counterfactual scene represents a communicative situation and interacts with the verbal part.
Invective:	The Germans are ignorant and stupid; they have a pseudo-culture.

Cartoon 28	30.12.1914
Heading:	*Dishonoured.*
Caption:	*Captain of the Emden: "Dirty work!"*
	(On the newspaper:) *SYDNEY PRESS - RAID ON SCARBOROUGH – KAISER'S FLEET SHELLS WOMEN AND CHILDREN*
Description:	A German marine captain is showing a defensive gesture with his cap in his left hand halfway behind his back. In front of him as if floating in the air there is an Australian newspaper.
Scenario 1:	The German military will support all the decisions of their leadership.
Scenario 2:	This German marine captain strongly disapproves of the shelling of women and children.
Explanation:	The two scenarios are contrasted. On December 16th 1914, three German warships appeared off the North-East coast of England and began shelling. They attacked several towns: Hartlepool, West Hartlepool, Whitby and Scarborough. More than 100 people were killed, and twice that number were injured. Several British destroyers which were dispatched to intercept the raiders came under fire; two were hit, and four seamen were killed. The raiders returned to Germany.
Type:	Non-combatant military scene interacts with the verbal part.

Invective: The Germans are cowards; even some high-ranking German militaries disapprove of the war atrocities.

Punch cartoon 29

Cartoon 29   30.12.1914
Heading: *The Iron Cross Epidemic.*
Caption: *Captain of a German cruiser, hurrying home after shelling health-resort, gives orders to lighten the ship for the sake of speed.*
Description: At the top left hand corner of the panel a war ship immersed deep in the water is moving forward. On the right hand side of the panel the same war ship is floating high on the water. Its personnel is on deck and many Iron Crosses have been thrown over board.
Scenario 1:   Military decorations are given sparsely and are held in high esteem.
Scenario 2:   The German military decorations are distributed in masses and thus are easily disposed of when necessary.
Explanation: The two scenarios are contrasted. Shelling health-resorts is a cowardly act, which does not deserve any military decorations. Hurrying home afterwards is another cowardly act.
Type: Counterfactual scene interacts with the verbal part.
Invective: The Germans are cowards.

Cartoon 30   Punch's Almanack for 1915
Heading: *News for German Consumption.*
Caption: *"The difficulties experienced in raising the much-vaunted 'Kitchener's army' are such that many of the recruits are mere children. Their equipment is of the most primitive description."*
Description: On a shopping street there are four small boys marching one after the other. The first is holding a toy sword in front of him; the others are carrying sticks over their shoulders like rifles. They are wearing paper hats. Several passers-by are watching them. In the background on the left, a suspicious looking man with large eyes, a dark hat and coat is taking notes. He is a German spy.
Scenario 1:   A spy provides relevant military information to his country.
Scenario 2:   This German spy mistakenly takes the play of children as an army drill.
Explanation: The two scenarios are contrasted.
Type: Everyday scene interacts with the verbal part.

Invective: The Germans are ignorant and stupid, e.g. this spy cannot tell the play of children from an army drill.

Cartoon 31	Punch's Almanack for 1915

Heading: *News for German Consumption.*
Caption: *"Signs are not wanting that women are being pressed into the service. Many, indeed, are already in uniform."*
Description: Two women wearing fashionable coats and hats are passing fashion shops on a shopping street. In the background on the right, a suspicious looking man with large eyes, a dark hat and coat is watching them. He is a German spy
Scenario 1:   A spy is able to differentiate fashion designs which are remotely similar to military uniforms and genuine uniforms.
Scenario 2:   This German spy is not able to make this distinction.
Explanation: The two scenarios are contrasted.
Type: Everyday scene interacts with the verbal part.
Invective: The Germans are ignorant and stupid, e.g. this spy cannot tell women's fashion designs from army uniforms.

Cartoon 32	Punch's Almanack for 1915

Heading: *News for German Consumption.*
Caption: *"In society the chief topics of conversation are the coming invasion and our mammoth howitzers."*
(Speech bubbles:) *I 'ear as 'ow these ere Germans 'ave got guns wot'll shoot all the way from Antwerk to Dover 'arbour. - Well! Well! Wot'll they be a'doing next?*
Description: Two elderly women are sitting on a bench talking. On the left a suspicious looking man with large eyes, a dark hat and coat is listening to them taking notes.
Scenario 1:   A spy is able to differentiate between curious gossip of elderly women and genuine concern of the population.
Scenario 2:   This German spy is not able to make this distinction.
Explanation: The two scenarios are contrasted. The dialect used depicts their lack of education; this is also shown by the fact that Antwerp is called 'Antwerk'.
Type: Everyday scene represents a communicative situation and interacts with the verbal part.
Invective: The Germans are ignorant and stupid, e.g. this spy cannot tell superficial gossip from serious talk about the apprehensions of the population.

Cartoon 33	Punch's Almanack for 1915

Heading: *News for German Consumption.*
Caption: *It would be impossible to give an adequate idea of the panic which the zeppelin menace has occasioned. Every night, in many of the principal thoroughfares, terror-stricken crowds may be seen gazing fearfully skywards.*
(Speech bubbles:) *Baby would enjoy this – There are the search lights – I wish a air-ship would come along – en farver! - You'll 'ave to be in bed afore then, my son - Don't they look pretty! - I 'ear as they're fifty million candle power, some of 'em. - Reelly!!*
Description: A crowd of adults and two children have gathered looking into the sky. In the right-hand corner a suspicious looking man with large eyes, a dark hat and coat is watching the scene taking notes.
Scenario 1:   A spy is able to differentiate between a crowd whose curiosity has been roused and one that is terror-stricken.

Scenario 2:   This German spy is not able to make this distinction.
Explanation: The two scenarios are contrasted.
Type: Everyday scene represents a communicative situation and interacts with the verbal part.
Invective: The Germans are ignorant and stupid.

Cartoon 34   Punch's Almanack for 1915
Heading: *The Spy Peril.*
Caption: *Are the automatic machines on pier-heads inspected often enough?*
CHOCOLATE - AUTOMATIC - DROP PENNY IN SLOT (written on the automatic machine)
Description: A stout German with small round glasses, a moustache, gaiters and a hat is standing on a pier in front of a chocolate vending-machine, in which another man is hiding. The first man reaches out his left hand backward and receives a letter from the man in the machine. Further down the pier two men are looking at the sea through telescopes.
Scenario 1:   Efficient spies find efficient ways of passing secret information.
Scenario 2:   These German spies do not work efficiently.
Explanation: The two scenarios are contrasted.
Type: Counterfactual scene interacts with the verbal part.
Invective: The Germans are ignorant and stupid.

Cartoon 35   Punch's Almanack for 1915
Heading: *The Last Line.*
Caption: *Germany calls out the old professors, who have been largely responsible for the war, to put their theories into practice.*
Description: Ten very old and ill-equipped soldiers are walking along a street. In the foreground on the right, three children are watching them. In the background, women are watching from the windows of their houses waving handkerchiefs.
Scenario 1:   In order to have an efficient army only young, healthy and strong men will be recruited.
Scenario 2:   Germany recruits old, weak and ill-equipped professors.
Explanation: The two scenarios are contrasted.
Type: Non-combatant military scene interacts with the verbal part.
Invective: The Germans are militarily inferior; they are also ignorant and stupid.

Cartoon 36   Punch's Almanack for 1915
Heading: *When William Comes to London.*
Upper panel
Caption: *When William comes with all his might*
And sets the river Thames alight;
I shouldn't be at all surprised
If London Town were Teutonised.
Bidding his band to play Te Deum
He'll occupy the Athenaeum,
And Pallas' Owl becomes a vulture
Under the new régime of culture.
Description: The German Kaiser is riding up the stairs of the Athenaeum. There is a brass band on either side playing and in front of him a girl is strewing flowers.
Scenario 1:   The Germans do not occupy London. The English keep the Athenaeum to themselves.
Scenario 2:   The German Kaiser occupies the Athenaeum with his noisy and pompous display of power.

Type: Counterfactual scene interacts with the verbal part.
                Lower panel
Caption: *Britons will have to pay a Mark*
                For leave to sit inside the park.
                And watch the noble Uhlans go
                Careering up and down the Row.
Description: In Hyde Park, a German official is selling tickets to two surprised
                visitors on a park bench. Proud German Uhlans are riding along Rotten
                Row. A German rider approaches a woman with two dachshunds with
                a ticket in his right hand. Marble Arch can be seen in the background.
Scenario 1:   The Germans do not occupy London. The English keep Hyde Park to
                themselves.
Scenario 2:   The Germans occupy London. The German Uhlans show their
                superiority in Hyde Park. The English have to pay money to the
                Germans to sit in their park.
Explanation: The two panels describe a hypothetical conceptual space of a German
                occupation of London, which contrasts with reality. The Athenaeum
                was a private club in Waterloo Place, which was founded in 1823 or
                1824 for the association of men of eminence and attainment in science,
                art and literature, and their patrons.
Type: Counterfactual scene interacts with the verbal part.
Invective: The Germans have a pseudo-culture. All it consists of is pompous and
                arrogant behavior, brass band music and charging money for the
                normal rights of the citizens. The authorities enforce this culture.

Cartoon 37   Punch's Almanack for 1915
Heading: *When William Comes to London.*
Caption: *A higher Art will mould our tastes*
                To Teuton wit and Teuton waists;
                And when their houris ply the hoof
                The house will rock from floor to roof!
Type: Counterfactual scene interacts with the verbal part.
Description: A fat German in a fancy uniform with a bearskin cap, which has a skull
                and cross bones symbol on it, is holding up a huge sausage. Behind
                him a choir of stout women in the similar uniform are singing. Each of
                them is holding a large stein in the hand.
Scenario 1:   The Germans are kept out of England. The English traditions are left
                untouched.
Scenario 2:   The Germans occupy London and import their culture to it, i.e.
                drinking lots of beer from large steins and eating huge sausages.
                Lower panel
Caption: *On Pilsen beer the Bosch will bloat,*
                Supplied by Herren Appenrodt.
                And German sausage be his joy
                At the new-christened Saveloy.
Description: There are Germans in a restaurant holding and waving over-sized beer
                steins and sausages. A waiter is carrying a tray full of beer steins.
                Sausages hang down from the tray. In the background, arrogant
                German military leaders are walking down some stairs pushing a
                pageboy to the side.
Scenario 1:   The Germans are kept out of England.
Scenario 2:   The Germans occupy London and import their beer-and-sausage
                culture to it.
Explanation: The two panels describe a hypothetical conceptual space of a German
                occupation of London, which contrasts with reality.
Type: Counterfactual scene interacts with the verbal part.

Invective: The Germans have a pseudo-culture. All it consists of is pompous and arrogant behavior, drinking lots of beer from large steins and eating huge sausages.

Punch cartoon 38

Cartoon 38   Punch's Almanack for 1915
Heading: *When William Comes to London.*
              Upper panel
Caption: *When William shoots at goal like this*
              There will be murder should he miss;
Description: The German Kaiser is running in a goose-step fashion to score a penalty at an empty goal. The goal posts are decorated with two eagles. Three soldiers on either side are saluting.
Type: Counterfactual scene interacts with the verbal part.
Scenario 1:   The English play soccer in a fair manner.
Scenario 2:   The German Kaiser plays soccer with German soldiers. He will be very angry if he misses.
              Lower panel
Caption: *When he plays what isn't cricket*
              God help the Hun that takes his wicket!
Description: The German Kaiser is holding an oversized cricket bat (three times the size of a normal one) in front of a wicket. A German soldier is about to pitch with a goose-step. He is carrying a rucksack and a rifle. Behind the Kaiser a stiff German soldier acts as the fielder behind the wicket. Four soldiers are saluting.

Scenario 1:   The English play cricket in a fair manner.
Scenario 2:   The German Kaiser plays cricket in a ridiculously distorted manner and will be very angry if he loses.
Explanation: The two scenarios are contrasted.
Type: Counterfactual scene interacts with the verbal part.
Invective: The Germans are militarists; therefore they are stiff, unfair and revengeful.

Cartoon 39   Punch's Almanack for 1915
Heading: *In the Champagne Country.*

Caption: *The Prussian officer, I hear,*
Is very good at lager beer,
But, when he goes for sweet champagne,
It makes him fuzzy in the brain.

That's, why, when he had had his glut,
Having absorbed it by the butt,
Our fellows found him where he lay.
Blind as a corpse in Epernay.

And when at last, a little pale,
He woke inside the prisoners' goal,
He still recalled that vintage-brand,
And murmured, "Hic! Der Vaterland!"

Upper left panel
Caption: *PROSIT* (written on the stein)
Description: A Prussian officer in a neat uniform is drinking beer from a large stein. On the table next to him on a plate, there is a sausage with a fork in it and a pretzel lying beside it.
Type: Everyday scene interacts with the verbal part.
Upper right panel
Caption:
Description: He is pouring champagne into a glass with a smile.
Type: Everyday scene interacts with the verbal part.
Lower left panel
Caption:
Description: He is lying on the floor with closed eyes and two empty champagne bottles in his arms. Another four empty champagne bottles are lying on the floor beside him.
Type: Everyday scene interacts with the verbal part.
Lower right panel
Caption:
Description: He is sitting with a hang-over on the floor of a cell. The window of the cell is barred. His cap is lying on the floor.
Explanation: There is a symbolic equivalence between the activities of the Prussian officer and the activities of the German army: as long as the Germans stay in Germany, they are ok, but as soon as they move into France, they encounter great difficulties and end up as prisoners of war.
Type: Everyday scene interacts with the verbal part.
Invective: The Germans are ignorant and stupid.

Cartoon 40   Punch's Almanack for 1915
Heading: *Herr Bethmann's Barty. (After 'Hans Breitmann.')*
Caption: *Herr Bethmann gife a barty;*

De Kaiser he vas dere;
De gompany made zo vine a noise
Ash efer sphlit de air;
De schampagne vlowed in poompers
Und all vas himmel-gay;
Dey drinks gonvusion to England,
Dey doasts de glorious Day.

Herr Bethmann gife a barty;
Vhere ish dat barty now?
Vhere is de poashted shblendour
Dat vlushed each varrior's prow?
Vhere ish de bromished trioomph
Of Deutschers, left und right?
All goned avay mit de eagle's tail
Avay in de Ewigkeit.

DER TAG (title of the musical note sheet on the piano)

Description: In the center of the cartoon, the Crown Prince is playing the piano. Drinking and singing German officers are standing behind it. In the foreground at the left, two officers are smoking. In front of them on the table lies an empty champagne bottle. In the background on the left, the German Kaiser is entering, surrounded by rays of light. He is greeted by three saluting officers and the German Chancellor, von Bethmann.

Scenario 1: There is a party going on, celebrating a glorious day for the German military.

Scenario 2: There is no party going on any more, because there is nothing to celebrate by the German military.

Explanation: The two scenarios are contrasted. The party which the Germans celebrate symbolizes their strong conviction that they will win the war. Thus this pictorial scenario and the sarcastic poem is similar to sayings such as the German *man kann das Fell des Bären erst verteilen, wenn man ihn hat* (you can only divide the skin of the bear, when you have it).

During the American Civil War, a journalist named Charles Godfrey Leland (1824-1903) began writing verses on the life and adventures of a fictitious German-American he called 'Hans Breitmann.' Hans Breitmann became a celebrity in both England and the United States. He was parodied, imitated and quoted everywhere; he was realized on the stage, memorized, and read voraciously. He brought laughter with his Teutonic philosophy, his beer drinking and his humorous German-English phrases. In 1871, the first complete edition of the ballads appeared, and in 1914 an edition was published with a historical-background introduction by Leland's niece, Mrs. Pennell.

Type: Non-combatant military scene interacts with the verbal part.

Invective: The Germans are ignorant and naïve, because they prematurely celebrate a victory of which they cannot be at all sure. They have a poor assessment of reality.

Cartoon 41   Punch's Almanack for 1915

Heading: *Special Booms in Berlin.*

Caption: *Though Teuton trade has had a slump,*
Scrap-iron's nicely on the jump;
It compensates for many losses –
This lovely boom in Iron Crosses.

Description: Several German soldiers are carrying scrap metal using the goose step.

Scenario 1:   There are efficient ways of carrying scrap metal.
Scenario 2:   The German soldiers are using the goose step.
Scenario 3:   Normal trading is going on.
Scenario 4:   Instead of normal trading the Germans produce an excess of Iron Crosses.
Explanation: The two scenarios are contrasted.
Type: Non-combatant military scene interacts with the verbal part.
Invective: The Germans are militarists. In addition, they are ignorant and stupid.

Cartoon 42   Punch's Almanack for 1915
Heading: *Special Booms in Berlin.*
Caption: *Stone-masons, too, are working hard,*
Sculpting St. William by the yard,
To occupy the empty pitches
Of prophets in Cathedral niches.

Description: Six stonemasons are working amongst several sculptures of William II.
Scenario 1:   Every sculpture of an emperor is a very important and unique artifact.
Scenario 2:   The sculptures of the German Kaiser are mass-produced.
Scenario 3:   The prophets and the Bible will give a nation its sense of direction.
Scenario 4:   The Kaiser gives the Germans their sense of direction.
Explanation: The two scenarios are contrasted. There is an excess of sculptures of the German Kaiser, which thus are devalued and not very important. As a consequence the German Kaiser is not very important.
The replacement of the sculptures of prophets in the niches of the cathedral by sculptures of William II means that the belief in the German Kaiser replaces the religious beliefs.
Type: Everyday scene interacts with the verbal part.
Invective: The Germans are ignorant and stupid, because they uncritically believe in their Kaiser.

Cartoon 43   Punch's Almanack for 1915
Heading: *Special Booms in Berlin.*
Upper panel
Caption: *Tailors are stitching overtime*
For Prussians who have passed their prime;
All day and night they readjust
Old tunics which have been and bust.
Description: Three tailors try to put uniforms, which are much too tight, on two very fat German soldiers. The uniform of the soldier in the center who is wearing a spiked helmet, which is also too tight, has burst open at several places.
Scenario 1:   A country is well advised to select young and fit men as soldiers.
Scenario 2:   Germany selects old and fat men as its soldiers.
Scenario 3:   The German tailors believe that the old uniforms still fit the soldiers.
Scenario 4:   The German soldiers are so fat that their uniforms do not fit.
Lower panel
Explanation: The first and second two scenarios are contrasted.
Type: Non-combatant military scene interacts with the verbal part.
Invective: The Germans are ignorant and stupid.

Cartoon 44   Punch's Almanack for 1915
Heading: *Special Booms in Berlin.*
Caption: *The Red Cross rage employs the hosier;*
I hear his chance was never rosier;
Behind this screen the gallant Hun
Can safely shoot at anyone.

Description:	In a busy marketplace a woman and a girl are selling Red Cross armlets and streamers to German men. In the right hand corner even a dachshund is wearing a Red Cross armlet round its neck.
Scenario 1:	People do not attack anybody behind the smokescreen of the Red Cross.
Scenario 2:	German men take the Red Cross as a smokescreen behind which they can shoot at other people.
Explanation:	The two scenarios are contrasted. The Germans support the Red Cross for selfish reasons. The kind of attack is not specified any further.
Type:	Everyday scene interacts with the verbal part.
Invective:	The Germans cannot be trusted, because they are bigoted.

Cartoon 45   Punch's Almanack for 1915

Heading:	*After the War.* Upper left panel
Caption:	*There will be no more late rising in the morning. We shall all spring out of the bed at reveille.*
Description:	A fat man in a nightdress is blowing a trumpet in front of the door of a bedroom. In the bed a disconcerted man is visible.
Scenario 1:	The English are no early risers. They like to take it easy in the morning.
Scenario 2:	The Germans are militarists; therefore they are early risers. In addition, they are noisy.
Explanation:	The two scenarios are contrasted.
Type:	Everyday scene interacts with the verbal part.
Invective:	The Germans are militarists; therefore they are insensitive and uptight.

Cartoon 46   Punch's Almanack for 1915

Heading:	*After the War.*
Caption:	*We shall know how to take cover against any projectile with soldierly adaptability.*
Description:	On a golf course three people are seeking cover on the ground. In the background a golfer has hit the ball, which is swirling towards the three people.
Scenario 1:	The English play golf in a relaxed manner.
Scenario 2:	The Germans play golf using military techniques.
Explanation:	The two scenarios are contrasted. The everyday scenario of playing golf is blended with a war scenario.
Type:	War scene interacts with the verbal part.
Invective:	The Germans are militarists; therefore they are stiff and insensitive.

Cartoon 47   Punch's Almanack for 1915

Heading:	*After the War.*
Caption:	*And when we can again find time for cricket we shall conduct ourselves with the precision of the parade ground.*
Description:	Cricket players and an umpire are marching onto the pitch. A player shouting commands is walking at their side. In the background there are spectators standing.
Scenario 1:	The English play cricket in a relaxed manner.
Scenario 2:	The Germans play cricket in a stiff military fashion.
Explanation:	The two scenarios are contrasted. The everyday scenario of playing cricket is blended with a war scenario.
Type:	War scene interacts with the verbal part.
Invective:	The Germans are militarists; therefore they are stiff and insensitive.

Cartoon 48	6.1.1915

Heading:

Caption: *German spy reports to headquarters: "Have visited army and navy stores. Find British forces being supplied with many useless articles calculated to embarrass their movements."*
INCANDESCENT GAS MANTLES (written on a large box)
EGGS (written on a small box)

Description: A man with a dark coat and hat is standing at one side of a room writing on a pad. In front of him on the floor, there are small household objects: a toy boat, a toy house, a teddy bear, two bird cages, a dog kennel, a lamp, a bowl with a goldfish, two lamps, a teapot and cups, champagne glasses, a small box, a large box, a pram, and a lawn mower. On the right a man is carrying two plants and in the background on the left, another man is moving some boxes.

Scenario 1: A spy should supply his country with reliable and relevant information and should be able to differentiate between a household store and an army and navy store.

Scenario 2: This German spy mistakenly takes a household store for an army and navy store.

Explanation: The two scenarios are contrasted.

Type: Everyday scene represents a communicative situation and interacts with the verbal part.

Invective: The Germans are ignorant and stupid, e.g. this German spy is hopeless.

Cartoon 49	13.1.1915

Heading: *A New British Explosive*

Caption: *Horror of German general staff on reading the following extract from notes of spy who, disguised as a highlander, has been listening near British lines: "we gave 'em wot 4 not 1/2."*

Description: Four German army officers are studying the notes of a British spy, which are on a table in front of them. The spy, who is disguised as a Highlander, is standing next to them.

Scenario 1: Army officers should be educated enough to be able to read an English text.

Scenario 2: The German officers think that this very simple colloquial text is the description of a new British explosive.

Explanation: The two scenarios are contrasted.

Type: Non-combatant military scene represents a communicative situation and interacts with the verbal part.

Invective: The Germans are ignorant and stupid, e.g. this German officer is unable to understand colloquial English..

Cartoon 50	13.1.1915

Heading: *The Enemy in our Midst.*

Caption: *Cultured Teuton training carrier pigeon, when off duty, to pose as a parrot.*

Description: A fat German man with glasses is standing in front of a pigeon sitting on a perch. He has pushed an artificial beak of a parrot over the one of the pigeon.

Scenario 1: It is obvious to everyone that the pigeon is only a fake parrot.

Scenario 2: The 'cultured Teuton' believes that no one will detect that the pigeon is only disguised as a parrot.

Explanation: The two scenarios are contrasted.

Type: Everyday scene interacts with the verbal part.

Invective: The Germans are ignorant and stupid, e.g. this German underrates the intelligence of the British.

Punch cartoon 50

Cartoon 51
Heading: *Subtleties of German Warfare.*
Caption: *Influencing public opinion.*
    DO NOT (written on a sheet of paper in the hand of the man, who is writing on the blackboard); ... *NEED YOU - DO NOT (JOIN) THE ARMY UNTIL THE WAR IS OVER.* (written on a poster on the wall)
Description: A man is writing on a blackboard copying from a sheet of paper. A second man is on the watch out. He is kneeling down and looking round the corner of the room.
Scenario 1:   Under cover agents in a foreign country should have a near-native command of the language. They should take efficient precautions not to be detected.
Scenario 2:   The German under cover agents have a poor command of English and act clumsily.
Explanation: The two scenarios are contrasted.
Type: Everyday scene interacts with the verbal part.
Invective: The Germans are ignorant and stupid, e.g. these German undercover agents are stupid and clumsy.

Cartoon 52   20.1.1915
Heading:
Caption: *British Tommy (returning to trench in which he has lately been fighting, now temporarily occupied by the enemy): "Excuse me – any of you blighters seen my pipe?"*
Description: Tommy is lying on the top of a trench occupied by three German soldiers. He talks to them, but they are so startled that they do not use the rifles in their hands.
Scenario 1:   When a soldier approaches a trench of the enemy, he must be extremely cautious.

Scenario 2:   This British soldier is indifferent to the possible danger.

Scenario 3:   When soldiers are in a trench, they must prevent an enemy from coming close.

Scenario 4:   These German soldiers are taken by surprise by a British soldier.

Explanation: The first and second two scenarios are contrasted.

Type: War scene represents a communicative situation and interacts with the verbal part.

Invective: The Germans are militarily inferior; therefore they do not have to be taken seriously.

Cartoon 53   27.1.1915

Heading:

Caption: *Nephew: "I'm reading a very interesting book, aunt, called 'Germany and the next war.' " Aunt: "Well, my dear, I should have thought they had their hands full enough with the present one."*

Description: A young man with a book in his right hand helps an elderly lady, who is knitting, into an armchair.

Scenario 1:   When the nephew mentions the fact that he is reading a book, he expects his aunt to be asked why he finds it interesting, e.g. the description of conditions, which might make Germany start another war.

Scenario 2:   The aunt skips this part of the exchange and remains with the fact that the war at hand has to be dealt with and finished first before a new one can be discussed.

Explanation: The two scenarios are contrasted. The aunt turns down her nephew's offer to learn something about Germany. There is a mild humor concerning the aunt's failure to differentiate between theoretical considerations and a concrete situation.

Type: Everyday scene represents a communicative situation and interacts with the verbal part.

Invective: The Germans are militarily inferior. In addition, they are militarists.

Punch cartoon 54

Cartoon 54   3.2.1915

Heading: *Hoch Aye!*

Caption: *Scene: A lonely part of the Scottish Coast.*
German spy (who has been signaling and suddenly notices that he is being watched) "Nein! Nein! Never shall you land on my beloved Shcotchland!"

Description: A man on the beach is signaling with both hands. A member of the British Navy, who is standing behind a large rock, is observing him.

Scenario 1: If a spy in a foreign country is detected, his command of the language should enable him to cover up his identity.

Scenario 2: When this German spy in Scotland is detected, his very poor command English betrays his identity immediately.

Explanation: The two scenarios are contrasted. The German spy uses German words *(Nein! Nein!)* and his German pronunciation of *Shcotchland* is inadequate.

Type: Everyday scene represents a communicative situation and interacts with the verbal part.

Invective: The Germans are ignorant and stupid, e.g. this German spy is stupid.

Cartoon 55   3.2.1915

Heading:

Caption: *In the order that no possible means of injuring England may be neglected, it is understood that the German professors of necromancy and witchcraft have been requested to make the best use of their magical powers.*
100 BEST CURSES – INVOCATIONS (book titles)
HOW TO MIX A HATE POTION. (title of a chapter in a book)

Description: In a large hall full of items of necromancy and witchcraft, four wizards are active. The one in the center is sticking long needles into a statue of John Bull.

Scenario 1: In trying to injure an opponent, rational and effective measures are used.

Scenario 2: Germany tries to deploy irrational means as used in necromancy and witchcraft to injure England. The effectiveness of these means is doubtful.

Explanation: The two scenarios are contrasted.

Type: Everyday scene interacts with the verbal part.

Invective: The Germans are ignorant and stupid, e.g. these German professors act irrationally.

Cartoon 56   3.2.1915

Heading: *The 'Kultur' Cut.*

Caption: *There is a strong patriotic movement towards a national ideal in tailorings.*
(Tags for the names of the models and the prices:)
HINDENBURG
M 65.50
BETHMANN HOLLWEG
M 60.25
FALKENHAYN
MOLTKE (crossed out)
M 70.50
TIRPITZ
INGENOHL(crossed out)
(price illegible)

VON KLUCK
M 55.50

Description:	A tailor is standing in front of his shop window, in which four male dolls with different dresses and hats are placed. They have name and price tags at the bottom. A very small assistant is moving a fifth mannequin, which has the name *Tirpitz* on it.

The names refer to the German Chancellor (until 1917), Theobald von Bethmann Hollweg, and high ranking militaries: Paul von Hindenburg had won the battles of Tannenberg and the Masurian Lakes against the Russians in 1914. Erich von Falkenhayn, Helmuth von Moltke, Alexander von Kluck, were generals and Friedrich von Ingenohl and Alfred von Tirpitz admirals.

Scenario 1:	The politicians and higher military ranks are expected to be role models with regard to rationality and efficiency.
Scenario 2:	In Germany the politicians and higher military ranks are most prominent as wearers of fashionable clothes.
Explanation:	The two scenarios are contrasted.
Type:	Everyday scene interacts with the verbal part.
Invective:	The Germans are militarily inferior, because their politicians and higher military ranks are concerned with idle preoccupations when more important things are occurring.

Cartoon 57   3.2.1915

Heading:	
Caption:	*"Oh, mother! How I wish I was an angel!"* *"Darling! What makes you say that?"* *"Oh, because then, mother, I could drop bombs on the Germans."*
Description:	A small girl is kneeling in front of her upper class mother who is sitting on a sofa reading a newspaper.
Scenario 1:	Small girls are not expected to be full of aggressions.
Scenario 2:	Even small British girls want to drop bombs on the Germans.
Explanation:	The two scenarios are contrasted.
Type:	Everyday scene represents a communicative situation.
Invective:	The Germans are abominable. This is proved by the fact that even small British children detest them.

Cartoon 58   17.2.1915

Heading:	*What our Enemy has to Put up with.*
	Left panel
Caption:	*1: "Ach! Himmel! – A shell!"*
Description:	A stout German soldier is looking up and has his arm raised in a defensive movement.
Type:	Non-combatant military scene represents a communicative situation and interacts with the verbal part.
	Middle panel
Caption:	*2. !!!*
Description:	He is hit by a ball at the side of his head, which almost makes him fall to the ground.
Type:	Non-combatant military scene interacts with the verbal part.
	Right panel
Caption:	*3: "Great Krupps! – What is it?"*
Description:	He is holding the ball at a thread of its seam, inspecting it quizzically.
Scenario 1:	An intelligent and sportsman-like soldier can distinguish a shell from a ball and react accordingly.
Scenario 2:	This German soldier is neither intelligent nor sportsman-like and is, therefore, surprised to be hit by the ball.

Explanation: The two scenarios are contrasted.
Type: Non-combatant military scene represents a communicative situation and interacts with the verbal part.
Invective: The Germans are ignorant and stupid, e.g. this German soldier cannot tell a ball from a shell. Therefore they are militarily inferior.

Cartoon 59   17.2.1915
Heading:
Caption: *Chorus from the trench: "What 'ave you got there, Tom?" Tom (bringing in huge Uhlan): "Souvenir"*
Description: 'Tom' or 'Tommy' the small British soldier with a flag and a rifle over his shoulders is leading a very tall German Uhlan past a trench with five laughing British soldiers. Tom is raising one hand to his lips as if telling a secret.
Scenario 1: Taking and guarding a prisoner of war is a serious and potentially dangerous activity.
Scenario 2: Tom takes this very lightly and jokes about it.
Explanation: The two scenarios are contrasted.
Type: Non-combatant military scene represents a communicative situation and interacts with the verbal part.
Invective: The Germans are militarily inferior. This is proved by the fact that British soldiers are in control and good-humored.

Cartoon 60   24.2.1915
Heading:
Caption: *Tirpitz's Dream: A submarine in Kensington Gardens.*
Description: A submarine with two sailors on top has surfaced in a pond of a park. A huge crowd of women, children and dogs are fleeing the scene. Some of the women are pushing baby strollers.
Scenario 1: A marine admiral should develop an effective military strategy to overcome a war enemy.
Scenario 2: Tirpitz is dreaming of scaring women, children and dogs in a park in the middle of London.
Explanation: The two scenarios are contrasted. It is impossible for a submarine to surface in the pond of a park. The first impression of the drawn scene is that of a military attack. Only later it becomes clear that the scenario is counterfactual.
Type: War scene interacts with the verbal part.
Invective: The Germans are militarily inferior, e.g. Tirpitz is dreaming instead of working hard.

Cartoon 61
Heading:
Caption: *Study of Prussian household having its morning hate.*
Description: A man, his wife, his three children and a dachshund are gathered around the table of their dining room. They are all staring indignantly ahead of themselves without any eye contact or interaction.
Scenario 1: A family interacts in a friendly and supportive way.
Scenario 2: A German family have regular sessions in the morning, when they all stare indignantly ahead of themselves without any eye contact or interaction.
Explanation: The two spaces are contrasted.
Type: Everyday scene interacts with the verbal part.
Invective: Germans hate the British. They behave in a weird and fanatic way.

Punch cartoon 61

Cartoon 62   24.2.1915
Heading: *Running Amok.*
Caption: *German bull: "I know; I'm making a rotten exhibition of myself; but I*
                shall tell everybody I was goaded into it."
                (TH)E NEUTRAL CHINA STORES (sign over the front of the building)
Description: A bull is attacking the shop window front of a building. The glass is
                bursting and china dishes are lying broken on the ground. Over the
                sign there are five national flags flying (countries from left to right:
                Sweden, Norway, Switzerland, USA and Netherlands)
Scenario 1:   Germany attacks neutral nations without being provoked.
Scenario 2:   Germany will say afterwards that it had been provoked.
Explanation: The two scenarios are contrasted. Germany is represented as a bull,
                which is an irrational and naturally aggressive animal.
Type: Metonymic scene represents a communicative situation and interacts
                with the verbal part.
Invective: The Germans try to mislead the public. They are irrational and
                naturally aggressive.

Cartoon 63   17.3.1915
Heading:
Caption: *Head of 'Punish England' bureau invents new 'stunt.' Edible fish to be*
                branded and returned to ocean to influence world opinion against
                England.
                PUNISH ENGLAND (written on eight fish and a crab in a basin and on
                the bottom of three stamps of different sizes)
Description: A stout German with small round glasses and a moustache is sitting in
                front of a table with a large pot. On the table there are branding
                utensils. He is branding a fish with a kind of stamp on which 'Punish
                England' is written. On his left there is a large glass basin with several

fish of different sizes and a crab, which have *Punish England* written on them.

Scenario 1: There are subtle means of influencing world opinion against England.

Scenario 2: Germany adopts a very primitive and unconvincing way of influencing world opinion against England.

Explanation: The two scenarios are contrasted.

Type: Everyday scene interacts with the verbal part.

Invective: The Germans are ignorant and stupid.

Cartoon 64   17.3.1915
Heading:
Caption: *What to do with our German helmets.*
Description: Different alternative uses of a German spiked helmet are presented. A woman is using it as a shopping basket, two helmets decorate the top of garden fence pillars; a man uses one as an ashtray, a horse has one fastened to its head as a food container; a housemaid is using one as a coal bucket; it is used as a flower pot and a salesman uses one as a bell.

Scenario 1: The military use of a German spiked helmet.

Scenario 2: Peaceful uses of a German spiked helmet.

Explanation: The two scenarios are contrasted.

Type: Everyday scene interacts with the verbal part.

Invective: The Germans are militarily inferior; therefore an alternative use for German helmets must be found.

Cartoon 65   7.4.1915
Heading: *A Great Naval Triumph.*
Caption: *German submarine officer: "This ought to make them jealous in the sister service. Belgium saw nothing better than this."*
Description: A naval officer is standing on the deck of a surfaced submarine looking down at drowning civilians. They are mainly women, who are desperate for help. His arms are clasped across his chest and there is a sneering grin on his face.

Scenario 1: For normal people this situation gives rise to feelings of pity and the willingness to help.

Scenario 2: For the naval officer this situation gives rise to feelings of triumph and pride.

Explanation: The contrast between the normal expectation and the actual behavior of the naval officer shows his cruel and unrelenting nature. He alludes to Belgium which here is a metonymy for the atrocities the Germans committed there at the beginning of the war. Another important point which the readers are reminded of is the fact that Germany's violation of Belgium had been the determinant of Britain's intervention in the war.

Type: Counterfactual scene represents a communicative situation and interacts with the verbal part.

Invective: The Germans are callous and cruel, e.g. the officers of the German navy have no regard for suffering and dying civilians.

Cartoon 66   7.4.1915
Heading:
Caption: *German composer seeking inspiration for melody to a 'song of hate'.*
Description: A man with round glasses and a moustache is looking out of an open window with his left hand behind his ear. With his right hand he is writing musical notes on a sheet of paper. On a roof in the background there are two cats fighting. A third cat is watching the two. The moon illuminates the scene.

Scenario 1:   Composing music is an activity of creative, joyful and culturally valuable inspiration.

Scenario 2:   This German composer tries to get his inspiration from the inharmonious noise of fighting cats.

Explanation: The two scenarios are contrasted. Instead of composing music as a creative, joyful and culturally valuable achievement, the German composer works on the basis of a 'culture of hatred'.

Type: Everyday scene interacts with the verbal part.

Invective: The Germans have a pseudo-culture, e.g. the famous German musical culture has negative roots and is prone to be abused.

Cartoon 67   7.4.1915

Heading: *The Reward of Kultur*

Upper left panel

Description: Two fat and aggressive German soldiers with swords in their hands are threatening a piglet, which is sitting on some cards.

Type: Counterfactual scene interacts with the verbal part.

Upper right panel

Caption: *GOTT STRAFE ENGLA ...(May God punish England)*

Description: The piglet is writing *Gott strafe England* on the ground.

Scenario 1:   No one would be aggressive to a piglet without a reason.

Scenario 2:   The two soldiers are threatening the piglet without any obvious reason and are happy when it shows aggression towards England.

Scenario 3:   Piglets cannot write and do not have any hatred of England.

Scenario 4:   This one can write and expresses a hatred of England.

Explanation: The two scenarios are contrasted.

Type: Counterfactual scene interacts with the verbal part.

Middle left panel

Description: The two soldiers are taking the piglet by the hand and happily walk away with it.

Type: Counterfactual scene interacts with the verbal part.

Middle right panel

Description: The two soldiers and the piglet are standing in front of the German Kaiser who is looking at them in a very strict manner.

Type: Counterfactual scene interacts with the verbal part.

Lower left panel

Caption: *GOTT STRAFE ENGLAN ...*

Description: The German Kaiser appears very pleasantly surprised when the piglet writes *Gott strafe England* on the ground again.

Type: Counterfactual scene interacts with the verbal part.

Lower right panel

Description: He decorates the piglet, which is held up by one of the soldiers, with an Iron Cross. The other soldier is saluting.

Scenario 1:   An emperor will not take the stunts of a piglet too seriously.

Scenario 2:   The German Kaiser enjoys the aggressive stunt of the piglet against England.

Scenario 3:   Piglets cannot write and do not have any hatred of England.

Scenario 4:   This piglet can write and expresses a hatred of England.

Explanation: The first and second two scenarios are contrasted.

Type: Counterfactual scene interacts with the verbal part.

Invective: Germans hate the British. They are abominable, i.e. naturally unfriendly and aggressive.

Cartoon 68   14.4.1915

Heading:

Caption: *"Please will yer do us a bit o'drill, sir, 'cos it's Bertram's birfday?"*

Description:	Two small children with toy swords are approaching a German spy from behind who is standing on the seacoast with binoculars. On the right a woman is pushing an even smaller child, who is sitting in a wooden box with wheels underneath.
Scenario 1:	A spy works so efficiently that children do not startle him.
Scenario 2:	The children are startling this German spy.
Scenario 3:	An adult (and the reader) will immediately recognize the man as a German spy and will not ask a German to give him a 'bit o'drill'.
Scenario 4:	The children do not recognize the man as a German spy and ask him, to give them a 'bit o'drill'.
Explanation:	The first and second two scenarios are contrasted.
Type:	Everyday scene represents a communicative situation and interacts with the verbal part.
Invective:	The Germans are ignorant, naïve and stupid, e.g. their spies are inefficient.

Cartoon 69   28.4.1915

Heading:	*Further Adventures of the Cultured Pig.*
	Upper left panel
Caption:	*DEUTSCHLAND UEBER ALLES* (written on cards on the ground)
Description:	Two German soldiers are laughing at what the cultured pig has written.
Scenario 1:	Pigs cannot write.
Scenario 2:	This pig has written something that pleases German soldiers.
Explanation:	The two scenarios are contrasted.
Type:	Counterfactual scene interacts with the verbal part.
	Upper right panel
Caption:	*DEUTSCHLAND UEBER ALLES* (written on cards on the ground)
Description:	The two German soldiers are embracing each other in fright (of a sudden attack). Also the pig looks afraid.
Scenario 1:	Soldiers are not afraid of fighting against a sudden attacker.
Scenario 2:	Little children embrace each other when they are afraid.
Explanation:	The two scenarios are contrasted. The German soldiers are scared like little children.
Type:	Counterfactual scene interacts with the verbal part.
	Middle left panel
Caption:	*DEUTSCHLAND UEBER ALLES* (written on cards on the ground but only partially visible)
Description:	The two German soldiers are showing their willingness to fight. The pig hides behind them. (In the next panel they are fleeing).
Scenario 1:	Soldiers who demonstrate their willingness to fight will do so.
Scenario 2:	The two German soldiers run away after their demonstration.
Explanation:	The two scenarios are contrasted.
Type:	Counterfactual scene interacts with the verbal part.
	Middle right panel
Caption:	*DEUTSCHLAND UEBER ALLES ALLES* (written on cards on the ground but only partially visible)
Description:	The two German soldiers are fleeing from British soldiers. The pig has taken its Iron Cross from its neck and is wearing it on its waist.
Scenario 1:	Pigs do not have foresight.
Scenario 2:	This pig adapts quickly to the new situation.
Explanation:	The two scenarios are contrasted.
Type:	Counterfactual scene interacts with the verbal part.
	Lower left panel
Caption:	*DEUTSCHLAND U ER ALLES* (written on cards on the ground) (Letters on unordered cards:) *N; S; E; B; A; M.*

Description:	The pig has taken away the *U* and the *E* from *UEBER* and is looking for an *N* and a *T* to change *UEBER* to *UNTER*.
Scenario 1:	Pigs cannot write and think ahead.
Scenario 2:	This pig can write and adapts quickly to the new situation.
Explanation:	The two scenarios are contrasted.
Type:	Counterfactual scene interacts with the verbal part.
	Lower right panel
Caption:	*DEUTSCHLAND UNTER ALLES* (written on cards on the ground)
Description:	The pig has written something that pleases the British soldiers. In the background soldiers guard the two captive German soldiers.
Scenario 1:	Pigs cannot think ahead.
Scenario 2:	This pig adapts quickly to the new situation.
Explanation:	The two scenarios are contrasted. It is a sign of intelligence to change sides when facing a superior force. This reflects the English saying 'if you can't beat them, join them'.
Type:	Counterfactual scene interacts with the verbal part.
Invective:	The Germans are ignorant and stupid, e.g. their soldiers have an insufficient comprehension and they are less intelligent than pigs. In addition, German soldiers are pompous cowards.

Punch cartoon 70

Cartoon 70	26.5.1915
Heading:	
Caption:	*German (as wind changes): "Gott strafe England!"*
Description:	A German soldier with a spiked helmet and bulging eyes is walking through gas fumes covering his nose with his hand.
Scenario 1:	The Germans use poisonous gas, which harms and kills the enemy.
Scenario 2:	The German soldiers are harmed by their own poisonous gas, because the wind changes.
Explanation:	The two scenarios are contrasted. In the second Battle of Ypres, which began on 22 April 1915, German troops used poison gas against Canadian troops.

Type: War scene represents a communicative situation and interacts with the verbal part.

Invective: The Germans are ignorant and stupid, e.g. they do not foresee that their weapons may damage themselves.

Cartoon 71   26.5.1915

Heading: *The While-you-wait-school of Hatred*
                  (Eleven panels in four rows)
                  First row left panel

Caption:

Description: A stout father with small round glasses and a hat is talking about his young son, who is standing next to him, to another stout man with small round glasses and a moustache.

Type: Everyday scene interacts with the verbal part.
                  First row middle panel

Caption: *ENGLAND* (written on a large doll on a stand)

Description: The man with the moustache is now alone with the boy. He points at a large doll, which represents England. The boy greets the doll politely by taking off his cap.

Type: Everyday scene interacts with the verbal part.
                  First row right panel

Caption: *ENGLAND* (written on the doll))

Description: The man is shouting at the boy and is about to slap him.

Type: Everyday scene interacts with the verbal part.
                  Second row left panel

Caption: *ENGLAND* (written on the doll)

Description: The man is slapping the boy holding him by the scruff of his neck.

Type: Everyday scene interacts with the verbal part.
                  Second row middle panel

Caption: *ENGLAND* (written on the doll)

Description: The man is hitting the boy with a cane. The boy is screaming.

Type: Everyday scene interacts with the verbal part.
                  Second row right panel

Caption: *ENGLAND* (written on the doll)

Description: The man has taken the boy by the feet is swinging him around. The boy is screaming.

Type: Counterfactual scene interacts with the verbal part.
                  Third row left panel

Caption: *ENGLAND* (written on the doll)

Description: The boy is lying on the floor still screaming. The man is kicking him.

Type: Counterfactual scene interacts with the verbal part.
                  Third row middle panel

Caption: *ENGLAND* (written on the doll)

Description: The boy is sitting on the floor, weeping and holding his backside. He is looking at the doll.

Type: Everyday scene interacts with the verbal part.
                  Third row right panel

Caption: *ENGLAND* (written on the doll)

Description: He is about to throw a bottle at the doll.

Type: Everyday scene interacts with the verbal part.
                  Fourth row left panel

Caption: *ENGLAND* (written on the doll)

Description: The bottle has burst and its content has splashed on the face of the doll. The boy is aggressively jumping at it with his head and a foot.

Type: Counterfactual scene interacts with the verbal part.
                  Fourth row right panel

Description:	The boy is jumping up and down on the doll. He has torn out its legs and is beating it. The two men are watching the boy. The father is jumping up with joy; the second man is bowing his head in a pleased and devoted gesture.
Scenario 1:	Everyone will appreciate a pleasant and polite boy.
Scenario 2:	A German boy who is pleasant and polite to anything English will be re-conditioned to be impolite and aggressive.
Explanation:	The two scenarios are contrasted.
Type:	Counterfactual scene interacts with the verbal part.
Invective:	The Germans hate the British.

Cartoon 72   9.6.1915
Heading:
Caption: *"My friend, I don't like the look of things. They mean business. No one in England now kicks the cricket-ball."*
Description: Two German men are sitting at a table in a *Biergarten*. Two large steins of beer are on the table. The man on the right is holding a newspaper in his hand.
Scenario 1:   The English continue playing cricket.
Scenario 2:   The English have stopped playing cricket.
Explanation: The fact that the English have stopped playing cricket means that they are now concentrating on fighting the Germans. The cricket ball is not kicked but thrown and batted.
Type: Everyday scene represents a communicative situation.
Invective: The Germans are ignorant and stupid, because they cannot differentiate between soccer and cricket. In addition, they are cowards.

Punch cartoon 73

Cartoon 73   16.6.1915
Heading:
Caption: (In a speech bubble:) *CUCK-OO*
                Artful device resorted to by a German sniper who thought he was observed.

Description:	A German soldier with a spiked helmet and a rifle is standing high up on a plank between two trees. He is keeping a slightly ducked position. His helmet covers his eyes.
Scenario 1:	An English sniper will not shoot at a cuckoo and the voice and the camouflage of a German soldier may be misleading him.
Scenario 2:	An English sniper will not shoot at a cuckoo, but the physical appearance of a German soldier cannot mislead him.
Explanation:	The two scenarios are contrasted.
Type:	Counterfactual scene represents a communicative situation and interacts with the verbal part.
Invective:	The Germans are ignorant and stupid, e.g. this German soldier behaves in a naïve and stupid way.

Cartoon 74   23.6.1915

Heading:	*Injured Innocence.*
Caption:	*Citizen of Karlsruhe: "Himmel! To Attack a peaceful town so far from the theatre of operations it is unheard of. What devil taught them this wickedness?"* *DIE ZEITU... - ZEPPELIN ... SOUTHEND ...* (on the front page of a newspaper) *(Airmen of the Allies have bombarded Karlsruhe, the headquarters of the 14th German Army Corps. The town contains an important arsenal and large chemical, engineering and railway works.)*
Description:	A man is blasted off his chair by an explosion. His table is falling over and the beer in the stein on it is spilt.
Scenario 1:	The Germans bombed British towns irrespective of military targets.
Scenario 2:	The British retaliated by bombing Karlsruhe, which is a military target because of its 'important arsenal and large chemical, engineering and railway works' - even if it is far from the theatre of operations.
Explanation:	On 15 June 1915, British aircraft bombed Karlsruhe. The German speaker complains about the British air raids forgetting that the Germans started air raiding British towns. Because of this fact and the principle 'an eye for an eye, a tooth for an tooth', the British are justified in air raiding German towns.
Type:	War scene represents a communicative situation and interacts with the verbal part.
Invective:	The Germans are ignorant and naïve, because they overlook the fact that they started the air raids and are ignorant of the principle 'an eye for an eye, a tooth for an tooth'.

Cartoon 75   23.6.1915

Heading:	
Caption:	*Ex-Policeman (finding Germans hiding in wood): "Now then - pass along there, pass along!"*
Description:	An English soldier is forcing two German soldiers forward at the point of the bayonet of his rifle. The German soldiers are cringing and wailing.
Scenario 1:	Prisoners of war retain their sense of pride.
Scenario 2:	These German soldiers lose their sense of pride.
Explanation:	The two scenarios are contrasted.
Type:	War scene represents a communicative situation and interacts with the verbal part.
Invective:	The Germans are cowards. In addition, they do not have a sense of pride.

Cartoon 76   30.6.1915

Heading:

Caption: *"What ho, Charlie! Another little gasometer?"*

Description: An English soldier with the bayonet on his rifle is escorting a big German prisoner of war. The German prisoner of war is holding his hands up. They are walking past a horse stable from which another English soldier is shouting something.

Scenario 1: Soldiers are physically fit and in good shape.

Scenario 2: This German soldier is neither physically fit nor in good shape.

Explanation: The two scenarios are contrasted.

Type: Non-combatant military scene represents a communicative situation and interacts with the verbal part.

Invective: The Germans are militarily inferior, because they are fat rather than fit.

Cartoon 77   28.7.1915

Heading: *Tactless Questions.*

Caption: *Court Dentist (to Kaiser): "Will the Most Omnipotent take gas?"*

Description:

Scenario 1: A dentist uses gas to prevent the patient from feeling pain.

Scenario 2: The Germans use gas as a weapon of war, i.e. to kill.

Explanation: The two scenarios are contrasted. In the context of the war, the German Kaiser, who knows about the practice of using gas as a weapon, interprets the meaning of 'gas' in the military and not in the medical context.

Type: Everyday scene represents a communicative situation and interacts with the verbal part.

Invective: The Germans are ignorant and stupid, e.g. the German Kaiser is stupid because he is not able to differentiate the two contexts appropriately.

Cartoon 78   28.7.1915

Heading: *A Friend in Need.*

Caption: *Germany: "Who said 'God punish England!'? God bless England, who lets us have the sinews of war."*
COTTON FOR HOLLAND; COTTON FOR SWEDEN; COTTON FOR NORWAY; COTTON FOR DENMARK (written on the cotton bales).

Description: A German official in a uniform is standing in front of bales of cotton in a harbor. He is smiling all over the face with open and raised arms.

Scenario 1: War enemies detest each other.

Scenario 2: Germany does not detest England, when it can profit from English wealth.

Explanation: The two scenarios are contrasted. On 8 March 1915, Great Britain barred cotton from Germany.

Type: Everyday scene represents a communicative situation and interacts with the verbal part.

Invective: The Germans are abominable, because they are bigoted.

Cartoon 79   25.8.1915

Heading: *The Achievement.*

Caption: *Count Zeppelin: "Stands London where it did, my child?" The child: "Yes, father; missed it again." Count Zeppelin: "Then you had no success?" The child: "Oh, yes, father; I've got home again."*

Description: An animated zeppelin is leaning on Count Zeppelin embracing him and weeping. Count Zeppelin is wearing three Iron Crosses. His top hat is lying on the ground. It also has an Iron Cross on it.

Scenario 1: Success of an air raid means killing people and destroying buildings.

Scenario 2:	Success of this zeppelin air raid means that the zeppelin itself was not destroyed.
Explanation:	The two scenarios are contrasted.
Type:	Metonymic scene represents a communicative situation and interacts with the verbal part.
Invective:	The Germans are militarily inferior, because their weapons are ineffective.

Cartoon 80   1.9.1915

Heading:	*The New 'Battle of the Baltic.'*
Caption:	*Tirpitz (after Nelson – with a difference): "I see no Russian victory!"*
Description:	Admiral von Tirpitz dressed like Nelson is standing on a wooden pier. He is holding a telescope to his right eye on which he is wearing a patch. In the background there are five ships that have sunk almost completely.
Scenario 1:	An admiral uses all his senses in order to assess the military facts correctly.
Scenario 2:	Admiral von Tirpitz uses a blind eye to look at the military facts.
Explanation:	The two scenarios are contrasted. On 20 March 1915, Berlin had to admit that Memel, the Prussian fort on the Baltic, was occupied by Russians.
Type:	War scene represents a communicative situation and interacts with the verbal part.
Invective:	The Germans are ignorant and naïve.

Cartoon 81   29. 9.1915

Heading:	*The 'U' Cure.*
Caption:	*We understand that the cure of Admiral von Tirpitz is taking the form of immersion in hot-water baths of special construction. The distinguished invalid, we hear, shows little improvement.* *BAD* (written on the matt in front of the tub) *HOT HOTTER* (written over the faucets)
Description:	Admiral von Tirpitz is lying in a bathtub with just his head and his toes showing. The tub has the shape of a 'U'.
Scenario 1:	The hot water cure in a U-shaped bath tub does not bring improvement to von Tirpitz as a 'distinguished invalid'.
Scenario 2:	The use of submarines does not bring success to von Tirpitz as Germany's most prominent admiral.
Explanation:	The two scenarios are set side by side. The text reads like a medical bulletin. The bath tub, which has the shape of a 'U', alludes to the German term *U-Boot*, anglicized as *U-boat*. A blending between a hydropathical treatment and the fight of the German submarines is evoked.
Type:	Metonymic scene interacts with the verbal part.
Invective:	The Germans are militarily inferior; therefore they will not succeed in their war efforts.

Cartoon 82   3.1.0.1915

Heading:	*The Ruling Passion.*
Caption:	*Even in the act of surrender the Landsturmer does not forget his commercial instincts, which have made him what he is.* *DECORATIONS BY 'HOHENZOLLERNS', EMPIRE BUILDERS & DECORATORS* (written on a poster).
Description:	A German soldier is raising his hands in surrender, stepping out of a trench. In front of him there is a poster. On either side of him there are

two other German soldiers about to surrender. The one on the right is
holding a poster in his hands.

Scenario 1:   Soldiers who have to surrender will feel dejected.
Scenario 2:   The German soldiers think of making money while surrendering.
Explanation: The two scenarios are contrasted.
Type: War scene interacts with the verbal part.
Invective: The Germans are abominable, e.g. the German soldiers have no sense
               of pride; they have a sense of making money instead.

Cartoon 83   10.10.1915
Heading: *A Hint to our Admiralty*
Caption: *Dummy baby design to tempt the German fleet to come out.*
Description: Behind the closed gates of a harbor, German war ships point their guns
               at a small vessel with a 'dummy baby'. An admiral is giving a sign to
               fire.
Scenario 1:   Innocent and helpless babies are no targets for a navy.
Scenario 2:   For the German navy innocent and helpless babies are favorite targets.
Explanation: Because of the cowardly nature of the German navy, only babies, i.e.
               defenseless targets, would lure them to come out into the open sea.
Type: Counterfactual scene interacts with the verbal part.
Invective: The Germans are cowards, e.g. the members of the German navy are
               afraid of the British fleet.

Punch Cartoon 83

Cartoon 84   10.10.1915
Heading:
Caption: *'Their Master's voice' record of the Kaiser's famous adaptation of the
               American poem (as applied to the Crown Prince): "I wish I'd raised
               my boy to be a soldier."*
Description: A group of smiling Germans is gleefully listening to a gramophone
               operated by William II in civilian clothes.
Scenario 1:   The Crown Prince has entered on an outstanding military career.
Scenario 2:   The military career of the Crown Prince is a deplorable failure.

Explanation: The title of the original song was 'I didn't raise my boy to be a soldier'.[1] The German Kaiser's adaptation turns the song into its opposite, i.e. the Kaiser regrets that the military career of the Crown Prince has turned out to be a failure.

Type: Everyday scene interacts with the verbal part.

Invective: The Germans are militarists, but inefficient ones.

Cartoon 85   1.12.1915

Heading:

Caption: *Tommy (finding a German prisoner who speaks English): "Look wot you done to me, you blighters! 'Ere - 'ave a cigarette?"*

Description: In a room with many German prisoners of war Tommy with a bandaged head is talking to a big German prisoner of war. The English soldier is pointing with his left hand at his head injury and with his right hand offers the German a cigarette.

Scenario 1:   A soldier who has been injured will be angry with the soldiers of the enemy.

Scenario 2:   German soldiers have injured this English soldier, but he is still friendly to the German prisoner of war.

Explanation: The two scenarios are contrasted. The body language of Tommy expresses the accusation. The fact that he has forgiven the Germans is given in the friendly (verbal) offer of a cigarette to the German prisoner of war. The two phases of the accusation and the forgiveness are integrated into one static drawing.
The invective is emphasized by contrasting the aggressive and unrelenting German soldiers with the forgiving English soldiers.

Type: Non-combatant military scene represents a communicative situation and interacts with the verbal part.

Invective: The Germans are abominable. The British retain a sense of fairness and friendliness.

Cartoon 86   15.12.1915

Heading:

Caption: *Tommy (to his prisoner): "Do you understand English?" German: "I a leedle undershdand." Tommy: "Well, then, blimey! You try an' 'op it, and you won't alf bloomin' well cop it!"*

Description: Tommy with the bayonet on his rifle is escorting a very tall German prisoner of war. The German is holding his hands up.

Scenario 1:   When a listener only has a restricted command of a foreign language, one should speak to him slowly and clearly and avoid a strong accent as well as dialect expressions.

Scenario 2:   Tommy uses a strong accent as well as dialect expressions in speaking to this German prisoner of war.

Explanation: The two scenarios are contrasted. The fact that the German prisoner of war has a poor command of English can be inferred from his strong accent. The cartoon also contains self-irony in that Tommy is presented as a little naïve but charming.

Type: Non-combatant military scene represents a communicative situation and interacts with the verbal part.

Invective: The Germans are militarily inferior. This is supported by Tommy's patronizing behavior.

---

[1] The song was composed by Al Piantadosi and the lyrics were written in 1915 by Alfred Bryan. It expressed Americans' resistance to be involved in World War I. (Cf. http://www.creativefolk.com/lyrics.html#anchor272658).

Cartoon 87   15.12.1915
Heading: *If we had been Prussians.*
Caption: *Scenes from a revised history of Great Britain. A sequel to the signing of Magna Charta.*
Description: In the foreground on the right, King John is tearing up the Magna Charta in front of his tent, while the barons are walking away in the background on the left.
Scenario 1:   In history, King John signed the Magna Charta and observed its rules.
Scenario 2:   In this 'revised history', King John is tearing up the Magna Charta ignoring its rules.
Explanation: The two scenarios are contrasted. The Germans sign treaties and then ignore them. If King John had behaved like the Germans, the British democracy could not have developed.
Type: Counterfactual scene interacts with the verbal part.
Invective: The Germans are abominable, because they have a bad character.

Cartoon 88   15.12.1915
Heading:
Caption: *Captured German officer (to English officer in charge of German prisoners): "You fight for money; we fight for honour." English officer: "Ah, well! Neither of us seems to get what we want, do we?"*
Description: A German officer on the left and an English officer are talking in the middle of destroyed buildings. In the background on the left, there are German prisoners of war facing another English officer.
Scenario 1:   The English soldiers fight for money and do not get it.
Scenario 2:   The German soldiers fight for honor and do not get it.
Explanation: The two scenarios are contrasted. This cartoon only entails the invective of the German officer that the British fight for money, which the English officer rejects.
Type: Non-combatant military scene represents a communicative situation and interacts with the verbal part.
Invective: The German soldier's attempt to paint a picture of moral superiority is rejected.

Cartoon 89   22.12.1915
Heading: *Christmas Amenities.*
Caption: *German sentry: "Shall we zing you zome carols to cheer you oop?"*
              English sentry: "Noa! Sing us something funny, sing us the "ymn of 'ate!"
Description: In the foreground on the right, there is a trench with four British soldiers. One is standing and shouting something, the others are sitting and smoking. In the background on the left, there is a German soldier with his head above the trench also shouting something. Between the two trenches there is barbed wire.
Scenario 1:   The 'hymn of hate' will annoy the people against which it is directed.
Scenario 2:   The English are amused by the German 'hymn of hate', which is directed against them.
Explanation: The two scenarios are contrasted. The German accent is parodied. On 25th December 1914 there was an unofficial Christmas truce initiated by the soldiers.
Type: War scene represents a communicative situation and interacts with the verbal part.
Invective: The Germans are militarily inferior; therefore the English need not take them seriously.

Cartoon 90   22.12.1915
Heading: *If we had been Prussians.*
Caption: *Scenes from a revised history of Great Britain. Edward III (to Queen*
                Philippa, after the taking of Calais): "Woman, you meddle. War is
                war! Besides, you are too late."
Description: Edward III is standing in front of the kneeling Philippa, holding her
                hand. He is pointing with his other hand to a tower with a gallows on
                which six people have been hanged. To the right of the couple, a
                kneeling man in armor is presenting two large keys on a cushion. On
                the left there are three guards.
Scenario 1:   After taking Calais, Edward III pardoned the defenders.
Scenario 2:   In the same situation, a Prussian king would have killed some of the
                defenders.
Explanation: The two scenarios are contrasted. There is a blending of a historical
                situation and the present time.
Type: Counterfactual scene represents a communicative situation and
                interacts with the verbal part.
Invective: The Germans are callous and cruel.

Punch Cartoon 91

Cartoon 91   22.12.1915
Heading: *The Saddest Sight of the War.*
Caption: *A German professor who has mislaid his beer ticket.*
                BIER HALLE (written over the entrance of a building)
Description: A prototypical stout German with round glasses, a moustache and a
                bow tie is standing in front of a building, searching the pockets of his
                suit with both hands. In the background to his left, a warden is standing
                in front of the entrance to the 'Bierhalle'. To his right, a similar
                looking man is walking towards the entrance with a smile on his face,
                holding up a ticket.
Scenario 1:   Professors spend all their energy on scientific endeavors.
Scenario 2:   The greatest concern of this German professor is his beer consumption.
Explanation: The two scenarios are contrasted.
Type: Everyday scene interacts with the verbal part.

Invective: The Germans are abominable, e.g. the German professors are lager louts.

Cartoon 92   29.12.1915
Heading: *Sweeping the North Sea.*
Caption: *Chorus of German admirals: "Still no sign of the British skulkers!"*
                DER TAG (name of the boat)
                Oscar II (name of the ship in the background)
Description: Five German admirals are in a small boat in a harbor. The harbor has large gates, which are slightly open. The *Oscar II* is the only ship to be seen on the horizon.
Scenario 1:   Admirals will prepare themselves seriously and conscientiously.
Scenario 2:   These five German admirals are fooling around like children. They are happy that they do not have to face the British fleet.
Explanation: The two scenarios are contrasted.
                In 1915 Henry Ford's 'Peace Ship', *Oscar II*, set sail for Norway on a pacifist expedition to end World War I.
Type: Counterfactual scene interacts with the verbal part.
Invective: The Germans are cowards, e.g. the German admirals are foolish and cowardly.

Punch cartoon 92

Cartoon 93   29.12.1915
Heading: *If we had been Prussians.*
Caption: *Scenes from a revised History of Great Britain.*
                Richard III (after that little affair of the Princes in the Tower) receives, at his own request, the Iron Cross.
Description: Richard III, sitting on his throne, receives an Iron Cross out of the hands of a bishop. In the background there are seven guards, some of whom are saluting and some of whom are playing fanfares.
Scenario 1:   Richard III covered up the presumed murder of two boys.

Scenario 2:	In the same situation a Prussian King would ask to receive an Iron Cross.
Explanation:	The two scenarios are contrasted. This means that there is not only an inflation of Iron Crosses, but also a reversal of the meaning of receiving one. During the reign of Richard III's two boys called 'Princes in the Tower' disappeared. Who they were and whether he was responsible for their deaths remains a puzzle to this day.
Type:	Counterfactual scene interacts with the verbal part.
Invective:	The Germans are callous and cruel.

Cartoon 94	Punch's Almanack for 1916

Left upper panel

Heading:	*The German hunt for metal*
Caption:	*Citizen having his heel-tips removed.*
Description:	A German soldier takes off the metal heel-tips of a civilian who is leaning against a fence. A second soldier is watching.
Scenario 1:	The German economy produces the raw materials for military goods efficiently.
Scenario 2:	These German soldiers acquire the raw materials for military goods in a very inefficient way from civilians.
Explanation:	The two scenarios are contrasted.
Type:	Everyday scene interacts with the verbal part.

Right upper panel

Caption:	*Dog's iron drinking-vessel being commandeered.*
Description:	A German soldier with his saber ready tries to take the drinking-vessel away from a dog. He looks apprehensive. Three other soldiers are watching the scene.
Scenario 1:	The German economy produces the raw materials for military goods efficiently.
Scenario 2:	This German soldier acquires the raw materials for military goods from dogs.
Explanation:	The two scenarios are contrasted.
Type:	Everyday scene interacts with the verbal part.

Middle panel

Caption:	*Confiscating child's tin trumpet by imperial decree.*
Description:	A German soldier takes away the tin trumpet from a child, who is crying. He looks apprehensive. Three other soldiers are watching the scene. One of them is holding the paper with the imperial decree.
Scenario 1:	The German economy produces the raw materials for military goods efficiently.
Scenario 2:	This German soldier acquires the raw materials for military goods from little children.
Explanation:	The two scenarios are contrasted.
Type:	Everyday scene interacts with the verbal part.

Lower panel

Caption:	*Removing articles of metallic substance by high velocity vacuum process.*
Description:	A German soldier operates a 'high velocity vacuum machine' which sucks the metal accessories from a civilian, who is kept by another soldier from being drawn into the machine. A German general is watching the scene.
Scenario 1:	The German economy produces the raw materials for military goods efficiently.
Scenario 2:	This German soldier acquires the raw materials for military goods from ordinary civilians by using a complicated machine.

Explanation:	The two scenarios are contrasted.
Type:	Counterfactual scene interacts with the verbal part.
Invective:	The Germans are ignorant and naïve, because their war efforts are inefficient.

Cartoon 95   Punch's Almanack for 1916

Heading:	*After the Conquest – Trafalgar Square.*
Caption:	*(Passed by the Imperial German Censor on the ground that the artist's attempted humour may be tolerated for the sake of his prophetic insight.)*
Description:	The scenario is Trafalgar Square with several statues of prominent Germans such as von Tirpitz and Zeppelin. Instead of the column with Nelson on top, the whole column is a longish statue of the German Emperor. German soldiers are parading between the lions.
Scenario 1:	Trafalgar Square as it used to be.
Scenario 2:	Trafalgar Square after the German occupation.
Explanation:	Every British reader will find Trafalgar Square after the German occupation an abominable sight.
Type:	Counterfactual scene interacts with the verbal part.
Invective:	The Germans are abominable, because they are pushy and meddlesome.

Cartoon 96   Punch's Almanack for 1916

Heading:	*Truth Mirrored in German Art.*
Caption:	*Scene showing the refined cruelty with which starving German prisoners are treated by the British.*
	(The above two pictures[1], the work of typical Berlin artists, have been substituted by the Imperial German Censor for an impossible cartoon in which doubt was cast upon the divinity of the Kaiser.)
Description:	A British soldier is marching past the barbed wire fence of a prisoner of war camp. Behind the fence many prisoners are watching him. He is carrying his rifle with a bayonet over his shoulder. With the bayonet, he has pierced a large sausage, which has six more sausage attached to it. Behind him two other soldiers are laughing at the prisoners.
Scenario 1:	The German prisoners of war are treated in a fair manner and neither tortured nor humiliated by the British.
Scenario 2:	The British torture and humiliate the German prisoners of war.
Scenario 3:	The 'Imperial German Censor' believes in the divinity of the Kaiser
Scenario 4:	The cartoonist doubts the divinity of the Kaiser.
Explanation:	The first and second two scenarios are contrasted. The 'Imperial German Censor', who believes in the divinity of the Kaiser, cannot be taken seriously. Therefore the picture which he has selected cannot represent the truth either.
Type:	Everyday scene interacts with the verbal part.
Invective:	The Germans try to mislead the public, e.g. the 'Imperial German Censor' is an obvious manipulator of the truth.

Cartoon 97   Punch's Almanack for 1916

Heading:	
Caption:	*The original arrangement of these two figures has been readjusted by the Imperial German Censor so as to present truth instead of falsehood. The legend has been suppressed.*

---

[1] The second panel was ignored because it did not concern Germans.

Description:	An unarmed German soldier is running from left to right. An armed British soldier to the right of him is running in the same direction. There is a vertical 'split screen line', i.e. an artificial rift in the middle of the cartoon, which shows that the original cartoon has been cut into two halves that have swapped places.
Scenario 1:	The German soldier is chasing the British soldier.
Scenario 2:	The British soldier is chasing the German soldier.
Explanation:	The scenario given in the cartoon is so obviously inconsistent that the viewer is provoked to identify two separate scenarios in the left and the right half of the cartoon, to swap the two halves and thereby rearrange the original single scenario of a British soldier chasing a German.
	This means that the readjustment of the two figures by the 'Imperial German Censor' is recognized as a very obvious and naive forgery of the original representation.
Type:	Counterfactual scene interacts with the verbal part.
Invective:	The Germans try to mislead the public, e.g. the 'Imperial German Censor' adulterates the facts. He is ignorant and naive because he believes that this obvious adulteration will not be noticed.

Punch cartoon 97

Cartoon 98	Punch's Almanack for 1916
Heading:	*Thoughts that Kill.*
Caption:	*German professor of chemistry thinking out a new poison-gas.*
	(Passed by the Imperial German Censor as an admissible compliment to German science.)
Description:	A bald, overweight German professor is sitting in an armchair smoking a pipe: Behind him a dog and a cat are lying dead on the floor and a parrot is falling off its perch dead. Small zigzag lines near the head of the professor indicate effusing poisonous gas.
Scenario 1:	Thoughts have no direct physical effect.
Scenario 2:	The thoughts of this German professor have a direct physical effect in reality, i.e. just thinking of a new poison-gas kills his pets.
Scenario 3:	Science should be constructive and invent useful things.
Scenario 4:	German Science is destructive and invents lethal weapons.
Explanation:	The first two and the second two scenarios are contrasted.

Type:	Counterfactual scene interacts with the verbal part.
Invective:	The Germans are callous and cruel, e.g. their scientists are perverted.

Cartoon 99	Punch's Almanack for 1916
Heading:	
Caption:	*Tommy (to new arrival at prisoners' camp): "What was your occupation?" German: "Army butcher." Tommy: "Cattle or babies?"*
Description:	Tommy is interviewing a German prisoner of war.
Scenario 1:	An army butcher slaughters animals for food.
Scenario 2:	An army butcher slaughters babies.
Explanation:	The term *butcher* is ambiguous because it has an everyday meaning and a metaphorical one.
Type:	Non-combatant military scene represents a communicative situation.
Invective:	The Germans are callous and cruel, because the Germans soldiers kill even babies.

Cartoon 100	Punch's Almanack for 1916
Heading:	
Caption:	*Ex-Policeman (recognising a peace-time acquaintance): "Lumme! It's you, is it? Still sneakin' abaht, are yer? I recollect warnin' you some time back abaht loiterin' in the Fulham Road!"*
Description:	A British soldier with a rifle and a bayonet on it is arresting a German soldier with a gaping mouth in a forest. The German is raising both arms in surrender.
Scenario 1:	As a policeman, the British man observed the German as a civilian 'sneaking about'.
Scenario 2:	As a soldier, the British man observes the German as a soldier also 'sneaking about'.
Explanation:	The British policeman/soldier does not see a difference between the two situations.
Type:	War scene represents a communicative situation.
Invective:	The Germans are militarily inferior.

Cartoon 101	Punch's Almanack for 1916
Heading:	*England under the Hun.*
Caption:	*Disastrous result of attempt of German officer to import the goosestep*
Description:	Doing the goosestep, a British soldier kicks the backside of the highest German military leader, i.e. the Kaiser who looks surprised.
Scenario 1:	The German soldiers follow the German military tradition subserviently by doing the goose-step.
Scenario 2:	The British soldiers use the German military tradition to get their revenge on the German Kaiser.
Explanation:	The two scenarios are contrasted.
Type:	Everyday scene interacts with the verbal part.
Invective:	The Germans are militarists. Their military tradition is pompous and stupid.

Cartoon 102	Punch's Almanack for 1916
Heading:	*Prussianised Sport.*
	Upper section, left panel
Caption:	*The Krupps' Long Driver Apparatus.*
Description:	A fat German golf player is about to strike the ball. On his back, he carries the 'Krupps' Long Driver Apparatus'.
Type:	Everyday scene interacts with the verbal part.
	Upper section, right panel

Caption:	*'Hate' on the green.*
Description:	A British golf player has putted the ball successfully. The German golf player shows a very angry reaction.
Scenario 1:	The German golf player is superior due to his 'Krupps' Long Driver Apparatus'.
Scenario 2:	The British golf player is superior in spite of the German's "Krupps' Long Driver Apparatus". He plays in a fair manner.
Explanation:	The two scenarios are contrasted.
Type:	Everyday scene interacts with the verbal part.
	Middle section, left and right panel
Caption:	*The new Potsdam putting.*
	Middle section, left panel
Caption:	*Kick your opponent in the stomach and - he won't know how you holed out.*
Description:	A German golf player kicks his British opponent in the stomach, who falls over backward.
Type:	Everyday scene interacts with the verbal part.
	Middle section, right panel
Description:	While the unfair player is proudly pointing at the hole, his opponent is holding his belly with pain.
Scenario 1:	The idea of golf is fair play.
Scenario 2:	The German golf player uses unfair means to win.
Explanation:	The two scenarios are contrasted.
Type:	Everyday scene interacts with the verbal part.
	Lower section, left panel
Caption:	*Handy magnet for drawing ball from bad lie.*
Description:	A German golf player uses a magnet behind his back to retrieve a ball from a bad position.
Scenario 1:	The idea of golf is fair play.
Scenario 2:	The German golf player uses unfair means to get an advantage.
Explanation:	The two scenarios are contrasted.
Type:	Everyday scene interacts with the verbal part.
	Lower section, right panel
Caption:	*Dealing with a caddy who will hand you the wrong club.*
Description:	A German golf player shoots a caddie with a pistol, who falls over backward.
Scenario 1:	There is a civilized way of dealing with the mistake a caddie makes.
Scenario 2:	The German golf player reacts inadequately to the mistake the caddie made.
Explanation:	The two scenarios are contrasted. The cartoon makes four similar points and invectives explicit. The upper and middle section with two panels each and the lower left panel and the lower right panel can be regarded as four paragraphs exemplifying a more general point referring to the unfair and even cruel way 'Prussians' play sports.
Type:	Everyday scene interacts with the verbal part.
Invective:	The Germans are militarists, e.g. they carry their militarism into sports.

Cartoon 103	Punch's Almanack for 1916
Heading:	*Prussianised Sport.*
	Upper panel
Caption:	*Asphyxiation on the soccer field.*
Description:	A soccer team with gas masks is running towards the opposite goal, spraying a large cloud of gas. The two front runners have gas cylinders on their backs. One player of the opposing team is lying on the ground, two are about to faint.

Scenario 1:	The British use fair play.
Scenario 2:	The Germans use poisonous gas, i.e. unfair means, to win in soccer.
Explanation:	The two scenarios are contrasted.
Type:	Counterfactual scene interacts with the verbal part.
	Middle panel
Caption:	*To brighten cricket. The explosive ball.*
Description:	The ball of a German-looking pitcher explodes at the bat of the batsman who is falling over backward. Four fieldsmen are watching with excitement.
Scenario 1:	The British use fair play.
Scenario 2:	The Germans use an explosive ball, i.e. unfair means, to win in cricket.
Explanation:	The two scenarios are contrasted.
Type:	Counterfactual scene interacts with the verbal part.
	Lower panel
Caption:	*Torpedoing salmon in the Highlands.*
Description:	A German on a boat is watching an explosion in the water which has ejected a salmon into the air. A Scottish angler in the water is watching the scene.
Scenario 1:	The British use sportsman-like means in angling.
Scenario 2:	The Germans use torpedoes, i.e. unfair means, in angling.
Explanation:	The two scenarios are contrasted.
Type:	Counterfactual scene interacts with the verbal part.
Invective:	The Germans are militarists, e.g. they carry their militarism into sports.

Cartoon 104   5.1.1916

Heading:	*The New Leaf.*
Caption:	*Fancy portrait of Prussian poet preparing to write a hymn of love - in case it should be wanted.*
Description:	A stout Prussian poet is sitting at a table in front of a statue of the German Emperor with a laurel wreath. On the floor there is a torn sheet of paper and a beer stein.
Scenario 1:	If a country loses a war, its citizens will be sad.
Scenario 2:	If the Germans lose the war, they will be bootlicking.
Explanation:	The two scenarios are contrasted.
Type:	Everyday scene interacts with the verbal part.
Invective:	The Germans are abominable, because they have a bad character.

Cartoon 105   19.1.1916

Heading:	*Prussian Dream of Peace in the Spring.*
Description:	A fat German hunter points his gun at a nest with very young birds and uses a branch to steady his shot. A child accompanying the hunter jumps up in excitement. A dachshund watches the hunter.
Scenario 1:	A normal dream of peace in the spring entails joyous, non-aggressive behavior in a natural surrounding.
Scenario 2:	A German dream of peace in the spring means aggressive behavior against young and defenseless birds in a natural surrounding.
Explanation:	The two scenarios are contrasted.
Type:	Counterfactual scene interacts with the verbal part.
Invective:	The Germans are callous and cruel.

Cartoon 106   2.2.1916

Heading:	*How a Prussian St. George would have done it.*
Caption:	*POISON LAID for DRAGONS* (written on a sign)
Description:	In the foreground a dead dragon is lying on its back. In the

165

background on the left, St. George is sitting on horseback looking at the dragon. On the right a woman is also looking at the dragon from behind a tree.

Scenario 1: St. George killed the dragon by fighting against him face to face.

Scenario 2: The 'Prussian St. George' killed the dragon by poisoning him with gas.

Explanation: The two scenarios are contrasted. Germans avoid fighting face to face and prefer perfidious means.

Type: Counterfactual scene interacts with the verbal part.

Invective: The Germans are cowards.

Cartoon 107   9.2.1916

Heading: *A German Holiday.*

Caption: *Child: "Please, sir, what is this holiday for?" Official: "Because our zeppelins have conquered England." Child: "Have they brought us back any bread?" Official: "Don't ask silly questions. Wave your flag."*

Description: In a town, a gloomy looking German official is distributing national German flags to children.

Scenario 1: Conquering England means having enough food and getting rid of the destitution and misery of the war.

Scenario 2: Since Germany has not conquered England, the destitution and misery of the war remain.

Scenario 3: The questions of children should be answered with patience and understanding.

Scenario 4: The German official does not answer the questions of the children, because in that case, he would have to admit that the Germany have not conquered England.

Explanation: The first and second two scenarios are contrasted. Conquering England means winning the war. But since Germany has not done that, there is no reason to celebrate.

Type: Everyday scene represents a communicative situation and interacts with the verbal part.

Invective: The Germans try to mislead the public, but they will not succeed, because even children can call attention to the falsehood of German propaganda.

Cartoon 108   9.2.1916

Heading: *Another Example of Prussian Effrontery.*

Caption: *Officer of zeppelin (in perfect English): "Would you kindly direct me to the War Office."*

Description: An officer of a German zeppelin is hovering in the air above a British policeman with a torch who is looking at him in surprise. The German is suspended by a belt and a rope.

Scenario 1: Any member of an enemy zeppelin will try to keep a low profile.

Scenario 2: The officer of the German zeppelin is asking the policeman openly to give him directions to find his target.

Explanation: The two scenarios are contrasted. The behavior of the German is extremely naïve.

Type: Counterfactual scene represents a communicative situation and interacts with the verbal part.

Invective: The Germans are militarily inferior. In addition they are naïve.

Cartoon 109   19.4.1916

Heading:

Caption: *Face massage specialist: "No doubt, sir, your speeches on* frightfulness have affected your expression." Prussian orator: "Well, you must do the best you can for me. Tonight I have to speak on 'our love for the smaller nations.'"

Description:	An elderly man is sitting in the chair of a face massage specialist, who is treating his face. The man has a disgruntled looking face with many wrinkles.
Scenario 1:	A disgruntled looking face reflects a disgruntled attitude.
Scenario 2:	A friendly looking face reflects a friendly attitude.
Scenario 3:	Speeches on frightfulness give an orator a disgruntled looking face and a disgruntled attitude.
Scenario 4:	The face massage specialist changes this disgruntled looking face into one with a friendly expression and a friendly attitude.
Explanation:	The first two and the second two scenarios are contrasted. The transition from the first two and the second two scenarios may be a little hard to follow.
Type:	Everyday scene represents a communicative situation and interacts with the verbal part.
Invective:	The Germans are abominable, because they are bad-tempered and disgruntled. In addition they are naïve.

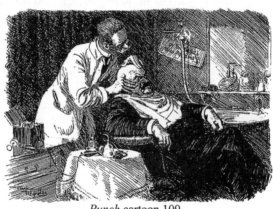

Punch cartoon 109

Cartoon 110	10.5.1916
Heading:	
Caption:	*Unfortunate position of once popular Berlin naval battle artist, whose occupation has vanished through his having rashly sunk the entire British fleet at an early stage of the war.*
Description:	An elderly man is sitting on the street in front of his sidewalk paintings. He is holding his hat in his hand.
Scenario 1:	A popular and successful naval battle artist is wealthy.
Scenario 2:	This German naval battle artist is shown as an extremely poor down-and-out.
Scenario 3:	In the picture, the entire British fleet is sunk.
Scenario 4:	In reality, the British fleet is superior to the German one.
Explanation:	The artist himself is responsible for this calamity. He failed to foresee that painting too many pictures of successful German ships sinking British ones, would cause the Germans to lose interest because they would believe that the British navy had been wiped out.

The picture scenario is a scenario of fantasy and invention and must not be confounded with reality.

Type: Everyday scene interacts with the verbal part.

Invective: The Germans try to mislead the public. Their propaganda is extremely exaggerated. Artists who work for the German propaganda machine are naive and shortsighted.

Cartoon 111 31.5.1916

Heading: *Injured Innocence*

Caption: *The German Ogre: "Heaven knows that I had to do this in self-defense; it was forced upon me." (aside) "Fee, fi, fo, fum!"*
Belgian Neutra(lity) (written on a torn sheet of paper under the left foot of the ogre) *Weltmacht oder Niedergang (world power or demise)* (written on a board)

Description: The German Chancellor, Hindenburg, is drawn like an ogre with two modern assets, i.e. the Iron Cross and the German spiked helmet. Under his left foot, there is a torn sheet of paper with 'Belgian Neutra(lity)' written on it. Corpses of children are lying on the ground.

Scenario 1: Hindenburg attacked Belgium in self-defense.

Scenario 2: Hindenburg attacked Belgium with premeditation.

Explanation: There is a blending of Hindenburg and an an ogre or a prehistoric fighter. The aggressive look, the cruelty against children and the aside betray Hindenburg's words as a lie. Germany violated the neutrality of Belgium and German soldiers committed atrocities against Belgians at the beginning of the war.

Type: Metonymic scene represents a communicative situation and interacts with the verbal part.

Invective: The Germans try to mislead the public. Hindenburg is aggressive, cruel and a liar.

Cartoon 112 14.6.1916

Heading: *Unconscious Candour.*

Caption: *German father: "Can't we see our victorious fleet?" Official: "No, you can't. Nobody can!"*
WILHELMSHAFEN - CLOSED TILL FURTHER NOTICE. (notice on the door)

Description: A German official is standing in front of a padlocked door with the above notice. He raises both hands to keep a German family (father, mother, child and dachshund) from entering.

Scenario 1: People are not allowed to see the victorious fleet, because of some unstated reason.

Scenario 2: People are not able to see the victorious fleet, because it does not exist/it was not victorious.

Explanation: The notice on the door 'Closed till further notice' evokes a conceptual space behind the door. The question of the German father refers to this space and presupposes a victorious German fleet in this space. In the first answer of the German official, this presupposition is not rejected, but in his second answer, the ambiguity of *nobody can,* meaning 'nobody is allowed to' and 'nobody is able to', is a denial that there is a victorious German fleet.

Type: Everyday scene represents a communicative situation and interacts with the verbal part.

Invective: The Germans try to mislead the public. German officials are stupid, because they fail to notice ambiguities where it would be essential to do so; Germans are easily impressed by their officials; they are stupid, because they also fail to notice ambiguities.

Punch cartoon 112

Cartoon 113   28.6.1916
Heading: *The Judgment of Paris.*
Caption: *Paris: "We've decided to keep the apple for ourselves." Germania:*
"Then what do I get?" Paris: "The pip!"
ECONOMIC CONFERENCE OF ALLIES (notice above the entrance) TRADE (written on the apple in the hand of Paris) KULTU(R) (written on the paper roll under the arm of Germania)
Description: Paris is walking down the steps of the building where the economic conference of the Allies has taken place. He is holding an apple in his left hand. At the bottom of the steps an ugly and disgruntled old woman, Germania, is waiting for him. Under her right arm, she carries a paper roll.
Scenario 1:   The Allies have planned a prosperous economic cooperation and future.
Scenario 2:   Germany will be excluded from this prosperous economic cooperation and therefore there will have a gloomy future.
Explanation: The apple symbolizes a prosperous economic future and the pip symbolizes a gloomy one.
Type: Metonymic scene represents a communicative situation and interacts with the verbal part.
Invective: The Germans are abominable; therefore it serves them right to be excluded from economic advantages.

Cartoon 114	5.7.1916

Upper left panel

Heading: *The War After The War. Details of the Coming German Attack. Mr. Punch's Solemn Warnings.*

Caption: *Subtle means will be used to render our health resorts unpopular, and thus drive us to Homburg and other German spas.*

Description: A German man is walking away from a park bench on which he has placed sharp pointed objects. In the background a man is jumping up with pain after having been pricked by one of these objects.

Scenario 1: Subtle means will not be noticed.

Scenario 2: The device the German man uses is very obvious.

Explanation: The two scenarios are contrasted.

Type: Counterfactual scene interacts with the verbal part.

Invective A: The Germans are abominable, because they are mischievous.

Upper right panel

Caption: *Good linguists (of the least obvious Teutonic type) will try to get into our Parliament: "I am for the subremacy of Pridish trade all der dime."*

VOTE FOR - TO CAPTURE GERMAN TRADE (posters)

Description: A fat man, representing the German ('Teutonic') stereotype, is standing behind a table giving a speech.

Scenario 1: Candidates for the British Parliament who do not look 'Teutonic' and who have an excellent command of the English language give speeches in public.

Scenario 2: A candidate for the British Parliament who represents the 'Teutonic' stereotype and who has a very poor command of the English language gives a speech in public.

Explanation: The two scenarios are contrasted. The caption in parentheses entails an obvious irony.

Type: Counterfactual scene interacts with the verbal part.

Invective B: The Germans are ignorant and naïve.

Lower left panel

Caption: *Self-constituted Bosch bodyguards will protect our free-trade legislators from the perils of the streets.*

Description: Three men are stopping a motorcar by raising both arms, so that a British gentleman with a top hat, an umbrella and a briefcase can cross the street safely.

Scenario 1: After the war, the Germans will keep a certain distance from the British.

Scenario 2: In this post war scene, the three Germans are behaving in a subservient manner to the British.

Explanation: The two scenarios are contrasted.

Type: Counterfactual scene interacts with the verbal part.

Invective C: The Germans are abominable, because they are bootlickers.

Lower right panel

Caption: *Attempts will be made to undermine our national physique by the lure of the health-sapping wood.*

Description: A man with an umbrella is offering two boy scouts cigars, which he is holding behind his back in a surreptitious way.

Scenario 1: It is to be expected that after the war, the Germans will keep a critical distance from the British.

Scenario 2: After the war, a German tries to tempt British children with cigars.

Scenario 3: Normal children will be tempted by the offer of a cigar.

Scenario 4: British children are not tempted by the offer of a cigar from a German.

Explanation: The first two and the second two scenarios are contrasted.

Type: Counterfactual scene interacts with the verbal part.
Invective D: The Germans are abominable, because behind a friendly and generous façade, they are mischievous.

Cartoon 115   5.7.1916
Heading: *The Chief Mourner.*
Caption: (Written on the tombstone:)

IN MEMORY OF
THE DECLARATION
OF
LONDON
2nd JUNE 1916
AGED ...
DEEPLY ...

Description: A dachshund is weeping on a tombstone.
Scenario 1: A dog may mourn the death of its owner at the grave.
Scenario 2: This dachshund mourns the end of the Declaration of London.
Scenario 3: A state should assess the advantages of treatises and keep them.
Scenario 4: Germany provoked the end of the Declaration of London and now sees that this was a grave mistake because of the repercussions against itself.
Explanation: There is a blending of human and animal 'mourning'.
The Declaration of London was an international code of maritime law related to war. It was proposed in 1909 and implemented in August 1914. There was a constant conflict about the British blockade of food and other material not directly related to war and armed British merchant ships on the one hand and German submarine attacks on the other. On 15 October 1916, Germany resumed its submarine attacks.
Type: Metonymic scene interacts with the verbal part.
Invective: The Germans are ignorant and stupid, because they are shortsighted.

Cartoon 116   9.8.1916
Heading: *Truthless Days.*
Caption: *English newspapers have now been excluded from Germany.*
THE WELL OF TRUTH (Written on the roof of the well)

THE FATHERLAND INVINCIBLE
NOT AN INCH OF GROUND LOST
OFFICIAL
(On a notice board attached to the well)

Description: A stout German soldier is sitting on a water well, which has been sealed with wooden boards. A cobweb at the top shows that the well has not been used for some time.
Scenario 1: The Germans used to be able to inform themselves about the truth through English newspapers.
Scenario 2: Now that English newspapers have been excluded from Germany, the Germans are cut off from the truth.
Scenario 3: It is known that Germany has suffered losses.
Scenario 4: The official notice states that this is not so.
Explanation: The first two and the second two scenarios are contrasted. There is a blending of receiving true information in English newspapers and getting water from a well.
The notice is so exaggerated that it obviously is not true. Since the

171

negative form of *true* is *untrue* the use of the uncommon derivative
truthless in the heading easily evokes the phonetically similar term
ruthless. The meaning is that the truth is being ruthlessly
suppressed by German officials.

Type: Metonymic scene interacts with the verbal part.
Invective: The Germans try to mislead the public.

Punch cartoon 116

Cartoon 117   16.8.1916

Heading: *The Detective on the German Spy-trail.*
                 Upper left panel

Caption: *Detective: "I'm afraid I'm on the wrong track. That doesn't look like a German."*

Description: A stout looking man with a hat and a walking stick is giving way to two women and a child on the sidewalk by partly stepping to the side. He is being followed by a British detective.

Scenario 1: A German behaves impolitely and does not give way to women and children.

Scenario 2: The man behaves politely and gives way to the women and the child.

Explanation: The two scenarios are contrasted, i.e. the detective watches the man and assesses how 'German', i.e. impolite and ruthless, his behavior is.

Type: Everyday scene represents a communicative situation and interacts with the verbal part.

Invective: The Germans are abominable, because they are impolite and ruthless.

Cartoon   Upper right panel

Caption: *"I hope I'm after the right man. He doesn't sound a bit like a German."*

Description: The same man is sitting at a table in a restaurant eating, i.e. he is putting a spoon in his mouth in a very orderly fashion. In the adjacent room the detective is listening intensely in the direction of the suspect with one hand behind his ear.

Scenario 1:	A German bmakes noises when eating.
Scenario 2:	The man does not make noises when eating.
Explanation:	The two scenarios are contrasted, i.e. the detective is listening in the direction of the suspect and tries to catch whether his table manners are 'German', i.e. uncouth.
Type:	Everyday scene represents a communicative situation and interacts with the verbal part.
Invective:	The Germans are abominable, because they are uncouth.
Cartoon	Lower left panel
Caption:	*"He gets less like a German every minute. But perhaps it's his artfulness."*
	GREAT BRITISH ADVANCE (written on a newspaper boy's broadside)
Description:	The man is buying a newspaper with the heading *Great British Advance* from a newspaper boy.
Scenario 1:	In England there is the tradition of buying evening papers.
Scenario 2:	The tradition of buying evening papers does not exist in Germany.
Scenario 3:	A German does not enjoy reports about British military advances.
Scenario 4:	A British person enjoys reports about British military advances.
Explanation:	The first and second two scenarios are contrasted. A man adhering to the tradition of buying evening papers and enjoying reports about British military advances is not likely to be a German spy.
Type:	Everyday scene represents a communicative situation and interacts with the verbal part.
Invective:	The Germans are abominable, because they do not have the charming British traditions.
	Lower right panel
Caption:	*"I'd better go home. This has been a wasted day."*
Description:	The man has dropped his jacket and is jumping over a railing into the sea to save a little girl who is crying for help. In the background a woman is raising her arms in despair. The detective is walking away with a straight face.
Scenario 1:	A German will not jump into the sea to save a little girl.
Scenario 2:	A British person will jump into the sea to save a little girl.
Explanation:	The two scenarios are contrasted. A man who jumps into the sea to save a little girl cannot be German. In the course of the events of this cartoon, the assumption that the suspect is a German spy is given up.
Type:	Everyday scene represents a communicative situation and interacts with the verbal part.
Invective:	The Germans are abominable. By contrast, the British are well-behaved, selfless and courageous.

Cartoon 118	6.9.1916
Heading:	*Berlin Official*
Caption:	*"Good news again this morning." "Ach! I grow weary of good news." "Come, come, my friend, we must be patient and bear our successes bravely."*
Description:	In a beer garden, a big man with a hat is sitting on a chair next to a table with a huge stein. He is holding a newspaper in his hands. On the right of the table, another fat and bald man is standing with a paper, his hat and an umbrella in his hand.
Scenario 1:	Everyone likes to listen to good news and everyone enjoys successes.
Scenario 2:	The reader of the newspaper does not like the good news and does not enjoy the reported successes, because they are just on paper and not true.

Explanation:	The contradiction is revealed through the incorrect collocation of *bear bravely* and *our successes*, which unmasks them as failures.
Type:	Everyday scene represents a communicative situation.
Invective:	The Germans are ignorant and naïve, because they are fooling themselves.

Cartoon 119   13.9.1916

Heading:	*The Spread of Kultur.*
Caption:	*Tennis-player (whose partner has sent a weak return): "Kamerad! Kamerad!!"*
Description:	In the foreground there is a tennis player, who is about to smash a ball that is over his head. On the other side of the net, his partner is squatting, raising both hands. In the background on the right, the female double partner of the squatting player is watching.
Scenario 1:	A German soldier who is in danger of being shot will surrender or ask clemency by shouting 'Kamerad! Kamerad!!'.
Scenario 2:	This British tennis player, who is in danger of being hit by the smash, is surrendering or asking clemency by shouting 'Kamerad! Kamerad!!'.
Explanation:	The two scenarios are contrasted. The squatting player is pretending to be a prototypical, surrendering German soldier, i.e. he is being ironic. Transferring such language to a civilian domain has a funny effect. An additional point is that since a language is an important part of a culture, it sheds a bad light on the culture, if that language is used in a disgraceful way.
Type:	Everyday scene represents a communicative situation.
Invective:	The Germans are cowards. They are uncultured.

Cartoon 120   13.9.1916

Heading:	*Meeting of Central Powers' Victories Committee.*
Caption:	*Agenda: To decide time and place of next success.*
	MORTGAGE (written on a roll of paper under the table)
Description:	The German Emperor with a patch on his uniform and a band-aid on his cheek is sitting on a box at a table, head in hand. Opposite him, the Austrian Emperor with a bandaged foot and a crutch is sitting on a chair with a broken leg that has been repaired with a string. The third man at the table is the Hungarian King with his head in both hands. To his right, the Bulgarian King is standing with his arm in a sling. All of them have an empty and staring gaze. At the entrance in the background on the right, the Turkish Sultan is sneaking in.
Scenario 1:	Military successes have to be fought for.
Scenario 2:	This victory committee wants to plan the next success instead of fighting.
Scenario 3:	Militaries should be quick and efficient.
Scenario 4:	This victory committee is very slow.
Explanation:	The first two and the second two scenarios are contrasted.The reason why the allies want to plan a victory rather than fight for it is because they have been badly defeated in the past.
Type:	Everyday scene interacts with the verbal part.
Invective:	The Germans are ignorant and stupid, because they are deluding themselves; and so are the Central Powers.

Cartoon 121   27.9.1916

Heading:	
Caption:	*Tommy: "Hello Fritz! Bound for England like myself?"*
	Fritz: "Ja wohl! Bot not mit a retorn teecket - tank gootness!"

Description:	The scenario is a battlefield with destroyed buildings. A German prisoner of war is lead by an armed British soldier. A wounded British soldier who is sitting on a heap of rubble addresses him.
Scenario 1:	German prisoners of war are deported to England against their will where they will want to return to Germany as soon as possible.
Scenario 2:	This German prisoner of war is happy to be deported to England where he wants to stay.
Explanation:	The German prisoner of war prefers England to Germany.
Type:	Non-combatant military scene represents a communicative situation.
Invective:	Life in Germany is deteriorating. This is proved by the fact that the German prisoner of war does not want to return.

Cartoon 122   27.9.1916

Caption:	*Tommy (to pal): "There you are, Bill, always the little gentleman. I wonder 'oo 'ad the sauce to capture 'im."*
Description:	A fat German prisoner of war of a higher military rank is posing in an arrogant and haughty way. He is turned away from the other German prisoners of war who are sitting or standing together. Two armed British soldiers are talking to each other. One of them is looking at him.
Scenario 1:	A prisoner of war interacts with the others like an equal, even if he is of a higher military rank.
Scenario 2:	This German prisoner of war behaves in an arrogant and standoffish manner.
Explanation:	The German prisoner of war ignores the new facts.
Type:	Everyday scene represents a communicative situation and interacts with the verbal part.
Invective:	The Germans are ignorant and stupid, e.g. this arrogant German officer is unable to assess the situation correctly, in which he finds himself.

Cartoon 123   27.9.1916

Heading:	*The Dope*
Caption:	*German citizen: "I used to swallow this stuff with a relish, but somehow it doesn't seem to go down quite so easily now."* *Victory Tonic; To be taken as before.* (written on the bottle)
Description:	There is a German with a wine glass in his right hand at which he looks with disgust and as if he was in pain. His left hand is touching his belly. On the table to his left is a bottle of 'Victory Tonic' next to which is a measuring jar. On the wall in the back are five more bottles of 'Victory Tonic'.
Scenario 1:	In the past Hindenburg drank the 'Victory Tonic' with a relish, i.e. he had no problems fooling himself about the German chances of winning the war.
Scenario 2:	Now he has developed a distaste for it, i.e. he has become more critical in his assessment of Germany's chances to win the war.
Explanation:	The German propaganda is so obviously false that the German leadership have difficulties in believing it themselves. The term *dope* is used ambiguously meaning 'drug' and 'stupid person'.
Type:	Everyday scene represents a communicative situation and interacts with the verbal part.
Invective:	The Germans try to mislead the public.

Cartoon 124   27.9.1916

Heading:	*John Bull Gets his Eye in.*
Caption:	
Description:	In the foreground John Bull is standing in an open field loading his

rifle. In the middle there are four destroyed zeppelins, which he has shot down. In the sky in the background, there are two zeppelins to be seen.

Scenario 1: The zeppelins are dangerous and effective military weapons.
Scenario 2: A civilian can easily shoot them down with a hunting rifle.
Explanation: The two scenarios are contrasted.
Type: Metonymic scene interacts with the verbal part.
Invective: The Germans are militarily inferior, because their zeppelins are ineffective.

Cartoon 125   11.10.1916
Heading: *Wartime Conundrums.*
Caption: *What should a particularly small 'bantam" do who has become separated from his unit and finds that half a company of large-size Prussian guards insist upon surrendering to him?"*
Description: A small British soldier with a rifle is approached by a group of big, unarmed German soldiers with their hands in the air, who are coming out of the cellar of a devastated building. In the background, there are more devastated buildings and trees.
Scenario 1: A majority of soldiers will always fight a minority of enemy soldiers.
Scenario 2: A majority of German soldiers surrenders to a single and particularly small British soldier.
Explanation: The two scenarios are contrasted. A 'bantam battalion' was a battalion of men below normal standard.
Type: Counterfactual scene interacts with the verbal part.
Invective: The Germans are cowards.

Cartoon 126   11.10.1916
Heading: *The New Super-hate.*
Caption: *German Dentist (to patient): "But your teeth are quite good. Why do you want them out?" Patient: "My youth, sir, was spent in England, and these teeth grew while I was there. I love my fatherland." Dentist (with emotion): "I understand."*
Description: An elderly man is sitting in a dentist's chair pointing at his teeth. A dentist is leaning forward looking at the patient.
Scenario 1: Teeth should be judged according to criteria of health by patients as well as by dentists.
Scenario 2: The German patient judges his teeth according to nationalist criteria.
Explanation: The two scenarios are contrasted.
Type: Everyday scene represents a communicative situation and interacts with the verbal part.
Invective: The Germans hate the British; they are chauvinists and anti-British.

Cartoon 127   18.10.1916
Heading:
Caption: *Whenever the telephone rings now, Count Zeppelin's domestic pets have a sense of impending disaster.*
Description: In the background, a man in uniform is phoning. In the foreground, a dachshund is creeping into a corner with his tail tucked between its legs and a cat is climbing up a cupboard in a move to escape.
Scenario 1: Because normal pet owners do not treat their pets as scapegoats, when bad news arrives, the pets do not react to the ringing of a telephone.
Scenario 2: Because Count Zeppelin treats his cat and dog as scapegoats, they panic at the ringing of the telephone, because they expect bad news.
Explanation: The two scenarios are contrasted. The cartoon is quite complex because it presupposes previous behavior of Count Zeppelin towards

Type:	his pets and also knowledge of stimulus and response behavior in pets.
	Everyday scene interacts with the verbal part.
Invective:	The Germans are militarily inferior; they react in an irrational and cruel way to this.

Cartoon 128   25.10.1916

Left panel

Heading:	
Caption:	*Special Constable: "What are you loitering about these buildings for? I don't like the look of you. You have a face like a German."*
	CINEMA WORK ... (written on the wall of a building)
Description:	A special constable and a grumpy looking man are meeting in front of a building.
Type:	Everyday scene represents a communicative situation and interacts with the verbal part.
	Right panel
Caption:	*John Smith: "Oh, that's my working-face, sir. I forgot to change it. I've been doing a Hun in the cinema."*
Description:	The man is smiling at the constable and doffs his cap. The constable is very astonished.
Scenario 1:	When actors leave the stage or studio they drop their role and behave normally again.
Scenario 2:	This actor retains the grumpy facial expression, after he has stopped playing a German.
Scenario 3:	The constable suspects every grumpy looking person of being a German.
Scenario 4:	This grumpy looking man is just an actor, who forgot to drop his German role.
Explanation:	The first two and second two scenarios are contrasted. This cartoon evokes the stereotype of the grumpy German who in addition lacks any sense of humor.
Type:	Everyday scene represents a communicative situation and interacts with the verbal part.
Invective:	The Germans are abominable, because they are grumpy by nature.

Cartoon 129   1.11.1916

Heading:	
Caption:	*Cockney Tommy: "Blow me if this ain't the old blighter who used to play 'I fear no foe in shining armour' dahn ahr street!"*
Description:	Six British soldiers are surrounding a stout German prisoner of war, who is holding his hands up. He looks very disconcerted.
Scenario 1:	A man should adhere to the principles he declares.
Scenario 2:	This German prisoner of war acts like a very fearful coward.
Explanation:	The two scenarios are contrasted.
Type:	Everyday scene represents a communicative situation and interacts with the verbal part.
Invective:	The Germans are cowards.

Cartoon 130   15.11.1916

Heading:	*The 'Independence' of Poland.*
Caption:	*CANNON-FODDER DEPARTMENT* (written over the building)
Description:	In the foreground on the left a huge German with a spiked helmet and a fur over one shoulder is standing on a hill. He looks like a giant caveman. In his right hand he is swinging a whip and his left hand is clenched to a fist. From the center to the background on the right a long line of men are moving towards the entrance of a building.

Scenario 1:	Independent people can go wherever they like.
Scenario 2:	A German brute coerces these Polish men with a whip to serve as cannon fodder for Germany.
Explanation:	The two scenarios are contrasted.
Type:	Metonymic scene interacts with the verbal part.
Invective:	The Germans are callous and cruel. The also cannot be trusted, because they do not keep their treatises.

Punch cartoon 131

Cartoon 131   29.11.1916

Heading:	
Caption:	*(News of the 'tanks' has just penetrated to East Africa.)* *Nervy Hun: "Kamerad! Kamerad!"*
Description:	A German soldier is kneeling in front of a hippo. It is nighttime with a full moon shining.
Scenario 1:	A tank is approaching the soldier who surrenders.
Scenario 2:	A hippo is approaching the soldier who surrenders.
Explanation:	The two scenarios are contrasted. On 15 September 1916, tanks were used by the British in combat for the first time. They introduced them to break the stalemate of the trench warfare in Belgium and France. It provided soldiers with armored support when advancing against enemy positions. The British kept this advantage over the Germans for roughly two years, but it was not a major factor in tipping the scales of the balance of power.
Type:	Counterfactual scene represents a communicative situation and interacts with the verbal part.
Invective:	The Germans are militarily inferior. The German soldiers are so frightened of the British tanks that their perception is inhibited.

Cartoon 132   29.11.1916

Heading:	*Hindenburgitis, or the Prussian Home Made Beautiful.*
Description:	An elderly couple is sitting in their living room. There are twenty-two images of Hindenburg on a glass, a lamp, the table cloth etc.
Scenario 1:	A normally furnished living room does not have an excess of images of Hindenburg.

Scenario 2:   This living room is overburdened with images of Hindenburg.
Explanation: The two scenarios are contrasted.
Type: Counterfactual scene interacts with the verbal part.
Invective: The Germans are ignorant and naïve; they are also politically fanatic
                and subservient.

Cartoon 133   6.12.1916
                Left panel
Heading:
Caption: *Herr Blumenzwiebel at the Grand Opera House, Berlin, a few seasons
                ago.*
Description: An opera singer in the dress of a Germanic warrior is singing on stage
                with both arms raised above his head. He is looking upward with a
                gaping mouth.
Type: Everyday scene interacts with the verbal part.
                Right panel
Caption: *Herr Blumenzwiebel at the theatre of war, somewhere in France, this
                season.*
Description: The same man in the uniform of a German soldier is standing in a
                trench with both arms raised above his head. He is looking upward with
                a gaping mouth. He looks rather concerned with both arms raised above
                his head.
Scenario 1:   In the make-believe context of an opera stage, this man is a hero.
Scenario 2:   In the real life context of the war, this man is a coward.
Explanation: The two scenarios are contrasted. The same movement and the same
                body position should not lead to any false conclusion. There is a word
                play on the expressions *Grand Opera House* and *theatre of war*.
Type: War scene interacts with the verbal part.
Invective: The Germans are cowards; they are heroes only in make-believe
                contexts.

Punch cartoon 133

Cartoon 134	13.12.1916
Heading:	*Levée en Masse*
Caption:	Crank: "Your Highness, I have here a scheme that will save many of your wonderful airships from destruction. It is a shell-proof envelope six inches thick." The Count: "Of what material?" The Crank: "Iron, your Highness." The Count: "Why, you idiot, do you expect the airship to rise?" The Crank: "It doesn't, your Highness. That is the sole purpose of my invention."
Description:	A man is standing in front of a desk, behind which Hindenburg is sitting. With his right hand he is pointing at a manuscript in his left.
Scenario 1:	A shell-protection for an airship in action is desirable.
Scenario 2:	A shell-protection for an airship which keeps it from rising is useless.
Explanation:	The two scenarios are contrasted.
Type:	Everyday scene represents a communicative situation and interacts with the verbal part.
Invective:	The Germans are ignorant and naïve, e.g. their inventers are unable to discriminate important facts from unimportant ones.
Cartoon 135	Punch's Almanack for 1917
Heading:	*A False Alarm.*
	Upper row, left panel
Caption:	*"Call me at seven sharp."*
Description:	A man with a candle is standing in front of a housemaid.
Type:	Everyday scene represents a communicative situation.
	Upper row, right panel
Caption:	*All ri –* (written in a speech bubble) *BOOM!*
Description:	He is lying in his bed sleeping.
Type:	Everyday scene interacts with the verbal part.
	Middle row, left panel
Caption:	*Ri –* (written in a speech bubble) *BANG!*
Description:	He is still in his bed sleeping.
Type:	Everyday scene interacts with the verbal part.
	Middle row, right panel
Caption:	*Thank you* (written in a speech bubble) *CRASH!*
Description:	He is whirled round. His bed has collapsed and disintegrated.
Type:	Everyday scene interacts with the verbal part.
	Lower row, left panel
Caption:	*"Oh, zepps?"*
Description:	He is kneeling on the destroyed bed.
Type:	Non-combatant military scene represents a communicative situation.
	Lower row, right panel
Caption:	*"I was afraid it was time to get up!"*
Description:	He has gone back to sleep on what remains of his bed.
Scenario 1:	An air raid by an enemy will make civilians panic.
Scenario 2:	An air raid by a German zeppelin does not bother this man.
Explanation:	The two scenarios are contrasted. Having to get up is more of a concern to this man than German zeppelins.
Type:	Non-combatant military scene represents a communicative situation.
Invective:	The Germans are militarily inferior. Therefore the zeppelin air raids need not be taken seriously.
Cartoon 135	Punch's Almanack for 1917
Heading:	*A False Alarm.*
	Upper row, left panel

Caption: *"Call me at seven sharp."*
Description: A man with a candle is standing in front of a housemaid.
Type: Everyday scene represents a communicative situation.
               Upper row, right panel
Caption: *All ri* – (written in a speech bubble)
               BOOM!
Description: He is lying in his bed sleeping.
Type: Everyday scene interacts with the verbal part.
               Middle row, left panel
Caption: *Ri* – (written in a speech bubble)
               BANG!
Description: He is still in his bed sleeping.
Type: Everyday scene interacts with the verbal part.
               Middle row, right panel
Caption: *Thank you* (written in a speech bubble)
               CRASH!
Description: He is whirled round. His bed has collapsed and disintegrated.
Type: War scene interacts with the verbal part.
               Lower row, left panel
Caption: *"Oh, zepps?"*
Description: He is kneeling on the destroyed bed.
Type: Everyday scene represents a communicative situation.
               Lower row, right panel
Caption: *"I was afraid it was time to get up!"*
Description: He has gone back to sleep on what remains of his bed.
Scenario 1: An air raid by an enemy will make civilians panic.
Scenario 2: An air raid by a German zeppelin does not bother this man.
Explanation: The two scenarios are contrasted. Having to get up is more of a concern to this man than German zeppelins.
Type: Non-combatant military scene represents a communicative situation.
Invective: The Germans are militarily inferior. Therefore the zeppelin air raids need not be taken seriously.

Cartoon 136   Punch's Almanack for 1917
Heading: *Fashions in the New Germany.*
Caption: *(Dr. Eugen Wolff has contributed to the 'Illustrirte* [sic] *Zeitung' an article on 'How we are to order our external life in the new Germany.' from which we cull the following selected passages.)*
               Upper panel
Caption: *'Let our women who look to Paris for their fashions, our men who look to London, remember that our physical form is not that of the English and French.'*
Description: The people in all the panels represent Germans. On the left, there is a rather stout, middle-aged woman wearing an expensive, elegant fur coat and high boots. Beside her, there is a well-fed girl with glasses, who also wears high boots. On the right, there is a fashionably dressed stout man with golf clubs and a well-fed and fashionably dressed boy with glasses, who carries a cricket bat on his shoulder and a ball in his left hand.
Scenario 1: 'Normally' dressed British people with a 'normal' weight.
Scenario 2: Overweight Germans dressed in traditional Bavarian clothing.
Explanation: The two scenarios are contrasted. Theodor Wolff was the publisher of the *Berliner Tageblatt.*
Type: Everyday scene interacts with the verbal part.
               Middle panel
Caption: *'Our physical form is not that of the English and French.'*

Description: On the left there is an elderly couple in traditional Bavarian dress. In the middle there is a stout soldier and a big army officer. On the right there is a very plump elderly woman with a dachshund.
Scenario 1:   'Normally' dressed British people with a 'normal' weight.
Scenario 2:   Overweight Germans dressed in traditional Bavarian clothing or uniforms.
Explanation: The two scenarios are contrasted.
Type: Everyday scene interacts with the verbal part.
              Lower panel
Caption: *'German clothes after the war must be modelled on some particular national costume noted for its ease and beauty.'*
Description: There is a middle aged couple in traditional Bavarian clothing with their three children and a dachshund. The children and even the dachshund are dressed in this style.
Scenario 1:   'Normally' dressed British people with a 'normal' weight.
Scenario 2:   Overweight Germans dressed in traditional Bavarian clothing.
Explanation: The two scenarios are contrasted.
Type: Everyday scene interacts with the verbal part.
Invective: The Germans have a pseudo-culture, because they are fat, smug and complacent.

Cartoon 137   3.1.1917
Heading:
Caption: *Gretchen: "Will it never end? Think of our awful responsibility before humanity." Hans: "And these everlasting sardines for every meal."*
Description: An elderly woman with glasses is sitting at a dining table. A very stout man is standing at the other side of it. Before the table there is a dachshund.
Scenario 1:   Responsibility to humanity precludes military aggression.
Scenario 2:   Boring food precludes military aggression.
Explanation: There is a contrast between the two scenarios.
Type: Everyday scene represents a communicative situation and interacts with the verbal part.
Invective: Life in Germany is deteriorating.

Cartoon 138   17.1.1917
Heading:
Caption: *Super-Boy: "But, father, if we have already conquered, why does the war go on?" Super-Man: "Be silent and eat your Hindenburg rock."*
Description: A fat German father is taking a walk in a park with his three children and a dachshund.
Scenario 1:   Germany has conquered England (or won the war), and therefore the war stops.
Scenario 2:   Germany has not conquered England (or won the war), and therefore the war goes on.
Scenario 3:   A father will give a child a rational explanation to his question.
Scenario 4:   This father evades the explanation, because there is none.
Explanation: The father wants to evade the question, because his answer can only be inconsistent.
Type: Everyday scene represents a communicative situation.
Invective: The Germans try to mislead the public. Only children believe in the German propaganda.

Cartoon 139   17.1.1917
Heading: *Force of Habit.*
Caption: *How an escaped prisoner of war betrayed himself.*

Description: In the center of the cartoon, there is a stout man standing in a street with raised arms, looking to his left, where a small child has triggered a toy rifle with a bang. In the background on the left, two elderly people and a police constable are looking suspiciously at the man.

Scenario 1:   Escaped prisoners of war will drop old habits in order not to be uncovered.

Scenario 2:   This German prisoner of war betrays himself, because he has retained his old habits.

Explanation: The two scenarios are contrasted. During the war the Germans have been forced so often to surrender that surrendering has become a deep-seated habit of theirs.

Type: Everyday scene interacts with the verbal part.

Invective: The Germans are ignorant and stupid. They are also cowards.

Punch cartoon 139

Cartoon 140   24.1.1917
Heading:
Caption: *Tube conductor: "Pass further down the car, please! Pass further down the car, please!! (in desperation) Any lady or gentleman present knows the German for 'pass further down the car'?"*

Description: In the middle of a London Underground car, a man is standing with a look of disbelief and surprise. He is stout and wears a top hat, striped trousers and gaiters. With his left hand he is holding on to a pole and in his right he is holding a newspaper. Behind him there is a dense throng of people, but in front of him there is some room. At the very far end of the car in the back, the head of the shouting tube conductor is visible.

Scenario 1:   In the crowd of a tube car a German will not be noticed.

Scenario 2:   The tube conductor notices this German in the crowded tube car from very far.

Explanation: The two scenarios are contrasted. The man is easily recognizable as a German, because he claims more space than the other passengers.

Type: Everyday scene represents a communicative situation and interacts with the verbal part.

Invective: The Germans are ignorant and stupid, because they believe that they are not easily recognizable by their looks and their egotistic behavior.

Punch cartoon 140

Cartoon 141   7.3.1917
Heading: *The Theatre of War.*
Caption: *TRENCH FULL.*
                                        NO MORE KAMERADS
                                           WANTED TODAY
                                    WAIT FOR THE NEXT RELIEF
                                          (written on a board)
Description: A happily smiling British soldier looking out of a trench is holding up
                 a board stuck on the bayonet of his rifle. Very far in the background
                 two men are running in the direction of the trench with raised arms.
Scenario 1:   The trench warfare is cruel, lethal and unrelenting.
Scenario 2:   The British soldier behaves as if this was a hotel in a holiday resort.
Scenario 3:   Soldiers will rather die than lose their honor and become prisoners of
                 war.
Scenario 4:   The German soldiers are more than happy to become prisoners of war
                 of the British.
Explanation: The first and second two scenarios are contrasted. The expression
                 trench full is reminiscent of a hotel sign and the expression *next relief*
                 implies a steady flow of German soldiers who surrender themselves to
                 the British.
Type: Counterfactual scene represents a communicative situation and
                 interacts with the verbal part.
Invective: The Germans are militarily inferior; therefore, they do not have to be
                 taken seriously. In addition, they have no sense of pride.

Cartoon 142   28.3.1917
Heading: *The Invaders*
Caption: *"I suppose old Hindenburg knows what he's about?" "Anyhow, every*
                 step takes us nearer the fatherland."
                 BAPAUME (written on a signpost)

Description:	An old German soldier and a young one are walking with their rifles and their backpacks in the opposite direction to which the signpost saying 'Bapaume' is pointing. The old one is bending forward, and the young one has a fearful look on his face.
Scenario 1:	The German soldiers are forced to retreat.
Scenario 2:	One of the soldiers believes that their march back to Germany is a planned action of Hindenburg's. The other does not care and is just happy to be heading home.
Explanation:	The two scenarios are contrasted.
Type:	War scene represents a communicative situation and interacts with the verbal part.
Invective:	The Germans are militarily inferior. This is proved by the fact that they are retreating.

Cartoon 143		28.3.1917
Heading:	*Some Catch: The Angler's Dream.*	
	First panel	
Caption:	*NOTICE* (written on a board)	
Description:	An angler is sitting and sleeping in his boat, which is floating on a river fastened to two poles.	
Type:	Everyday scene interacts with the verbal part.	
	Second panel	
Caption:	*U88* (written on the submarine)	
Description:	In his dream he is terrified when he notices that there is a German submarine the size of his boat on the hook of his fishing line.	
Type:	Counterfactual scene interacts with the verbal part.	
	Third panel	
Caption:	*NOTICE* (written on the board) *U88* (written on the submarine)	
Description:	He is standing on the bank of the river talking to a policeman. In the background the submarine lies near the bank fastened to a tree.	
Type:	Counterfactual scene interacts with the verbal part.	
	Fourth panel	
Caption:	*THE FIRST MAN ON SHORE GETS THE BEER* (written on the board) *U88* (written on the submarine)	
Description:	The angler is standing on the bank behind the submarine holding up a sign. The policeman is watching from the bank.	
Type:	Counterfactual scene represents a communicative situation and interacts with the verbal part.	
	Fifth panel	
Caption:	*THE FIRST MAN ON SHORE GETS THE BEER* (written on the board) *U88* (written on the submarine)	
Description:	Four German sailors are hastening toward the angler. The captain is shouting at them from the turret of the submarine, threatening them with his fist.	
Type:	Counterfactual scene represents a communicative situation and interacts with the verbal part.	
	Sixth panel	
Caption:	*NOTICE* (written on the board) *U88* (written on the submarine)	
Description:	The angler is standing on the submarine holding the signpost in his hand. The policeman is guarding the sailors in the background.	
Type:	Counterfactual scene interacts with the verbal part.	
	Seventh (insert) panel	

Description: Back in the real world, the angler is disappointed at his catch on the hook, which is just a tiny fish.
Scenario 1:   An angler should watch his fishing rod and not sleep.
Scenario 2:   This angler sleeps and has dreams.
Scenario 3:   Sailors should be concerned about their submarine when an enemy traps it.
Scenario 4:   The German sailors are merely concerned about getting beer as quickly as possible.
Explanation: The first and second two scenarios are contrasted.
Type: Everyday scene interacts with the verbal part.
Invective: The Germans are militarily inferior, because they are more interested in beer than in fighting.

Cartoon 144   28.3.1917
Heading:
Caption: *Fond Teuton Parent (to super-tar home on leave): "And you like your ship, Fritz?" Fritz: "I love her! She's a wonder! Such speed! Whenever we race back to port she's been first every time."*
Description: In a living room the old parents of a young sailor, who is standing on the right, are sitting on chairs. A boy, a girl, a housemaid and a dachshund are also in the room.
Scenario 1:   In a competition ships are racing back to port to see which is the fastest.
Scenario 2:   Fritz' ship is racing back to port, because the opponent chases it back home.
Explanation: Fritz does not understand that the 'race back to port' is a flight.
Type: Everyday scene represents a communicative situation and interacts with the verbal part.
Invective: The Germans are ignorant and naïve, because they fail to see the real meaning of what is happening. The members of the German marine are cowards.

Cartoon 145   28.3.1917
Heading:
Caption: *Karl: "What worries me is the fact that we want more men for the navy. What I should like to know is, where are they to come from?" Gretchen: "Be calm, Karl. Doubtless our glorious professors of chemistry will invent a substitute."*
Description: In a living room an elderly woman is sitting half asleep in an armchair. Her husband is walking up and down.
Scenario 1:   Human parents procreate human offspring.
Scenario 2:   Human offspring is procreated by chemical means.
Explanation: The two scenarios are contrasted.
Type: Everyday scene represents a communicative situation.
Invective: The Germans are ignorant and naive.

Cartoon 146   11.4.1917
Heading:
Caption: *"You wouldn't think it to look at 'im, but when I says ' 'ands up,' 'e answers back in puffick English, 'steady on with yer blinkin' toothpick,' 'e sez 'and I'll come quiet."*
Description: A German prisoner of war is standing on the left half turning back. Behind him is a British soldier with a bayonet on his rifle who is talking to two Scottish soldiers.
Scenario 1:   German prisoners of war have a very poor command of English.

186

Scenario 2:	This German prisoner of war speaks a very colloquial English vernacular.
Scenario 3:	A bayonet is a lethal weapon.
Scenario 4:	The German prisoner calls the bayonet 'blinkin' toothpick'.
Explanation:	The first and second two scenarios are contrasted. The strong accent of the British soldier is funny.
Type:	Everyday scene represents a communicative situation and interacts with the verbal part.
Invective:	The Germans are militarily inferior; they can be surprisingly funny, though.

Cartoon 147   25.4.1917

Heading:	*Cannon-fodder - and after*
Caption:	*Kaiser: (to 1917 recruit) "And don't forget that your Kaiser will find a use for you - alive or dead." KADAVERVERWERTUNGS(AN)STA(LT) (corpse-conversion factory)* (sign on the building)
Description:	Standing in front of a recruit and briefing him, the German Kaiser points at a 'corpse-conversion factory'.
Scenario 1:	When soldiers are killed they are buried honorably.
Scenario 2:	When German soldiers are killed their remains are sent to a 'corpse-conversion factory'.
Explanation:	The German Kaiser has absolute power over his subjects and will use it unscrupulously. The Germans would treat any enemy in the same brutal way or even worse. That the Germans had corpse-conversion factories was one of the myths during the First World War.
Type:	Everyday scene represents a communicative situation and interacts with the verbal part.
Invective:	The Germans are callous and cruel, e.g. their Kaiser has no regard for his own soldiers.

Cartoon 148

Heading:	*The Waning of Faith.*
Caption:	*Guardian of statue: "You wish to hammer another nail into the Colossus of our Hindenburg?" Ex-enthusiast: "No; I want my old one back."*
Description:	A man with pliers in his left hand and an umbrella in his right is leaning towards a uniformed guard, pointing at him. The guard is about to open the door. In the background, there is the colossus of Hindenburg
Scenario 1:	Germans showed their enthusiasm for Hindenburg by hammering a nail into the Hindenburg colossus.
Scenario 2:	This German shows his disillusion with Hindenburg and the war by wanting his nail back.
Explanation:	The two scenarios are contrasted.
Type:	Everyday scene represents a communicative situation and interacts with the verbal part.
Invective:	Life in Germany is deteriorating. Therefore the faith of the Germans in their leadership is diminishing.

Cartoon 149   9.5.1917

Heading:	*Donnerwetter.*
Caption:	*Hindenburg: "Whichever comes out, it's rotten weather for me!" WESTERN FRONT WEATHER COTTAGE* (written on the weather-box)

Description:	Hindenburg, who is wearing a uniform with an Iron Cross and a spiked helmet, is standing in front of a weather cottage. In the left door there is a British soldier under a British flag holding a rifle with a bayonet and in the right door there is a French soldier under a French flag also holding a rifle with a bayonet.
Scenario 1:	A weather cottage has a figure indicating fair weather in one door and another indicating bad weather in the other.
Scenario 2:	This weather cottage has two figures both indicating bad weather.
Explanation:	The two scenarios are contrasted. The figures represent the British and the French army, which Hindenburg and the German army are facing. Whichever army the Germans meet, there will be a negative outcome for them.
Type:	Metonymic scene represents a communicative situation and interacts with the verbal part.
Invective:	The Germans are militarily inferior.

Cartoon 150   16.5.1917

Heading:	*The Bribe.*
Caption:	*"Who goes there?" "K - Kamerad - mit souvenirs."*
Description:	In the foreground on the right, the silhouette of a British soldier is to be seen from behind. He is looking out of a trench at the silhouette of a German soldier who is holding five spiked helmets in his hands.
Scenario 1:	Soldiers in the trenches are expected to fight relentlessly.
Scenario 2:	This German soldier is thinking of making money out of the death of his fellow soldiers and/or making a deal by surrendering.
Explanation:	The two scenarios are contrasted.
Type:	War scene represents a communicative situation and interacts with the verbal part.
Invective:	The Germans are abominable, e.g. the German soldiers have neither a sense of pride nor of piety; instead they have a sense of making money and securing advantages for themselves.

Cartoon 151

Heading:	
Caption:	*British Officer (interrupting carousal in Bosch dug-out): "Time, gentlemen, please!"*
Description:	Seven German soldiers are drinking champagne in a dug-out. Two of them are so drunk that they are hardly able to sit upright. A British officer is standing at the entrance with his pistol in hand. Behind him there are another two British soldiers.
Scenario 1:	Soldiers in the trenches are expected to be on the alert at any time.
Scenario 2:	These German soldiers are not at all on the alert but drunk.
Scenario 3:	The landlord of a pub says 'Time, gentlemen, please!' when the guests have to stop drinking and leave.
Scenario 4:	This British officer says 'Time, gentlemen, please!' when the party of the German soldiers is over. They have to stop drinking and leave for a prisoners of war camp.
Explanation:	The first and second two scenarios are contrasted. The British officer uses this announcement ironically. He can do this because he need not take the German soldiers seriously.
Type:	War scene represents a communicative situation and interacts with the verbal part.
Invective:	The Germans are militarily inferior, because their soldiers are silly drunkards. Therefore they are no match for the British soldiers.

188

Cartoon 152   11.7.1917

Heading:	*The Tuber's Repartee.*
Caption:	*German pirate: "Gott strafe England!" British potato: "Tuber über alles!"*
Description:	An anthropoid potato on a cliff overlooking the sea is bamboozling the captain of a surfaced German submarine, who looks surprised and very annoyed.
Scenario 1:	The captains of German submarines try to starve Britain by their blockade.
Scenario 2:	The British potatoes make up for the loss and thus undermine the aim of German submarine warfare.
Explanation:	The two scenarios are contrasted. The happy people who can eat the potatoes are replaced by a happy anthropoid potato
Type:	Metonymic scene represents a communicative situation and interacts with the verbal part.
Invective:	The Germans are callous and cruel; but they will not succeed in their attempts to starve Britain.

Cartoon 153   18.7.1917

Heading:	
Caption:	*Teuton writes: "I am sad at heart, dear Gretchen. Despite my weak sight they have for some reason drafted me into the shock troops."*
Description:	A small, fat soldier with round glasses is sitting on a stone writing a letter. A drop of sweat is visible on his forehead.
Scenario 1:	Only the fittest soldiers will be drafted into the shock troops.
Scenario 2:	The soldier is a pitiful sight and not at all fit to be drafted into the shock troops.
Explanation:	The two scenarios are contrasted.
Type:	Non-combatant military scene represents a communicative situation.
Invective:	The Germans are ignorant and naïve, because they have a poor sense of judgment.

Cartoon 154   18.7.1917

Heading:	
Caption:	*Grandpa (to small Teuton struggling with home lessons): "Come, Fritz, is your task so difficult?" Fritz: "It is indeed. I have to learn the names of all the countries that misunderstand the All-Highest." DIE WELT (THE WORLD)* (on the map on the wall)
Description:	A boy is sitting over a book at his desks. An old man is standing next to him. On the wall there is a map and behind the desk a globe.
Scenario 1:	Normally there are only a few misunderstandings between countries.
Scenario 2:	Very many countries misunderstand the German Emperor.
Explanation:	The term *misunderstand* is a euphemism for military aggression. Children should learn something useful. Fritz does not understand the fatal background of his task.
Type:	Everyday scene represents a communicative situation and interacts with the verbal part.
Invective:	The Germans are abominable, but try to blame the other nations.

Cartoon 155   12.9.1917

Heading:	*The Reverse of the Medal.*
Caption:	*Optimistic German (reading paper): "This is kolossal! Our irresistible airmen have again, for the twentieth time, destroyed London." Gloomy ditto: "That being so, let's hope they'll stop those cursed British airmen from bombing our lines every day and night."*
Description:	Two Germans are sitting with their beer steins at a table in a beer

garden. The 'optimist' on the left is a stereotypical fat German; the 'pessimist' on the right is rather slim. He is leaning forward with both arms between his legs looking shocked. Both have a little flag with *Riga* written on it in the buttonhole of their jackets. In addition the man on the left has another two flags in his left hand and on his hat. He is holding a newspaper in the other hand.

Scenario 1:	A town can be destroyed only once.
Scenario 2:	The newspaper claims that London has been destroyed for the twentieth time.
Scenario 3:	If the German air force has destroyed London, they can start defending Germany against British air raids.
Scenario 4:	This is not the case.
Explanation:	The first and second two scenarios are contrasted.
Type:	Everyday scene represents a communicative situation and interacts with the verbal part.
Invective:	The Germans try to mislead the public. The German newspaper reports are just lies.

Cartoon 156		3.10.1917
Heading:	*A Place in the Moon.*	
Caption:	*Hans: "How beautiful a moon, my love, for showing up England to our gallant airmen!" Gretchen: "Yes, dearest, but may it not show up the fatherland to the brutal enemy one of these nights?"*	
Description:	An elderly couple is walking down an alley under a full moon.	
Scenario 1:	The moon lights the scene of German air raids.	
Scenario 2:	The moon also lights the scene of British air raids.	
Explanation:	The two scenarios are contrasted. The moonshine is of equal advantage to the German and the British air raid pilots.	
Type:	Everyday scene represents a communicative situation and interacts with the verbal part.	
Invective:	The Germans are ignorant and naïve, e.g. Hans believes that the moon is partial.	

Cartoon 157		10.10.1917
Heading:	*A Birthday Greeting for Hindenburg.*	
Caption:	*F.M. Sir Douglas Haig (sings) "O I'll tak' the high road an' ye'll tak' the low road...."*	
	(The enemy has been fighting desperately to prevent us from occupying the ridges above the Ypres-Menin road, and so forcing him to face the winter on the low ground.)	
	To my dear Field-Marshal on his 70ᵗʰ Birthday. William (written on a label attached to the sculpture)	
Description:	Hindenburg is sitting in front of a dugout with a sculpture of the head of William II in his hands. At the top of the trench, Marshal Haig is singing, holding a sheet of music in front of him.	
Scenario 1:	Hindenburg wanted the German army to occupy the ridges above the Ypres-Menin road.	
Scenario 2:	Marshal Haig triumphantly reminds Hindenburg with his song that this plan has failed.	
Scenario 3:	The army leaders of opposing armies do not communicate by singing to each other as if they were on an opera stage.	
Scenario 4:	In this cartoon, Haig and Hindenburg do this.	
Explanation:	The first and second two scenarios are contrasted. William II gives idolatrous presents to his Field Marshal.	
Type:	Metonymic scene represents a communicative situation and interacts with the verbal part.	

Invective:	The Germans are militarily inferior. They are on the road to defeat. The German Kaiser is an idolater of himself.
Cartoon 158 Heading:	31.10.1917
Caption:	*Tommy: " 'Ands up, all of yer. I'm goin' on leave termorrer. Ain't got no time to waste."*
Description:	Tommy is moving quickly towards a dilapidated building in which four German soldiers are about to surrender. His rifle has a bayonet on it and on his back he is carrying a large backpack.
Scenario 1:	When a single soldier takes several soldiers of the enemy prisoner, he will proceed extra carefully and not think of his leave the next day.
Scenario 2:	Tommy goes about the job very lightly, because he is more concerned with his leave the next day and has no time to lose.
Explanation:	The two scenarios are contrasted. The accent of Tommy is funny.
Type:	War scene represents a communicative situation and interacts with the verbal part.
Invective:	The Germans are militarily inferior, because their soldiers are cowards Therefore they need not be taken seriously.

Cartoon 159 Heading:	31.10.1917
Caption:	*Prisoner (on his dignity): "But you vos not know vot I am. I am a sergeant-major in der Prussian guard." Tommy: "Well, wot abaht it? I'm a private in the West Kents."*
Description:	A very tall and arrogant looking German prisoner of war is standing on one side of a barbed wire fence looking indignantly at Tommy.
Scenario 1:	The German prisoner of war claims respect because of his high military rank in spite of the fact that his function has been withdrawn from him.
Scenario 2:	Although he is only a private soldier Tommy shows a very natural and parochial sense of pride.
Explanation:	The two scenarios are contrasted. Whereas the German prisoner of war shows arrogance because of his military rank, Tommy, the simple British soldier, has a very natural sense of pride. Arrogant Germans are wrong in thinking that they can impress people simply by mentioning their (high) military rank.
Type:	Non-combatant military scene represents a communicative situation and interacts with the verbal part.
Invective:	The Germans are militarists. It is arrogant and naïve of them to underestimate the simple British soldier and his natural and parochial sense of pride.

Cartoon 160 Heading:	Punch's Almanack for 1918
Caption:	*Over-zealous Tommy (far in advance of his objective): "Orl right. Don't get nasty. I must 'ave come a bit too far. We're not expected here till next week. See you later. So long!"*
Description:	Tommy is kneeling on top of a trench with his rifle on the ground in front of him. In the trench there are five German soldiers, two of whom are pointing their weapons at him. Another two are hesitant and the fifth is throwing his arms up in surrender.
Scenario 1:	When a single soldier approaches an enemy trench by mistake, he will retreat immediately or surrender.
Scenario 2:	Tommy takes his mishap very lightly, because he is sure of victory.
Explanation:	The two scenarios are contrasted. Tommy's accent is funny.

Type: Counterfactual scene represents a communicative situation and interacts with the verbal part.
Invective: The Germans are militarily inferior, because most of the German soldiers are cowards. Therefore they need not be taken seriously.

Cartoon 161   Punch's Almanack for 1918
Heading: *Germany and the Next War (Commercial).*
Caption: *Combing out the army for overseas commercial travelers. Likely members of the Prussian guard unlearning the goose-step.*
Description: The legs of the members of the Prussian guard, who are walking, are fettered by short chains, which restrict their stride.
Scenario 1: The goose-step is such an unnatural way of walking that no special unlearning program is necessary.
Scenario 2: The members of the Prussian guard have internalized the goose-step so intensely that for them an unlearning program is necessary if they want to return to a normal life.
Explanation: The two scenarios are contrasted. It is remarkable that in these cartoons of the Almanack for 1918 there is a post-war perspective, even if a following 'commercial war' is envisaged.
Type: Everyday scene interacts with the verbal part.
Invective: The Germans are abominable, because they are stiff and very formal.

Cartoon 162   Punch's Almanack for 1918
Heading: *Germany and the Next War (Commercial).*
Caption: *Hun Polyglot preparing commercial travellers for a descent on London.* (Written on the blackboard in the center:) *Putrid weather. - This is OK. - This is a bit of all right - Care for a gasper? - damrot – It's a dud - What about a spot of mother's ruin with a dash of angostura? – Here's a top notcher. - Try (von) one of my kill-me-quicks. - Then it's a wash-out. - A topping bit of fluff* (Written on the blackboard on the left:) *pint of bubbly - ...ldn't be amiss - any old time - decent of you - old thing*
Description: A fat German teacher is teaching English to a group of German adults. He is pointing at a phrase on the blackboard.
Scenario 1: The British are easy going and thus their phrases are very informal.
Scenario 2: The German adults look very formal. They show a stunned reaction.
Explanation: The Germans will have great difficulties learning these phrases.
Type: Everyday scene interacts with the verbal part.
Invective: The Germans are abominable, because they are stiff and very formal.

Cartoon 163   Punch's Almanack for 1918
Heading: *Germany and the Next War (Commercial).*
Caption: *The bravest man that ever lived. The first Bosch to try and do a deal with England.* *MADE IN GERMANY* (written on seven tags on household goods) *LONDON - DOVER - SOUTHEND* (written on signposts on the coast)
Description: A prototypical German is approaching the white cliffs of Dover in a small row boat filled with household goods.
Scenario 1: A self-critical man knows that the British will not buy German goods during the war.
Scenario 2: This German believes that he can sell his German goods in England during the war.
Explanation: The two scenarios are contrasted.
Type: Everyday scene interacts with the verbal part.
Invective: The Germans are ignorant and naïve, because they ignore the facts.

Punch cartoon 163

Cartoon 164	Punch's Almanack for 1918
Heading:	*Germany and the Next War (Commercial).*
Caption:	*Training commercial travellers for little set-backs in their overseas campaigns.*
Description:	There is scaffolding with stairs leading up on the left and stairs leading down on the right. On the top platform of the scaffolding, there is a big boot fastened to a long spring. Four Germans are waiting on the staircase on the left in order to move up. One German has been catapulted down by the boot and is flying through the air with a briefcase in his hand. He is about to land on a mattress at the bottom of the stairs on the right. Another man, who has obviously just landed on the mattress, is crawling towards the stairs on the left in order to move back up again.
Scenario 1:	Commercial travelers will be trained rhetorically so that they can convince potential customers better.
Scenario 2:	The German commercial travelers are trained physically so that they can cope with being kicked out better.
Explanation:	The two scenarios are contrasted.
Type:	Counterfactual scene interacts with the verbal part.
Invective:	The Germans are abominable. Therefore the British dislike them.

Cartoon 165	Punch's Almanack for 1918
Heading:	*The Propagandists (It is quite probable that when peace comes the Central Powers will begin active propaganda with the object of getting into the good graces of their late enemies.)*
Caption:	*Kindness to British children.*
Description:	German men and women distribute sweets and toys among British children, who look surprised.
Scenario 1:	The Germans attacked Belgium, France and the soldiers of the Allies and caused death, damage and grief.
Scenario 2:	The German men want to make the British believe that they are true demonstrators of peace.
Explanation:	The two scenarios are contrasted. The British find it difficult to trust the Germans and their demonstration of good will and friendship.
Type:	Everyday scene interacts with the verbal part.

Invective:	The Germans cannot be trusted, because they are subservient hypocrites.

Cartoon 166   Punch's Almanack for 1918
Heading: *The Propagandists (It is quite probable that when peace comes the Central Powers will begin active propaganda with the object of getting into the good graces of their late enemies.)*
Caption: *A demonstration by members of the 'Germanic League of Love.'*
(Sign held by demonstrators:) *FRATERNITY - FRATERNITY - FRATERNITY - WE LOVE YOU ALL - KIND HEARTS ARE MORE THAN GOTHAS*
Description: German men and women parade with flags demonstrating their peaceful and friendly intentions. A dachshund is watching the parade suspiciously.
Scenario 1:   The Germans attacked Belgium, France and the soldiers of the Allies and caused death, damage and grief.
Scenario 2:   The Germans love the British and are their brothers.
Explanation: The two scenarios are contrasted. The British find it difficult to trust the Germans and their demonstration of good will and friendship. *Gothas* are large German airplanes.
Type: Everyday scene interacts with the verbal part.
Invective: The Germans cannot be trusted, because they are subservient hypocrites.

Cartoon 167   Punch's Almanack for 1918
Heading: *The Propagandists.*
Caption: *The free restaurant.*
FREE - FREE SCHULTZ RESTAURANT (written on the building)
(Illegible words at the side of the entrance:) *SOUPS*
(Posters on the shop window:) *FREE BEER - FREE DINNER - FREE CIGARS - ENGLISH SPOKEN - FREE FOOD*
Description: A German landlord invites passers-by into his free restaurant in an overly polite and subservient manner. Through the door of the restaurant, a young man can be seen carving a turkey. There are many large sausages hanging from the ceiling.
Scenario 1:   The Germans attacked Belgium, France and the soldiers of the Allies and caused death, damage and grief.
Scenario 2:   The Germans love the British so much that polite and subservient German landlords open free restaurants for them.
Explanation: The two scenarios are contrasted. The British find it difficult to trust the Germans and their demonstration of good will and generosity.
Type: Everyday scene interacts with the verbal part.
Invective: The Germans cannot be trusted, because they are subservient hypocrites.

Cartoon 168   Punch's Almanack for 1918
Heading: *The Propagandists.*
Caption: *Propaganding by poster*
PEACEFUL WILHELM - THE HAPPY HOHENZOLLERN - LOVE AND JOY AND SWEET CONTENT (on the first poster)
GOTT S(TR)AFE ENGLAND, WHY BEAR MALICE? - WE BEAR NONE! (on the second poster; the letters in parentheses have been crossed out.)
LE(S)T (WE) US FORGET - KIPLING. - WAR IS FOOLISHNESS. (on the third poster; the letters in parentheses have been crossed out.)
Description: Several people look at three posters. In the one on the right there is a

man dancing and playing the flute. He wears Lederhosen. Two sheep are dancing next to him. In the poster in the middle, there is a German man with open arms and his hat in his left hand. In the poster on the left, there is a German dressed like an angel who is hovering over demolished cannons. He is blowing a trumpet and strewing roses.

Scenario 1: The Germans attacked Belgium, France and the soldiers of the Allies and caused death, damage and grief.

Scenario 2: The Germans love the British.

Explanation: The two scenarios are contrasted. The British find it difficult to trust the Germans and their demonstration of love and good will.

Type: Everyday scene interacts with the verbal part.

Invective: The Germans cannot be trusted, because they are subservient hypocrites.

Cartoon 169   2.1.1918

Heading: *An Easy Conundrum.*

Caption: *First watcher on the Rhine: "These accursed British, our so peaceful and cultured Mannheim to bomb!" Second ditto: "What devil taught them this frightfulness?"*
Mannheim (on a signpost)

Description: Inside a building, two men are kneeling on the floor, looking out at a heap of debris and destroyed buildings.

Scenario 1: The Germans bombed British towns such as London in a non-peaceful and uncultured way before the British bombed German towns.

Scenario 2: The British retaliated by bombing German towns such as Mannheim.

Explanation: The Germans complain about the British air raids forgetting that they started air raiding British towns. Remembering this fact and the principle 'an eye for an eye, a tooth for an tooth', is the easy solution to this 'easy conundrum'.

Type: War scene represents a communicative situation and interacts with the verbal part.

Invective: The Germans are ignorant and naïve.

Cartoon 170   9.1.1918

Heading:

Caption: *Private Sloggins (to German officer who has demanded an escort of equal rank): "That's wot we've 'alted for. Duggy 'aig's comin' over special. I seed 'im myself this mornin' an' arranged it."*

Description: An infuriated big German officer is stepping out of a long line of prisoners of war approaching a British guard, who looks at him in surprise.

Scenario 1: General Haig is much too busy to deal with such unimportant matters such as escorting a German prisoner of war of whatever rank.

Scenario 2: General Haig comes and escorts the German officer.

Explanation: The two scenarios are contrasted. The strong accent and the dialect of the British soldier are funny. What Private Sloggins says is so obviously a lie that it has to be taken as irony. This is also indicated by the fact that he refers to Sir Douglous Haig as *Duggy 'aig.* General Haig was the commander of I Corps of the British Expeditionary Force (BEF).

Type: Everyday scene represents a communicative situation and interacts with the verbal part.

Invective: The Germans are abominable, because they are arrogant and pompous. They have to be paid back in kind.

Cartoon 171   6.2.1918
Heading:
Caption: *Private Smith (late assistant to palmist, etc. Bond Street): "Who 'd have thought it? They seem to know me."*
Description: A British soldier, who is holding a rifle with a bayonet, is standing in front of a dugout, in which several German soldiers are surrendering with their hands up in the air. Eleven hands are visible.
Scenario 1:   A normal soldier will interpret the gesture of soldiers raising their hands in the air as surrender.
Scenario 2:   This British soldier interprets this gesture as the soldiers showing their hands to him as a palmist.
Explanation: The two scenarios are contrasted. For Private Smith, the fact that so many German soldiers surrender to a single British one must have a different reason than their cowardice.
Type: Counterfactual scene represents a communicative situation and interacts with the verbal part.
Invective: The Germans are cowards.

Cartoon 172   20.3.1918
Heading: *The Bomberang*
Caption: *Hans of Coblenz (during reprisal): "I am disappointed in the British!"*
Description: A man is running away from falling debris after an explosion.
Scenario 1:   The Germans bombed British towns.
Scenario 2:   The British retaliated by bombing German towns.
Explanation: The German complains about the British air raids, forgetting that the Germans started air raiding British towns. Because of this fact and the principle 'an eye for an eye, a tooth for an tooth', there is no reason to be disappointed in the British. There is a blending of 'bomb' and 'boomerang'.
Type: War scene represents a communicative situation and interacts with the verbal part.
Invective: The Germans are ignorant and naïve.

Cartoon 173   12.6.1918
Heading: *A German 'Peace' - for the Instruction of our Pacifists.*
Caption:
Description: A German soldier with a rifle in his left and a whip in his right arm is whipping a Ukrainian couple. The farmer's wife is pulling a plow, and the husband is walking behind it. He protects his face with his right arm against the whip.
Scenario 1:   In a just peace, there is no oppression.
Scenario 2:   A German peace includes oppression and cruelty against civilians.
Explanation: There is a contrast between the normal and the German concept of peace. The cartoon alludes to the fact that Germany marched into the Ukraine after it had concluded a peace treaty with it.
Type: Everyday scene interacts with the verbal part.
Invective: The Germans cannot be trusted, because they are liars; they are cruel.

Cartoon 174   26.6.1918
Heading: *A Pitiful Pose.*
Caption: *Teuton crocodile: "I do so feel for the poor British wounded. I only wish we could do more for them." ("We Germans will preserve our conception of Christian duty towards the sick and wounded." – From recent remarks of the Kaiser reported by a German correspondent.)*
Description: In the foreground a crocodile with a spiked helmet is raising its head, weeping. In the background two German fighter planes are

bombarding a Red Cross station, killing two members of the Red Cross.

Scenario 1: Germany says it feels for the British wounded.

Scenario 2: Germany air-raids British Red Cross stations.

Explanation: Germans say one thing and do another. The cartoon is a pictorial translation of the expression 'to weep crocodile tears'. The meaning of this expression originates from the fact that crocodiles sometimes secrete a fluid from their eyes when they kill prey.

Type: Metonymic scene represents a communicative situation and interacts with the verbal part.

Invective: The Germans cannot be trusted, because they are liars and hypocrites.

Cartoon 175   3.7.1918

Heading: *The Blond Beast's Burden.*

Caption: *German citizen: "And they tell me this may go on for years and years and years!" (Herr von Kuehlmann, in his original speech before the Reichstag, while insisting on the victorious achievements of the German army, hinted at the possibility of a Thirty Years' War.)*
VICTORY (on the foot of the statue)

Description: A stout German with a cap is almost collapsing under the weight of the statue of victory he is carrying. The statue is taller than he.

Scenario 1: A victory is won at a certain point in time.

Scenario 2: The German conception of victory is equivalent to a long stretch of time.

Explanation: The two scenarios are contrasted. Richard von Kuehlmann (1873 – 1948) was a German diplomat. As foreign secretary he led the delegation that negotiated the Treaty of Brest-Litovsk in March 1918. In July 1918, army leaders forced his removal from office for publicly declaring that the war could not be ended by military action alone and without recourse to diplomacy.

Type: Metonymic scene represents a communicative situation and interacts with the verbal part.

Invective: The Germans are ignorant and naïve, because they are fooling themselves.

Cartoon 176   24.7.1918

Heading:

Caption: *Gallant Berliner: "Alas, noble lady, the bow to which you are entitled I cannot perform, my linoleum trousers not permitting." (People in the towns are having to resort to garments made of window-blinds, curtains, etc. such is the shortage of clothing material in Germany. – Vide Daily Press).*

Description: In a park a stout German man is greeting a stout German woman, who is holding a sunshade, by doffing his hat.

Scenario 1: Germans show a stiff and formal behavior towards women.

Scenario 2: This German retains his stiff and formal behavior in spite of the wartime circumstances.

Explanation: The two scenarios are contrasted.

Type: Everyday scene represents a communicative situation and interacts with the verbal part.

Invective: The Germans are abominable, because they are stiff, formal and inflexible.

Cartoon 177   7.8.1918

Heading: *The Chastened Mood.*

Caption: *Hindenburg (to Germania): "You've not quite caught the idea,*

madam. What I rather want is an expression of calm and serene
patience." (Hindenburg has confided to a newspaper correspondent
that the German people need to develop the virtue of patience).

Description: A woman with a helmet and a trident is sitting in an armchair. She has
an expression of insane exuberance on her face. Between her legs, a
dachshund is sitting holding a coat of arms with its paws. On the right
Hindenburg is leaning on his camera, looking at Germania.

Scenario 1: Every normal person is able to put an expression of calm and serene
patience on his or her face.

Scenario 2: Germania is only able to put an expression of guilt or insane
exuberance on her face.

Explanation: The two scenarios are contrasted. The heading gives the reason for the
expression on Germania's face. The facial expression is difficult to
interpret.

Type: Metonymic scene represents a communicative situation and interacts
with the verbal part.

Invective: The Germans are abominable, because they lack serenity and
calmness.

Cartoon 178   7.8.1918
Heading:
Caption: *German Prisoner: "Vy vos you spare mine life?"*
British Tommy: "'Cause ye're so much like a little gal-friend o' mine
as I left behind me down Whitechapel Way."

Description: A very tall and big German soldier is standing in front of a British
soldier with a helmet and a backpack, who is holding a rifle with a
bayonet. In the background there are some explosions.

Scenario 1: The British soldier has spared the life of the German prisoner for
humanitarian reasons or compassion.

Scenario 2: The British soldier has spared the life of the German prisoner, because
he resembles the little girlfriend of the British soldier.

Explanation: The two scenarios are contrasted. The strong accent of the German and
that of the British soldier is funny. What the British soldier says is so
obviously a lie that it has to be taken as irony.

Type: Everyday scene represents a communicative situation and interacts
with the verbal part.

Invective: The Germans are abominable, because they are ugly and speak with a
funny accent.

Cartoon 179   7.8.1918
Heading: *The River Season.*
Caption: *Fritz: "They told me to cross the Marne, and I've done it – both ways.*
Now where's this Aisne they talk about?"

Description: A German soldier with a rifle but without a helmet is running forward.
He has a stare on his face. Behind him on the left, there is a huge
explosion. On the right there is the rubble of destroyed houses.

Scenario 1: A soldier who has occupied foreign territory and lost it again will
develop a critical assessment, when he is again ordered to occupy
foreign territory.

Scenario 2: This German soldier goes about occupying foreign territory again
without further reflection.

Explanation: The two scenarios are contrasted. The German soldier is presented as
following any order without thinking.

Type: War scene represents a communicative situation and interacts with the
verbal part.

Invective: Germans are ignorant and stupid, because they do not think for themselves, but just follow orders.

Cartoon 180   7.8.1918
Heading:
Caption: *Tommy: "Nah then, 'indenburg, not so much of this war of movement."*
Description: A British soldier in combat gear is chasing a fleeing German soldier through a partly destroyed village.
Scenario 1:   In a war of movement soldiers make deliberate tactical moves in a well-planned fashion.
Scenario 2:   The movement of the German soldier is a precipitate flight.
Explanation: The term *war of movement* obviously does not apply to the drawn scene. The British soldier coins a new name for German soldiers by calling them 'Hindenburg'.
Type: War scene represents a communicative situation and interacts with the verbal part.
Invective: The Germans are cowards.

Cartoon 181   14.8.1918
Heading: *Von Pot and von Kettle.*
Caption: *German general: "Why the devil don't you stop these Americans coming across? That's your job." German admiral: "And why the devil don't you stop 'em when they* are *across? That's yours."*
Description: A German general and a German admiral are shouting at each other furiously.
Scenario 1:   The leadership of the army and the navy should cooperate in an efficient manner.
Scenario 2:   The leadership of the German army and navy are exchanging angry reproaches.
Explanation: The two scenarios are contrasted. The combination of the German marker of nobility, *von*, with the name of a household utensil pokes fun at the fact that very many German members of the upper echelons of the military had such names because they belonged to the nobility.
Type: Everyday scene represents a communicative situation and interacts with the verbal part.
Invective: The Germans are militarily inferior. They are desperate and about to lose the war.

Cartoon 182   21.8.1918
Heading:
Caption: *"Himmel! The All-highest has the truth spoken - ... the worst* is *behind us."*
Description: Several German soldiers are running away in a headlong flight. They have lost or thrown away their weapons and are being chased by a British tank and British soldiers.
Scenario 1:   The expression *the worst is behind us* has a metaphorical meaning that better times are ahead.
Scenario 2:   In this context the expression adopts a literal meaning.
Scenario 3:   The predictions of the German Emperor may come true but have to undergo critical judgment.
Scenario 4:   The predictions of the German Emperor are wishful thinking. Nevertheless, the Germans believe in them at the cost of misinterpretation.
Explanation: The first and second two scenarios are contrasted. The speaker holds the naive belief that the German Emperor always tells the truth,

thereby ignoring the difference between the actually intended and the current meaning of a saying, which are contradictory. The speaker uses a funny and incorrect German word order in his English.

Type: War scene interacts with the verbal part.
Invective: Germans are ignorant and naïve. Therefore they follow their Kaiser blindly. In addition, they are cowards.

Cartoon 183   28.8.1918
Heading:
Caption: *Gretel: "Have you ever contemplated what would happen to us all should the enemy triumph?" Hansel: "Don't, Gretel – don't! Fancy being forced to play cricket!"*
Description: An elderly stout couple is sitting in their living room at a table. In the background there is a bust of Hindenburg. The man is propping his head in the palm of his left hand in despair. In his other hand is a newspaper.
Scenario 1: Losing a war has many negative implications.
Scenario 2: For this German the worst consequence is having to play cricket.
Explanation: The two scenarios are contrasted.
Type: Everyday scene represents a communicative situation and interacts with the verbal part.
Invective: The Germans are ignorant and stupid, because they are inflexible.

Cartoon 184   4.9.1918
Heading: *In Reserve.*
Caption: *German Eagle (to German Dove): "Here, carry on for a bit, will you? I'm feeling rather run down."*
Description: An eagle with a spiked helmet and his wings stretched out is walking on the ground looking at a dove, which is perched on top of its open cage. It is wearing the cap of a German official.
Scenario 1: A country should seek peace at all times.
Scenario 2: Germany seeks peace because their military forces have been beaten.
Explanation: The two scenarios are contrasted.
Type: Metonymic scene represents a communicative situation and interacts with the verbal part.
Invective: The Germans are militarists.

Cartoon 185   16.10.1918
Heading: *The German Angel of Peace.*
Caption:
Description: A dark and uncouth female figure with wings is walking through a destroyed landscape. Her eyes and her mouth are wide open. She is raising her left hand in which she is holding a palm leaf. In her right hand she is holding a burning torch, and at her side she is carrying a sword, the grip of which has the form of the German Eagle.
Scenario 1: An angel of peace carries a palm leaf and moves through an untarnished countryside.
Scenario 2: The German angel of peace carries a palm leaf in her left hand and a torch in her right hand and moves through the countryside, burning buildings and leaving a path of destruction.
Explanation: There is an obvious contradiction between the peaceful intentions Germany claims and its actual aggressive behavior.
Type: Metonymic scene interacts with the verbal part.
Invective: The Germans are callous and cruel; they are destructive liars.

Cartoon 186   23.10.1918

Heading:

Caption: *Bosch (suddenly appearing over the top): "Kamerad! Kamerad!"*
Briton: "Lor', my son, you did give me a turn. I thought you was an
enemy."

Description: A British soldier in combat gear is standing in a trench looking up. An unarmed German soldier is lying over the top of the trench, fearfully looking at the British soldier. The German is making a defensive movement with his hands.

Scenario 1:   An enemy appearing at the top of a trench would mean severe danger and alert the soldiers in the trench.

Scenario 2:   The German soldier appearing at the top just startles the British soldier who does not take him seriously as an enemy.

Explanation: The German soldiers are very keen to get away from the theater of war.

Type: War scene represents a communicative situation and interacts with the verbal part.

Invective: The Germans are cowards, e.g. their soldiers are willing to surrender at any time. Therefore they need not be taken seriously.

Cartoon 187   30.10.1918

Heading: *Everything in its Proper Order.*

Caption: *Hun prisoner: "Und ven comes der peace of vitch dey vos talk?"*
Tommy: "One thing at a time, Fritz. We've got to finish the war first."

Description: A German prisoner of war with his hands in his pockets is standing next to a British soldier in combat gear, who has just lit a cigarette. Far in the background there are some soldiers moving about.

Scenario 1:   The German prisoner expects a peace treaty on equal terms.

Scenario 2:   The British soldier predicts a peace treaty after Germany has lost the war.

Explanation: The two scenarios are contrasted. Tommy makes a distinction between 'peace' and 'finishing the war', which means that he wants to win the war in any case. The strong accent of the German is funny.

Type: Everyday scene represents a communicative situation and interacts with the verbal part.

Invective: The Germans are militarily inferior. They are desperate and about to lose the war.

Cartoon 188   6.11.1918

Heading: *Essence of Parliament.*

Caption for   *Inconveniences of the war.*
both panels:

                     Left panel

Caption: *Shortage of Feeding-stuffs in Ireland.*

Description: An Irishman with a dejected expression on his face is standing in a strut with his left hand in his pocket. On the palm of his right hand he holds an emaciated weeping piglet.

Type: Everyday scene interacts with the verbal part.

                     Right panel

Caption: *Only a half-bottle of wine for Hun officer prisoners.*

Description: A stout German prisoner of war officer is standing in a strut with his left hand in his pocket. On the palm of his right hand, he holds a small-sized bottle of wine. He has an irritated expression on his face.

Scenario 1:   The Irish, who are not responsible for the war, have difficulties getting enough food for themselves. They calmly accept this.

Scenario 2:   The German prisoner of war officers, who are responsible for the war, get the luxury of a small-sized bottle of wine, with which they are dissatisfied.

Explanation:	The two scenarios are contrasted.
Type:	Everyday scene interacts with the verbal part.
Invective:	The Germans are abominable, because they are arrogant and demanding.

Cartoon 189   13.11.1918

Heading:	*Surrender de luxe.*
Caption:	*Tommy: "Wot the dooce are you?" Hun: "I vos the servant of Leutnant Graf von Spitsburg. In a moment he arrive."*
Description:	A British soldier in combat gear is waiting for an unarmed big German soldier who is about to cross some planks over a trench. He is carrying the luggage of his lieutenant, i.e. a large backpack and three large bags, under his arm and on his shoulder. Instead of raising his hands in surrender, he is holding a stick with an artificial hand over the upper bag.
Scenario 1:	When a lieutenant becomes a prisoner of war, he will expect very modest accommodation with little personal space.
Scenario 2:	The German lieutenant moves from the front into a British prisoner of war camp as if he were moving house or moving into a luxury accommodation with lots of personal space.
Explanation:	The two scenarios are contrasted.
Type:	War scene represents a communicative situation and interacts with the verbal part.
Invective:	The Germans are abominable, because they are arrogant and demanding.

Punch cartoon 189

4. Results

The differences between the British and the German cartoons are quite striking, but it seemed difficult to specify this intuitive impression in any precise way. Therefore, we have subjected the cartoons to our analytic framework and can now look at these features and compare them. One of them concerns the different types of scenes of chapter 3.1, which include the interaction between the verbal and pictorial parts. We have also compared the invectives in order to see which of them feature most prominently in the two groups of cartoons.

4.1 Scenes

As was stated above, every panel of a cartoon presents a specific scene as a starting point, providing the anchoring ground for the heading and the captions. Whereas the German cartoonists use everyday scenes in just one third of their cartoons (32.7 %) as their point of departure, the British cartoonists do so in almost half of their cartoons (47.0 %), i.e. this type of scene is the main device of the British cartoonists. This explains the fact that the British cartoons have a more down to earth or matter of fact character, while the German cartoons seem more 'poetic' and erudite.

Non-combatant military scenes are used to an equally low degree in both *Simplicissimus* (6.7 %) and *Punch* (9.0 %). In such scenes the war is commented by members of the military or by members of the two warring factions, e.g. a German prisoner of war and his British guard. War scenes are shown by the German cartoonists more reluctantly (6.7 %) than by the British (10.9 %). The British cartoonists deal with the war in a lighthearted fashion, which emphasizes their message of being the superior nation.

In the British cartoons there are twice as many counterfactual scenes to be found (24.4 %) than in the German ones (11.1 %), i.e. they transport a greater sense of the unreal which again communicates a sense of light heartedness as well as of the absurd, which also nowadays is regarded as typical of British humor.

The greatest difference discloses when one regards metonymic scenes, which are the favorites of the German cartoonists (42.8 %). The percentage of this type in British cartoons is 9.0 %, i.e. the German cartoonists use it more than four times as often. This explains the impression that German cartoons are less direct, because their point requires some cultural background knowledge, e.g. when figures and names such as Aegir, the God of the ocean in Norse mythology, Charon, the son of Erebus and Nyx (Night) in Greek mythology, Napoleon and Albion, the earliest-known name for the islands of Britain, are used in the cartoons. Diagrams 1 and 2 compare the results and give a graphic account of them. They are followed by table 10 which contains the absolute figures and exact percentages of the scene types.

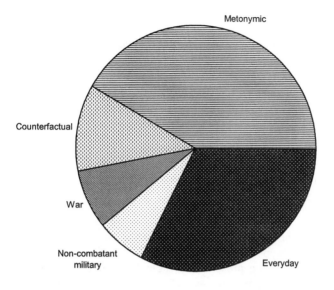

Diagram 1: Distribution of scene types in *Simplicissimus*

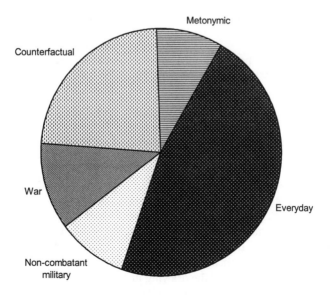

Diagram 2: Distribution of scene types in *Punch*

Types of scenes	Simplicissimus	Punch
1. Everyday scenes:	68 = 32.7 %	125 = 47.0 %
2. Non-combatant military scenes:	14 = 6.7 %	24 = 9.0 %
3. War scenes:	14 = 6.7 %	29 = 10.9 %
4. Counterfactual scenes:	23 = 11.1 %	65 = 24.4 %
5. Metonymic scenes:	89 = 42.8 %	24 = 9.0 %
Panels overall:	208 = 100 %	266 = 100 %

Table 10: Types of scenes in Simplicissimus and Punch.

The next question to be asked is how *Simplicissimus* and *Punch* compare with regard to the three subtypes of the scenes which specify the verbal-pictorial interaction. These results are presented in table 11. The absolute figures and exact percentages of the scene types as well as their subtypes can be found in appendix 2.

Pictorial and verbal elements	Simplicissimus	Punch
Communicative situation:	86 = 41.3 %	22 = 8.3 %
Interaction with the verbal part:	75 = 36.1 %	147 = 55.3 %
Communicative situation and interaction with the verbal part:	47 = 22.6 %	97 = 36.5 %
Panels overall:	208 = 100 %	266 = 100 %

Table 11: Pictorial and verbal elements in Simplicissimus and Punch

Whereas 41.3 % of the German cartoons simply show a situation, in which communication is taking place, this type makes up the smallest section of the British cartoons (8.3 %). This means that two fifth of the German cartoons rely on the verbal communication between speakers, while the pictorial part just serves to present them. It is left to the reader to identify them and to decide who is saying what. This also means that the medium is not used to the full because the point is made verbally and the drawing just has a supportive function.

An interaction between the drawing and the verbal part of a cartoon is contained in more than half of the British cartoons (55.3 %). This is the case in just over one third of the German cartoons (36.1 %). The following example from *Punch* cartoon 96 illustrates that the readers are presented with an interpretation of what they see in the drawing: *Scene showing the refined cruelty with which starving German prisoners are treated by the British.* In these cases the captions support the drawing, which has a relevant function for the point.

In just over a third of the British cartoons (36.5 %) and about one fifth of the German ones (22.6 %) a communicative situation is presented and also verbal elements are given, which interact with the pictorial elements in the cartoon. The British cartoonists tend to give the reader more information about the speakers and their specific roles, e.g. *Tommy (to new arrival at prisoners' camp): "What was your occupation?" German: "Army butcher." Tommy: "Cattle or babies?"* (*Punch* cartoon 99). This means that the British cartoonists want to be certain that their point is understood and therefore give the reader pictorial as well as verbal information.

What can also be interpreted from these figures is that the British cartoonists present humorous and ironical scenarios pictorially in more than 90 % of the cases whereas the Germans only reach half that figure. The bar chart in diagram 3 gives a comparative account of the results. They reflect the fact that *Punch* had a much broader and less elitist clientele of readers than *Simplicissimus* which - before WW 1 - was read by the liberal middle class as the symbol of a new anti-establishment mood.

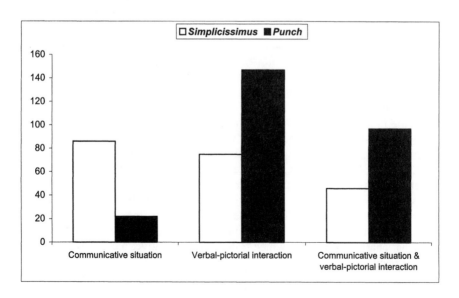

Diagram 3: Pictorial and verbal elements in *Simplicissimus* and *Punch*

4.2 Invectives

Of the 352 cartoons under scrutiny there are only five which do not have a clear-cut invective directed at the war opponent. This applies to cartoons 6 and 88 from *Punch* and to cartoons 25, 126 and 162 from *Simplicissimus*. Unlike cartoons with invectives, they are either humorous in a general way, show self-irony or are neither humorous nor ironical.

In *Punch* cartoon 6 the general question of how to deal with German nationals living in England is touched upon, but it is presented from the point of view of a small child and thus does not contain a criticism but rather shows a childlike over-generalization, which gives rise to laughter: *Ethel in apprehensive whisper which easily reaches her German governess, to whom she is deeply attached: "Mother, shall we have to kill Fräulein?"*.

In *Punch* cartoon 88 the question of moral superiority is discussed with the British officer denying the claim of his German counterpart: *Captured German Officer to English Officer in charge of German prisoners: "You fight for money; we fight for honor." English Officer: "Ah, Well! Neither of us seems to get what we want, do we?"* The issues of German moral superiority and British greed are topicalized, but do not have the quality of an invective.

Three *Simplicissimus* cartoons have no direct invective, i.e. nos. 25, 126 and 162. Cartoon 25 contains an ironical remark of a member of the German military leadership, which simply expresses their resolve to continue the war with England, but is clearly not an invective against the British: *Sylvester Punch. "Scarborough and Hartlepool shelled! Let us drink to a further German-English approximation, hurrah, hurrah, hurrah!"*. Cartoon 126 contains a self-ironical remark pointing at the Germans' love of beer: *The Worst. "They keep sayin': God punish England ... no diluted beer they don't have to drink!"*. Finally, cartoon 162 is a warning that the attitude of superiority towards the British is ill-founded and may have negative repercussions: *The German Gentleman. "So what if they came; then we would finally have the chance to play football with a genuine Englishman." - "Or the genuine Englishman with him?"*. This warning is not surprising because the cartoon was published on October 22nd 1918, when Germany was already facing political unrest, mutiny in the navy and starvation. With the economy in ruins and mounting defeats on the battlefield it must have been obvious to anyone that the war was lost. A few weeks later, i.e. in November of the same year, the German generals requested armistice negotiations with the Allies and soon afterwards the war was over. The distribution of the invectives in *Simplicissimus* and *Punch* is given in table 12 The bar chart in diagram 4, which follows table 12, gives a comparative account of the results.

Invectives	*Simplicissimus*	*Punch*
1. They are abominable.	11 = 6.6 %	39 = 17.9 %
2. They are stupid, ignorant, naïve.	32 = 19.3 %	59 = 27.1 %
3. They are callous, cruel.	31 = 18.7 %	15 = 6.9 %
4. They cannot be trusted, are bigoted.	15 = 9.0 %	8 = 3.7 %
5. They are cowards.	9 = 5.4 %	15 = 6.9 %
6. They are militarily inferior.	35 = 21.1 %	32 = 14.7 %
7. Life is deteriorating.	4 = 2.4 %	3 = 1.4 %
8. They mislead the public, abuse the press etc.	21 = 12.6 %	20 = 9.2 %
9. The Germans are militaristic.	-	18 = 8.3 %
10. The Germans have no culture.	-	4 = 1.8 %
11. The Germans hate the British.	-	4 = 1.8 %
12. The British are responsible for (the continuation of) the war.	8 = 4.8 %	-
Overall:	166 = 100 %	218 = 100 %

Table 12: Invectives in *Simplicissimus* and *Punch*

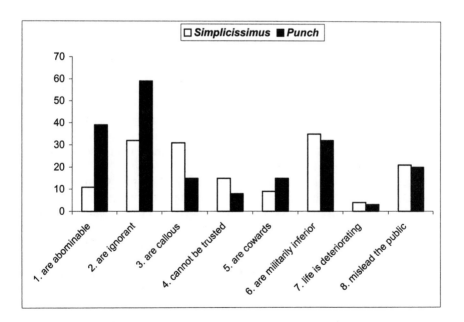

Diagram 4: Invectives in *Simplicissimus* and *Punch*

Two of the invectives on each side show a considerable difference. The British cartoonists stress the first two, i.e. that the Germans are abominable and that they are stupid. For the first invective the ratio is 17.9 % : 6.6 %, which means that the British call the Germans abominable almost three times as often. The cartoons repeat and entrench the image of the 'ugly' German who is insensitive, impolite, aggressive etc. With regard to the second invective the difference is not as pronounced: 27.1 % : 19.3 %, i.e. the British brandish the Germans as stupid in just over a quarter of their cartoons, whereas the Germans do this in just one fifth of theirs. It is the most frequent British invective and has the advantage that it ridicules the opponent and still has a humorous value. Since intellectual underachievements build the cornerstone of jokes and humor, this fact explains the overall impression that the German cartoons are less 'funny' than the British ones. The most frequent invectives employed by the Germans are that the British are militarily inferior and that they are callous and cruel. The ratio of the former invective is 18.7 % : 6.9 % and that of the latter is 21.1 %. 14.7 %. By presenting the enemy as militarily inferior the cartoonists encourage their readers to believe in an easy military victory rather than raise a critical voice against the war.

The invective that the members of the other side are callous and cruel is meant to undermine the moral stance of the enemy and it also justifies the war. It reflects a traditional stereotype of the callous British monger and profiteer who exploits people of other nations, e.g. the ones of the British empire. In this way the Germans can blame the war on the negative nature of the British, who let other nations fight for them, and can thus avoid any mention of their own responsibility for initiating it.

Whereas the British laugh about the mental insufficiency of the Germans in a very general way, the Germans try to undermine the trustworthiness of the British by presenting them as unreliable. Unreliability and callousness or cruelty are obviously connected. The percentage of the German cartoons carrying the message that the British cannot be trusted (9 %) is more than twice as high as that of the analogous British ones (3.7 %).

Three types of invectives are used by the British against the Germans without any 'retaliation' by their opponents: The Germans are portrayed as militaristic (8.3 %), as having no culture or only a pseudo-culture (1.8 %) and of harboring an 'irrational hatred' of the British (1.8 %). The Germans have only one invective, which is not reciprocated, i.e. that the British are responsible for (the continuation of) the war, which amounts to 4.8 %. It is hard to believe that this invective occurs at all in the light of the historical fact that Germany provoked Britain to declare war because Germany had invaded Belgium, thereby breaking its neutrality.

The three final mutual invectives in the list rise to a similar level. The percentage of the accusation that the enemy is cowardly is 6.9 % in

Simplicissimus and 5.4 % in *Punch*. That life is deteriorating in a war is to be expected, still this is used as an invective with a certain schadenfreude value on an equally low level of 2.4 % in *Simplicissimus* and of 1.4 % in *Punch*. It is directly connected with the war and is intended to undermine the morale of the enemy and to boost one's own. A bigger difference is given in the invective that the other side is misleading the public. 12.6 % of the German cartoons make this claim and 9.2 % of the British ones. With the news agency Reuter the British had a powerful tool of influencing public opinion, so it was only natural that the Germans tried to undermine the reliability and effectiveness of it. The news policy was a major concern for the Germans because very early in the war the British had severed the German transatlantic cable and thus more or less had a news monopoly in the USA.

It has to be kept in mind that the main function of the cartoons is not to amuse but to ridicule and denigrate the enemy. The cartoons differ in the way they achieve this and the ones in *Punch* adopt a more light hearted approach. The invectives function as an argumentative war propaganda, i.e. they make up a fabric of arguments and – with minor differences - are used by both sides. The argumentative structure is not linear but multi-layered. The most prominent arguments concerning the British are formulated below:

1. The British are simply abominable *because* they are stupid, ignorant, naïve, callous, cruel, bigoted and cannot be trusted.
2. They are cowards and are *therefore* militarily inferior.
3. *Therefore* life is deteriorating.
4. *Therefore* they have to mislead the public.
5. They are responsible for the war. *Therefore* they have to mislead the public
6. They mislead the public. *Therefore* they cannot be trusted.
etc.

In turn, the most prominent arguments concerning the Germans can be formulated as follows:

1. The Germans are simply abominable *because* they are stupid, ignorant, naïve, callous, cruel, bigoted and cannot be trusted.
2. They are cowards and are *therefore* militarily inferior.
3. *Therefore* life is deteriorating.
4. *Therefore* they have to mislead the public.
5. They are militarists, have no culture and hate the British. *Therefore* they have to mislead the public.
etc.

A regular reader of these cartoons who identifies with these invectives and the underlying stereotypes is faced with the incremental nature of these argumentative contents. We do not claim that the readers are immediately affected by these arguments because research on newspapers does not support any such inference, but the total lack of a self-critical function of any kind in the cartoons must have corroborated the self-fulfilling prophecy that the war was unavoidable.

4.3 The Cartoonists
It is quite revealing to look at the cartoonists who created the 163 German and the 189 British cartoons which were selected for this study. The names of the ten most productive *Punch* cartoonists and all the ten *Simplicissimus* cartoonists can be found in part 1 of table 13 below. The figure following the names indicates the number of the cartoons they contributed.

No.	Simplicissimus	Punch
1.	Blix: 31	L. Raven-Hill: 30
2.	O. Gulbransson: 30	G. Morrow: 24
3.	Th.Th. Heine: 29	F. Reynolds: 18
4.	E. Thöny: 26	F.H. Townsend: 18
Sum:	116 of 163 = 71.2 %	90 of 189 = 47.6 %
5.	W. Schulz: 14	G.L. Stampa: 12
6.	E. Schilling: 12	B. Partridge: 11
7.	E.D. Petersen: 9	E.H. Shephard: 9
8.	K. Arnold: 5	L. Baumer: 8
9.	F. Sedlacek: 2	R. Brook: 8
10.	K.W. Boehmer: 1	A.W. Mills: 8
Sum:	163 = 100 %	146 of 189 = 77.2 %

Table 13, part 1: German and British cartoonists

The remaining twenty-five *Punch* cartoonists are listed in part 2 of table 13 below. In four of the German cartoons and in one of the British ones it was not possible to identify the cartoonists because they had not signed them or their names were illegible.

No.	Simplicissimus	Punch
11.		C. Harrison: 5
12.		C.A. Shepperson: 4
13.		G.D. Armour: 3
14.		C. Grave: 3
15.		A.W. Lloyd: 3
16.		'Fougasse' (K. Bird): 2
17.		A. Moreland: 2
18.		P.T. Reynolds: 2
19.		J.A. Shephard: 2
20.		A. Bailey: 1
21.		N. Barker: 1
22.		W. Bird: 1
23.		L.R. Brightwell: 1
24.		R. Bull: 1
25.		G. Davey: 1
26.		L. Edwards: 1
27.		T. Evans: 1
28.		D. German: 1
29.		W.A. Howells: 1
30.		F.G. Lewin: 1
31.		E.A. Morrow: 1
32.		E. Noble: 1
33.		G. Simmons: 1
34.		B. Thomas: 1
35.		J. Wingat: 1
Illegible:	4	1
Total:	163 = 100 %	189 = 100 %

Table 13, part 2: German and British cartoonists

More than two thirds (116 = 71.2 %) of the German cartoons were drawn by only four cartoonists: Blix, O. Gulbransson, Th.Th. Heine and E. Thöny. The four most productive British cartoonists produced just half of the *Punch* cartoons (90 = 47.6 %): L. Raven-Hill, G. Morrow, F. Reynolds and F.H. Townsend. Whereas ten cartoonists produced all the *Simplicissimus* cartoons, the ten most productive *Punch* cartoonists contributed a total of 146 cartoons, i.e. just over three quarters (77.2 %) of that part of the corpus. The remaining twenty five British cartoonists shared the rest of forty three cartoons. Sixteen of them produced only one cartoon each, four produced two cartoons, three created three, one was responsible for four and another one for five. This means that in

Germany the intellectual effort rested on the shoulders of only a few specialists whereas in Great Britain it rested on many more. Because of this much broader basis in *Punch*, one might expect a greater diversity of styles and invectives than can actually be found, As was demonstrated, the differences between *Simplicissimus* and *Punch*, on the other hand are clear-cut.

4.4 Stereotypes then and now

As was mentioned above, the invectives we found in the cartoon corpus strongly rely on stereotypical judgments and it is interesting to look at what has remained of them three quarters of a century later. Keller (1991) asked German and English pupils to assess the other nation on the basis of a list of 178 judgments. In it there were several negative ones which correspond to the invectives found in the cartoons. In table 14 below we have listed these correspondences.

Invectives	Stereotypes
1. are abominable	revanchists, unfaithful, exploiters, dirty, boastful, avoiding hard work, obstinate, mistrustful, religious intolerance, servile, envious, vain, lazy, miserly, unsociable, arrogant, miserly, snobs
2. are ignorant	primitive, unsophisticated, too trusting, stolid, awkward, shallow, superstitious
3. are callous, cruel	brutal, nation of businessmen
4. cannot be trusted	unreliable, hypocrites
5. are cowards	cowardly, timid
8. mislead the public	deceitful, corruptible
9. are militaristic	military nation, accepting authority
10. have no culture	uncultured
11. have an irrational hatred of the British (Germans)	vengeful, fanatical, impulsive

Table 14: Corresponding invectives and stereotypes

The cartoon invectives concerning military inferiority (6), the deterioration of the living conditions (7) and the blame that one party is responsible for (the continuation of) the war (12) have no correspondences in Keller's list, because they are directly related to the war. It is a trivial fact that most of these labels have a relative value and that they can easily be interpreted in a derogatory way. Among these are *national pride, proud, strong willed, extremely patriotic, class-conscious, disciplined, reserved, unemotional* and *class distinction*. But such a negative meaning was not intended in Keller's study.

In a second step Keller (1991: 121 f.) reduces the number of characteristics to those which were mentioned by at least 40 % of his British and German subjects. The list of characteristics attributed by the British to the Germans which passed this mark contains nineteen labels and is placed on the left hand side of table 15. The corresponding list of characteristics which were attributed by the Germans to the British contains twenty-four labels and is placed on the right hand side of table 15.

The Germans judged by the British	The British judged by the Germans
1. national pride	1. bound by tradition
2. hard-working	2. national pride
3. skilled craftsmen	3. polite
4. well-built	4. class-conscious
5. conscious of duty	5. disciplined
6. intelligent	6. gentlemen
7. proud	7. reserved
8. good scientists	8. correct
9. strong willed	9. freedom-loving
10. extremely patriotic	10. tactful
11. good technicians	11. cultured people
12. sport-loving	12. unemotional
13. progressive	13. conventional
14. clean	14. reserved with foreigners
15. military nation	15. self-confident
16. glory-seeking	16. conscious of duty
17. hardy	17. sport-loving
18. musical	18. good politicians
19. anti-semitic	19. proud
--	20. hospitable
--	21. nation of businessmen
--	22. class distinction
--	23. good democrats
--	24. snobs

Table 15: The British image of Germans and vice versa

It shows that the young generations in Germany and Great Britain do not cling to the old stereotypes handed down by their forefathers because only one in each list corresponds to the list of invectives found in the cartoons. Germany is still seen as a military nation (no. 15) and the British are still assessed as snobs (no. 25). Whereas it is an obvious fact that Great Britain still has a class society which reveals itself to the general public in institutions such as public schools, elite colleges within the universities, the gentry, the House of Lords etc. the military do not play a major role in the public and political life of Germany. But Prussian militarism dates back to the 19th century and thus has a very long tradition in the consciousness of the British. It may take a few more peaceful decades to eradicate it

In a different study, Hortmann (1992) investigated the effects a stay in Germany has on the German stereotypes, which British students have internalized. Her results are quite similar. In a list which presents the twenty one characteristics which were mentioned most often there are three which might be regarded as hyponyms of *abominable: materialistic, authoritarian, arrogant* and *pushy*. They occur as no. 5, 6, 8 and 10 in table 16. But as can be seen, the assessments are also quite positive, overall.

West Germans[1] in the eyes of British exchange students

1. efficient	8. arrogant	15. helpful
2. competitive	9. frank	16. broad-minded
3. self-assertive	10. pushy	17. polite
4. career-minded	11. pleasure-loving	18. considerate
5. materialistic	12. nationalistic	19. inhibited
6. authoritarian	13. outgoing	20. humorous
7. reliable	14. generous	21. easy-going
7. earnest		

Table 16: The British image of West Germans

The constant reproduction of negative stereotypes in the media defines and entrenches ethnic character and national identity. On the one hand, this entails the simplification which is typical of stereotypes and a system of bipolar, i.e. black and white oppositions, according to which the outgroup is characterized, on the other. It also means that the whole system of oppositions which serves to separate the outgroup from the ingroup is invoked again and again and thus reproduced and also that possible inaccuracies and contradictions are not dealt with in more complex discourse structures in which the opposite pole of the black and white structure would enter the conceptualizations. But this does not suggest that these images are directly translated into everyday life, in which personal experiences play just as important a role. It is easier to judge figures of a text world in a negative way than real world people, because the latter can be friendly, charming and helpful.

---

[1] Most of the research was carried out before the reunification of Germany in 1989.

5. Conclusion

At the end of his book on World War I, John Keegan (1998: 456) concludes, "... the First World War is a mystery. Its origins are mysterious. So is its course. Why did a prosperous continent, at the height of its success as a source and agent of global wealth and power and at one of the peaks of its intellectual and cultural achievements, choose to risk all it had won for itself and all it offered to the world in the lottery of a vicious and local internecine conflict? Why, when the hope of bringing the conflict to a quick and decisive conclusion was everywhere dashed to the ground within months of its outbreak, did the combatants decide nevertheless to persist in their military effort, to mobilize for total war and eventually to commit the totality of their young manhood to mutual and existentially pointless slaughter?"

Before 1914 the cartoonists had dealt critically with the topic of a possible war, but once the conflict had begun, they were drawn between their own critical intelligence and the patriotic impulse toward unquestioning national solidarity. Critical judgment of the war hysteria of 1914 was subdued. And during the war, when their countries' international security and prestige was concerned any criticism was regarded as subversive and even traitorous, no matter how reasonable it may have been. Thus the cartoons are not critical of the war as such, they simply target inconsistencies, illogicalities and flaws of the enemy. They seemed not to believe any more in humor, irony and sarcasm as forces in social and political change but were in line with the newspapers of the time, which contained the self-fulfilling prophecy that war was inevitable and unavoidable. The cartoons do not question its political background, which corroborates the fact that at the beginning of the 20th century wars were regarded as natural events between countries which were seen as being involved in a Darwinian struggle of a survival of the fittest.[2]

The common ground of political cartoons is normally made up of recent political issues. In our corpus, there are only very few which allude to a specific historical incident, such as the sinking of the *Lusitania*. The vast majority stay on a general level of allusion, that is to say that the correlation between the topics of the cartoons and their historical background is rather loose. It is left to the readers to fill in the gaps not only intellectually but also emotionally. In this way, the cartoonist can use a simplified model of the world, which in turn facilitates irony and sarcasm, because the simple elements and rules of the discourse world(s) are presupposed as given: 'soldiers must be courageous', 'politicians must be wise, must never contradict themselves' etc. Another aspect which belongs to the simplified world model pertains to the fact that both British and German cartoonists enhance a polar conceptualization of THEM versus US

---

[2] Reumann (1969: 70 ff.) points out that, if cartoons have an effect at all, it is that of consolidating given attitudes.

which they employ for categorizing two groups of people. THEM are the enemies and their allies who are different in some significant way which the invectives specify. The difference that becomes focal in this case is the presence or absence of the characteristic(s) that would make THEM be like US. This polar system reflects the stereotypes and is used by both sides with the function of enhancing solidarity of the respective nations.

The invectives are not normally made explicit but have to be inferred by the reader, which acts as an intellectual challenge in a culture of humor, irony and sarcasm. As we demonstrated, the invectives, i.e. the critiqued behavior can be generalized under different headings, but they not only constitute an attack; some of them have the function of blurring historical 'facts'. Thus, when Great Britain is made the culprit for letting soldiers of other nations die for its own selfish interests, the historical fact is blurred that it was Germany which attacked Belgium and France and that only afterwards the British Expeditionary Force (BEF) was sent across the Channel to help fight the aggressor.

Before the war *Simplicissimus* had been engaged in a liberal fight against all kinds of orthodoxies, i.e. the bureaucracy of an authoritarian state, militarism and imperialism. During the war years, both *Simplicissimus* and *Punch* refrained from criticizing the orthodoxies and authorities in their own countries. Their attacks were launched solely on the orthodoxies and authorities of the enemy, thus remaining loyal to their own governments.

A second 'mystery' concerns the difference between British and German humor. The main aim of political cartoons is a serious attack of criticism and denigration. Therefore the cartoonists employ humor and irony not for the sake of mirth but to soften the blow of the invective and render it less blunt and heavy-handed. The British cartoonists do this more often than the Germans. Since the aim of both is to demonstrate the superiority of their own side, the British cartoonists prove this point by showing that the Germans are stupid and clumsy, while the German cartoonists point out the educational and moral inferiority of the British. Since a moralizing stance suppresses a humorous context much more than laughing playfully at something silly, the German cartoons seem less 'funny' and even today the Germans come up against the prejudice of being without humor.

Further research lanes which open up from here might lead to the analysis and comparison of comparable cartoons from the USA, Russia, France, Austria and other countries which were involved in the First World War, for that would complete the picture of a European and world wide retrospective in this area.

Appendix 1: The Cartoon Corpus

This appendix contains two lists of the cartoons from *Simplicissimus* and from *Punch*, which we have analyzed in this book. They are ordered and numbered according to their date of publication with the following information added: the heading or - if there is none - the first part of the first caption, the volume of *Simplicissimus* or *Punch*, the page where they appeared and the name of the cartoonist.

1. Cartoons from *Simplicissimus* 1914 - 1918

Simplicissimus, Volume 19, Issue Numbers 1 – 26, 1914

No.[1]	Heading/Caption	Cartoonist	No.[2]	Date	Page[3]
1	*Der Hüter des Völkerrechts*	O. Gulbransson	20	17.8.1914	328
2	*Der englische Geschäftskrieg*	E. Thöny	21	25.8.1914	331
3	*Englands Schmerz*	Th.Th. Heine	23	8.9.1914	FP
4	*Der Gentleman in deutscher Gefangenschaft*	O. Gulbransson	24	15.9.1914	362
5	*Englands wilde, verwegene Jagd*	E. Thöny	25	22.9.1914	FP
6	*Das fromme England*	E. Thöny	25	22.9.1914	370
7	*Die Lügenzentrale*	Th.Th. Heine	25	22.9.1914	372

Simplicissimus, Volume 19, Issue Numbers 27 – 52, 1914/15

No.	Heading/Caption	Cartoonist	No.	Date	Page
8	*Der Engländer und seine Weltkugel*	Th.Th. Heine	28	13.10.1914	FP
9	*Aus unserem Verbrecheralbum: Winston Churchill, Seeräuber*	O. Gulbransson	28	13.10.1914	390
10	*England braucht Geld*	Blix	28	13.10.1914	394
11	*Die Saat geht auf*	W. Schulz	28	13.10.1914	406
12	*Von der Waterkant*	E.D. Petersen	28	13.10.1914	414
13	*Britische Gerechtigkeit*	Blix	32	10.11.1914	430
14	*Die Spionenfurcht in London*	Th.Th. Heine	32	10.11.1914	431
15	*Englische Regel*	E. Thöny	33	17.11.1914	442
16	*Die Belgier in London*	Blix	33	17.11.1914	449
17	*Prince of Wales*	E.D. Petersen	35	1.12.1914	472
18	*Ein Bild aus dem englischen Familienleben*	Th.Th. Heine	35	1.12.1914	474

---

[1] The figures in this column refer to the numbers of the *Simplicissimus* cartoons in our corpus.
[2] The figures in this column refer to the issue numbers.
[3] 'FP' means front page.

Simplicissimus, Volume 20, Issue Numbers 1 – 26, 1915

Simplicissimus, Volume 20, Issue Numbers 27 – 52, 1915/16

Simplicissimus, Volume 21, Issue Numbers 1 – 26, 1916

Simplicissimus, Volume 21, Issue Numbers 27 – 52, 1916/17

Simplicissimus, Volume 22, Issue Numbers 1 – 26, 1917

No.	Heading/Caption	Cartoonist	No.	Date	Page
114	*Der Weltbefreier*	O. Gulbransson	3	10.4.1917	FP
115	*Ums Heiligste*	Th.Th. Heine	4	17.4.1917	FP
116	*Die Deutschen im Atlantic*	W. Schulz.	4	17.4.1917	42
117	*John Bull, Tod und Teufel*	F. Sedlacek	4	17.4.1917	50
118	*Deutschen-Progrom*	O. Gulbransson	5	1.5.1917	61
119	*Der große 'Durchbruch'*	O. Gulbransson	6	8.5.1917	FP
120	*Im englischen Kriegslaboratorium*	Blix	6	8.5.1917	79
121	*Das Ende der Tanks*	E. Thöny	6	8.5.1917	80
122	*Wer andern eine Grube gräbt*	Blix	7	15.5.1917	FP
123	*Die Sorge des Landesvaters*	Blix	8	22.5.1917	102
124	*Britische Rote-Kreuz-Munition*	E. Schilling	8	22.5.1917	103
125	*Pharao John Bulls Traum*	E. Schilling	8	22.5.1917	107
126	*Das Ärgste*	E. Thöny	10	5.6.1917	119
127	*Englische Landwirtschaft*	Blix	11	12.6.1917	136
128	*Lloyd George*	O. Gulbransson	12	19.6.1917	141
129	*Der britische Seelöwe*	E.D. Petersen	12	19.6.1917	155
130	*Flandern*	Th.Th. Heine	13	26.6.1917	FP
131	*Siegesfanfaren*	Th.Th. Heine	17	3.7.1917	FP
132	*Lloyd George*	O. Gulbransson	19	7.8.1917	248
133	*Ihre Antwort*	E. Thöny	20	14.8.1917	250
134	*Wenn der Feind bei uns herrschte*	Th.Th. Heine	20	14.8.1917	251
135	*In Flandern*	Th.Th. Heine	22	28.8.1917	FP
136	*Aus der Rede des Lloyd Guck in die Luft*	E. Schilling	23	4.9.1917	295
137	*Lloyd George*	E.D. Petersen	24	11.9.1917	299
138	*Divisionen des Todes in Flandern*	E. Schilling	25	18.9.1917	319
139	*Im demokratischen England*	Th.Th. Heine	26	25.9.1917	335

Simplicissimus, Volume 22, Issue Numbers 27 – 52, 1917/18

No.	Heading/Caption	Cartoonist	No.	Date	Page
140	*Freiheit die Ich meine*	K. Arnold	29	16.10.1917	367
141	*Im englischen Parlament*	E. Thöny	29	16.10.1917	375
142	*See-Jägerlatein*	E. Schilling	31	30.10.1917	391
143	*Der Mannschaftsersatz in England*	(no signature)	36	4.12.1917	463
144	*Die Tuchknappheit in London Westend*	(no signature)	36	4.12.1917	463
145	*Die Kartoffelnot in England*	(no signature)	36	4.12.1917	463
146	*Englisches Kriegsbrot*	(no signature)	36	4.12.1917	463
147	*Lloyd George der Redestratege*	E. Schilling	37	11.12.1917	467
148	*Cant*	E. Thöny	38	18.12.1917	487

Simplicissimus, Volume 23, Issue Numbers 1 – 27, 1918

Simplicissimus, Volume 23, Issue Numbers 27 – 52, 1918/19

2. Cartoons from *Punch* 1914 - 1918

Punch, Volume 147, 1914

No.[1]	Heading/Caption	Cartoonist	Date	Page
1	*A Quick Change of Front*	C. Harrison	19.8.1914	159
2	*"It's an ill wind ...*	G.D. Armour	19.8.1914	165
3	*To Paris as the crow flies ....*	A.W. Lloyd	26.8.1914	180
4	*The Triumph of 'Culture.'*	B. Partridge	26.8.1914	185
5	*Special constables who can speak ...*	A.W. Mills	2.9.1914	193
6	*"Mother shall we have to kill ...*	C.A. Shepperson.	2.9.1914	202
7	*For Neutral Consumption*	A.W. Lloyd	2.9.1914	206
8	*Ex-Teuton (to landlady): "Ach! ...*	L. Raven-Hill	2.9.1914	209
9	*Teutonic Barber: "Shafe sir?"*	F.H. Townsend	16.9.1914	239
10	*The Wolff: "Good morning my dear ...*	A.W. Lloyd	23.9.1914	266
11	*Youthful Patriot: "Oh Mummy, you ...*	C.A. Shepperson	30.9.1914	280
12	*Unreported Casualty to the Football ...*	E.H. Shephard	7.10.1914	298
13	*Facts from the Front. We learn ...*	E.H. Shephard	21.10.1914	318
14	*Why Have we no Supermen like ...*	L. Baumer	21.10.1914	337
15	*Facts from the Front. Storm of ...*	E.H. Shephard	21.10.1914	338
16	*"Pfutsch! Dey vas just a few tings ...*	P.T. Reynolds	21.10.1914	342
17	*Forewarned*	L. Raven-Hill	4.11.1914	371
18	*Facts from the Front. Tactical use ...*	E.H. Shephard	4.11.1914	378
19	*Latest Device of the Enemy*	G. Morrow	4.11.1914	387
20	*How to Bring up a Hun*	A.W. Mills	11.11.1914	394
21	*A Prussian Court-Painter ...*	E.A. Morrow	11.11.1914	401
22	*Owing to the outcry against ...*	C. Grave	9.12.1914	469
23	*The Master Word*	G.L. Stampa	9.12.1914	477
24	*The Zeppelin Menace*	L. Baumer	9.12.1914	478
25	*"Run avay you leedle poys ...*	P.T. Reynolds	9.12.1914	483
26	*Unrecorded Events in the History ...*	G. Morrow	16.12.1914	498
27	*Language-Kultur*	G.D. Armour	16.12.1914	507
28	*Dishonoured*	L. Raven-Hill	30.12.1914	518
29	*The Iron Cross Epidemic*	C. Graves	30.12.1914	526

---

[1] The figures in this column refer to the numbers of the *Punch* cartoons in our corpus.

Punch, Volume 148, 1915

No.	Heading/Caption	Cartoonist
	Punch's Almanack for 1915	
30	*News for German Consumption: "The difficulties ...*	L. Baumer
31	*News for German Consumption: "Signs are not wanting ...*	L. Baumer
32	*"In society the chief topics ...*	L. Baumer
33	*"It would be impossible ...*	L. Baumer
34	*The Spy Peril*	C. Harrison
35	*The Last Line*	C. Harrison
36	*When William Comes to London. When William comes with all his might ...*	F.H. Townsend
37	*A higher art will ...*	F.H. Townsend
38	*When William shoots ...*	F.H. Townsend
39	*In the Champagne Country*	L. Raven-Hill
40	*Herr Bethmann's Barty*	C.A. Shepperson
41	*Special Booms in Berlin. Though Teuton trade ...*	E.H. Shephard
42	*Stone-masons, too ...*	E.H. Shephard
43	*Tailors are stitching ...*	E.H. Shephard
44	*The Red Cross rage ...*	E.H. Shephard
45	*After the War. There will be no more late rising ...*	A.W. Mills
46	*We shall know how to take cover ...*	A.W. Mills
47	*And when we can again find time ...*	A.W. Mills

No.	Heading/Caption	Cartoonist	Date	Page
48	*German spy reports to headquarters ...*	G. Morrow	6.1.1915	20
49	*A New British Explosive*	T. Evans	13.1.1915	30
50	*The Enemy in our Midst*	R. Brook	13.1.1915	34
51	*Subtleties of German Warfare*	G. Morrow	13.1.1915	40
52	*British Tommy (Returning to trench ...*	D. German	20.1.1915	54
53	*Nephew: "I'm reading a ...*	F.H. Townsend	27.1.1915	65
54	*Hoch aye!*	E. Noble	3.2.1915	81
55	*In the order that no possible means ...*	G. Morrow	3.2.1915	87
56	*The 'Kultur' Cut*	E.H. Shephard	3.2.1915	89
57	*"Oh, Mother! How I wish I were ...*	L. Baumer	3.2.1915	90
58	*What our enemy has to put up with*	F. Reynolds	17.2.1915	134
59	*Chorus from the trench: "What 'ave you ...*	R. Bull	17.2.1915	135
60	*Tirpitz's Dream*	G. Morrow	24.2.1915	145
61	*Study of Prussian Household ...*	F. Reynolds	24.2.1915	150

Punch, Volume 149, 1915

Punch, Volume 150, 1916

Punch, Volume 151, 1916

No.	Heading/Caption	Cartoonist	Date	Page
126	*The New Super-hate*	G. Morrow	11.10.1916	276
127	*Whenever the telephone rings ...*	G. Morrow	18.10.1916	292
128	*Special constable: "What are you ...*	W. Bird	25.10.1916	293
129	*Cockney Tommy: "Blow me ...*	A. Bailey	1.11.1916	319
130	*The 'Indepence' of Poland*	B. Partridge	15.11.1916	344
131	*News of the 'tanks' ...*	J.A. Shephard	29.11.1916	376
132	*Hindenburgitis, or the Prussian home ...*	F. Reynolds	29.11.1916	380
133	*Herr Blumenzwiebel at the Grand Opera ...*	C. Harrison	6.12.1916	400
134	*Levée en Masse*	G. Morrow	13.12.1916	420

Punch, Volume 152, 1917

No.	Heading/Caption	Cartoonist
	Punch's Almanack for 1917	
135	*A False Alarm*	G.L. Stampa
136	*Fashions in the New Germany*	F. Reynolds

No.	Heading/Caption	Cartoonist	Date	Page
137	*Gretchen: "Will it never end?"*	F. Reynolds	3.1.1917	8
138	*Super-boy: "But, Father ...*	F. Reynolds	17.1.1917	40
139	*Force of Habit*	G. Morrow	17.1.1917	48
140	*Tube conductor: "Pass further down ...*	F.H. Townsend	24.1.1917	63
141	*The Theatre of War*	F.H. Townsend	7.3.1917	152
142	*The Invaders*	L. Raven-Hill	28.3.1917	191
143	*Some Catch: The Angler's Dream*	L. Raven-Hill	28.3.1917	206
144	*Fond Teuton Parent*	F. Reynolds	28.3.1917	209
145	*Karl: "What Worries me ...*	F. Reynolds	28.3.1917	209
146	*"You wouldn't think it ...*	R. Brook	11.4.1917	247
147	*Cannon-Fodder - and after*	L. Raven-Hill	25.4.1917	267
148	*The Waning of Faith*	B. Partridge	25.4.1917	273
149	*Donnerwetter*	L. Raven-Hill	9.5.1917	299
150	*The Bribe*	"Fougasse"	16.5.1917	313
151	*British officer (interrupting carousal ...*	B. Thomas	13.6.1917	388

Punch, Volume 153, 1918

No.	Heading/Caption	Cartoonist	Date	Page
152	*The Tuber's Repartee*	L. Raven-Hill	11.7.1917	19
153	*Teuton writes: "I am sad at heart ...*	R. Brook	18.7.1917	33
154	*Grandpa (to small Teuton ...*	F. Reynolds	18.7.1917	45
155	*The Reverse of the Medal*	F.H. Townsend	12.9.1917	185
156	*A Place in the Moon*	L. Raven-Hill	3.10.1917	233
157	*A Birthday Greeting for Hindenburg*	B. Partridge	10.10.1917	
158	*Tommy: "'ands up, all of yer ...*	G.L. Stampa	31.10.1917	299
159	*Prisoner (on his dignity): "But you ...*	L. Raven-Hill		307

Punch, Volume 154, 1918

No.	Heading/Caption	Cartoonist
	Punch's Almanack for 1918	
160	*Over-zealous Tommy*	L. Raven-Hill
161	*Combing out the Army ...*	F.H. Townsend
162	*Hun polyglot preparing commercial ....*	F.H. Townsend
163	*The bravest man that ever lived*	F.H. Townsend
164	*Training commercial travellers ...*	F.H. Townsend
165	*Kindness to British children*	G. Morrow
166	*A demonstration by members of the 'Germanic League of Love.'*	G. Morrow
167	*The Free Restaurant*	G. Morrow
168	*Propaganding by Poster*	G. Morrow

No.	Heading/Caption	Cartoonist	Date	Page
169	*An Easy Conundrum*	L. Raven-Hill	2.1.1918	3
170	*Private Sloggins*	A. Moreland	9.1.1918	21
171	*Private Smith*	G.L. Stampa	6.2.1918	85
172	*The Bomberang*	L. Raven-Hill	20.3.1918	179
173	*A German 'Peace'*	L. Raven-Hill	12.6.1918	371
174	*A Pitiful Pose*	L. Raven-Hill	26.6.1918	403

Punch, Volume 155, 1918

No.	Heading/Caption	Cartoonist	Date	Page
175	*The Blond Beast's Burden*	B. Partridge	3.7.1918	9
176	*Gallant Berliner: "Alas, noble lady ...*	J.A. Shephard	24.7.1918	56
177	*The Chastened Mood*	F.H. Townsend	7.8.1918	83
178	*German Prisoner: "Vy vos you spare ...*	F.G. Lewin	7.8.1918	84
179	*The River Season*	B. Partridge	7.8.1918	89
180	*Tommy: "Nah then, 'indenburg ...*	L. Edwards	7.8.1918	92
181	*Von Pot and von Kettle*	B. Partridge	14.8.1918	105
182	*"Himmel! The All-highest has ...*	A. Moreland	21.8.1918	123
183	*Gretel: "Have you ever contemplated ...*	F. Reynolds	28.8.1918	136
184	*In Reserve*	L. Raven-Hill	4.9.1918	153
185	*The German Angel of Peace*	B. Partridge	16.10.1918	253
186	*Bosch (suddenly appearing ...*	'Fougasse'	23.10.1918	272
187	*Everything in its Proper Order*	L. Raven-Hill	30.10.1918	279
188	*Essence of Parliament*	F.H. Townsend	6.11.1918	302
189	*Surrender de luxe*	G.L. Stampa	13.11.1918	312

Appendix 2 Table of Scenes

Types of scenes	Simplicissimus	Punch
1. Everyday scene - overall	68 = 32.7 %	125 = 47.0 %
Communicative situation	42 = 20.2 %	16 = 6.0 %
Interaction with the verbal part	18 = 8.6 %	65 = 24.4 %
Communicative situation and interaction with the verbal part	8 = 3.8 %	44 = 16.5 %
2. Non-combatant military scene - overall	14 = 6.7 %	24 = 9.0 %
Communicative situation	10 = 4.8 %	5 = 1.9 %
Interaction with the verbal part	0 = 0 %	10 = 3.8 %
Communicative situation and interaction with the verbal part	4 = 1.9 %	9 = 3.4 %
3. War scene - overall	14 = 6.7 %	29 = 10.9 %
Communicative situation	7 = 3.4 %	1 = 0.4 %
Interaction with the verbal part	3 = 1.4 %	11 = 4.1 %
Communicative situation and interaction with the verbal part	4 = 1.9 %	17 = 6.4 %
4. Counterfactual scene - overall	23 = 11.1 %	65 = 24.4 %
Communicative situation	4 = 1.9 %	0 = 0 %
Interaction with the verbal part	13 = 6.2 %	53 = 19.9 %
Communicative situation and interaction with the verbal part	6 = 2.9 %	12 = 4.5 %
5. Metonymic scene - overall	89 = 42.8 %	24 = 9.0 %
Communicative situation	23 = 11.1 %	0 = 0 %
Interaction with the verbal part	37 = 17.8 %	9 = 3.4 %
Communicative situation and interaction with the verbal part	29 = 13.9 %	15 = 5.6 %
Panels overall	208 = 100 %	266 = 100 %

Table 17 Types of scenes and types of pictorial-verbal interaction

Appendix 3: Chronology of the First World War

1914

June 28	Assassination of Archduke Franz Ferdinand, heir to the throne of the Austro-Hungarian empire, and the Duchess of Hohenberg in Sarajevo, Bosnia, by the Bosnian student, Gavro Princip. Austria suspects Serbia of aiding the plot.
July 28	Austria-Hungary declares war on Serbia, accusing Serbia of provoking the assassination. The hostilities begin after Germany and Austria-Hungary refuse England's invitation to a conference.
Aug. 1	Germany declares war on Russia.
Aug. 3	Germany declares war on France.
Aug. 4	Germany invades Belgium, a neutral country.
Aug. 4	England declares war on Germany.
Aug. 7	Great Britain's Expeditionary Force (BEF) lands at Ostend, Calais and Dunkirk.
Aug. 17	Russia invades East Prussia.
Aug. 23	Austria-Hungary invades Russian Poland (Galicia).
Sept. 5	The 'Pact of London' is concluded. England, France and Russia agree not to sign a separate peace.
Sept. 5-10	First Battle of Marne halts the German advance, resulting in stalemate and trench warfare.
Sept. 14	First battle of Aisne and of Ypres begins.
Oct. 29	Turkey enters the war on the side of the Central Powers.
Nov. 9	The Australian cruiser *Sydney* wrecks the German cruiser *Emden*.
Dec. 2	Austrian forces move into and occupy Belgrade, Serbia.
Dec. 8	British and German naval forces engage near the Falkland Island. The British sink the German cruisers *Scharnhorst, Gneisenau, Nürnberg* and *Leipzig*.
Dec. 21	First German air raid on Britain.
Dec. 25	Soldiers' unofficial Christmas truce.

1915

Jan. 19	First German zeppelin attack on England.
Jan. 23	A British squadron sinks the German cruiser *Blücher* in a sea battle at Dogger Bank.
Feb. 2	Great Britain places all goods on contraband list.
Feb. 4	Germany proclaims the waters around Great Britain, including the whole English Channel, a war zone after February 18.
Feb. 10	United States warns Great Britain and Germany not to abuse flag nor to attack American ships.
Feb. 18	Germany begin submarine blockade by sinking a British collier without warning.
March2	Great Britain declares virtual blockade of German coast.
March 8	Great Britain bars cotton from Germany.
April 11	The German ambassador calls upon the American people to stop the export of arms to the Allies.

April 22	The Germans use poison gas for the first time in an attack on Canadian soldiers at Ypres, Belgium.
April 26	The Allies land armies at the Dardanelles.
April 26	Great Britain, Russia, France and Italy sign a secret treaty in London. Italy is to receive the Trentino, South Tyrol, Trieste, Istria, Gorizia, Gradisca, Saseno, the Dodecanese Islands; potential territory or concessions in Adalia, Rritrea, Somaliland, and Libya. Italy is to begin hostilities within a month.
May 7	The British Cunard liner *Lusitania* is sunk by a German submarine off Kinsale Head, at the Irish coast; more than a thousand passengers are killed or drown. Among them are more than a hundred Americans.
May 13	President Wilson sends a stern note to Germany demanding reparation for the loss of American lives on the *Lusitania* and insists that submarine attacks on merchant vessels carrying non-combatants must stop at once.
June 4-6	German aircraft bomb English towns.
June 15	Allied aircraft bomb Karlsruhe in retaliation.
Aug. 4	The British reply to the American protest against the blockade. They insist that the blockade is strictly within international law, but are prepared to submit disputed cases of seizure to arbitration.
Sept. 1	Germany agrees to sink no more liners without warning.
Oct. 2	Agreement between Bulgaria and the Central Powers. Bulgaria is to enter the war on the 15th.
Oct. 13	London is bombarded by zeppelins; 55 persons are killed and 114 injured.
Dec. 4	Henry Ford, with large party of peace advocates, sails for Europe on a chartered steamer, *Oscar II*, with the object of ending the war.
Dec. 22	Henry Ford leaves his peace party at Christiania and returns to the United States.

1916

January	The first Military Service Act is passed in Great Britain. It calls for the compulsory enlistment of unmarried men between the ages of 18 and 41.
Jan. 29-31	German zeppelins bomb Paris and towns in England.
Feb. 10	British conscription law goes into effect.
March 16	Admiral von Tirpitz, the head of the German navy, retires.
March 24	Commander Herbert Pustkuchen of the U-29 torpedoed the Channel steamer *Sussex*. The commander mistook the *Sussex* for a mine layer and ordered it to be sunk. The blast only damaged the ship, but of the 325 passengers aboard, of whom 25 were Americans, 80 were killed or injured, 4 Americans being among the latter.[1]
April 19	President Wilson sends an ultimatum by wireless publicly warning Germany not to pursue its submarine policy.
May	The second Military Service Act is introduced in Great Britain. All men regardless of marital status between the ages of 18 and 41 have to enlist.
May 5	The German reply to Wilson's ultimatum says that the illegal U-boat methods will cease if the United States force Great Britain to raise the blockade of Germany.

---

[1] Cf. King (1972: 276).

May 31	Jutland naval battle (Battle of the Skaggerak); the British and German fleets suffer heavy losses. The fact that the smaller German fleet is not defeated is a relative success.
June 5	Earl Kitchener, the British Secretary of War, loses his life when the British cruiser *Hampshire*, on which he was voyaging to Russia, is sunk off the Orkney Islands, Scotland.
June 21	Allies economic conference agrees on boycott of Germany after the war.
Aug. 29	Field Marshal von Hindenburg becomes Chief of Staff of the German armies, succeeding General von Falkenhayn.
Sept. 15	British break third German line north of the Somme. For the first time tanks are used in a battle.
Oct. 15	Germany resumes submarine attacks.
Nov. 23	German warships bombard the English coast.
Nov. 28	First German airplane (as opposed to zeppelin) air-raid on Britain.
Dec. 6	David Lloyd George replaces Asquith as British Prime Minister.
Dec. 12	Germany and its allies propose peace.
Dec. 14	Entente allies demand reparation, restitution and adequate security for the future, it is announced in British Parliament.
Dec. 18	Lloyd George announces in Parliament that the Allies reject the German peace proposal; reparation and restitution are the only basis on which they will negotiate a peace.
Dec. 18	President Wilson invites the belligerents to announce the terms on which peace might be concluded.
Dec. 26	Germany replies to Wilson's note suggesting that direct discussion between the belligerents in some neutral country seems the best road to peace. No terms are stated.
Dec. 30	The Allies turn down the German peace proposals; the proposals are described as sham proposals, lacking all substance and precision. They are less an offer of peace than a war manoeuvre.

1917

Jan. 10	Statement of the Allied war aims: the restoration of Belgium, Serbia, and Montenegro; the evacuation of invaded territories in France, Russia and Rumania; the restitution of "provinces formerly torn from the Allies by force"; the liberation of Italians, Slavs, etc.; the "turning out of Europe of the Ottoman Empire"; the reorganization of Europe, guaranteed by a "stable regime and based at once on respect for nationalities and the right of full security and liberty of economic development" etc.
Jan. 22	President Wilson in address to the Senate outlines a program for a "peace without victory."
Jan. 29	German peace terms are sent for the private information of President Wilson: Restitution to France of the part of Alsace occupied by Germany; the acquisition of a strategic and economic frontier zone separating Germany and Poland from Russia; the restitution of colonial conquests, securing to Germany colonial territory compatible with its population and economic interests; the restoration of occupied France, subject to certain strategic and economic modifications and financial compensation; renunciation of economic obstacles to normal commerce; compensation for German undertakings and civilians

damaged by the war; economic and financial salvaging of territory invaded by both sides; and the placing of the freedom of the sea on a secure foundation.

Feb. 1   Germany resumes unrestricted submarine warfare in zones surrounding the coasts of the Entente Powers.

Feb. 3   The United States severs diplomatic relations with Germany.

Feb. 26   President Wilson signs the order for arming merchantmen.

Feb. 26   The 'Zimmerman Telegram', Germany's note to Mexico proposing a German-Mexican alliance, is intercepted and published by the British naval intelligence. Germanny will support Mexico in regaining its lost territory in Texas, New Mexico and Arizona. Mexico is to persuade Japan to change sides in the war. There is a strong reaction in the United States.

March 11   Secret agreement between France and Russia. Russia is to support French demands for Alsace-Lorraine, and the left bank of the Rhine is to become a neutral state. In return, France "recognizes Russia's complete liberty in establishing its Western Frontiers."

March 12   The Russian Revolution begins; a provisional government is formed.

April 2   President Wilson asks the Congress for an army of 500,000.

April 6   President Wilson signs a resolution declaring a state of war.

Dec. 15   A formal armistice between Russia and the Central Powers is signed at Brest-Litovsk. Germany is to gain immensely large territories in the east.

1918

Jan. 8   President Wilson's address to Congress outlines an American peace program enumerating the 'fourteen points'.

Jan. 26   Ukraine declares its complete independence.

Feb. 9   Ukraine signs a peace treaty with the Central Powers at Brest-Litovsk.

Feb. 10   Russian government declares the war at an end and orders demobilization.

Feb. 3   Treaty of Brest-Litovsk concluded by the Bolsheviks and the Central Powers.

March 21   Great German offensive begun from Arras to La Fere along 50 miles of the British and French line.

March 29   French General Ferdinand Foch made commander in chief of the Allied forces in France.

July 18   The great offensive of the Allies and the Americans begins.

Sept. 29   Bulgaria surrenders.

Oct. 6   Germany and Austria address pleas for armistice to President Wilson.

Oct. 14   Turkey appeals to President Wilson for armistice.

Oct. 30   Turkey accepts the conditions imposed by the Allies and signs the armistice.

Nov. 3-5   Mutiny spreads in the German fleet and naval bases, beginning at Kiel.

Nov. 4   Austria-Hungary withdraws from the war.

Nov. 8   German plenipotentiaries receive armistice proposals from Foch at Senlis.

Nov. 9   Chancellor Maximilian von Baden announces the abdication of the Kaiser and the Crown Prince and the appointment of Friedrich Ebert, vice-president of the Socialist Democratic Party, as chancellor pending the creation of a 'constitutional German national assembly'.

Nov. 10   Kaiser William II flees to Holland.

Nov. 11   Armistice signed at Senlis at 5 a.m.; the hostilities are to cease at 11 a.m.

List of Cartoons from *Simplicissimus* and *Punch* reproduced in this book:[1]

[1] In the column *cartoon* 'S' stands for *Simplicissimus* and 'P' for *Punch*. The figures refer to the numbers in chapters 3.3 and 3.4 and appendix 1.

237

References

Abret, H. & A. Keel
1985   *Die Majestätsbeleidigungsaffäre des 'Simplicissimus'-Verlegers Albert Langen.* Franfurt: Verlag Peter Lang.
Allen, A.T.
1984   *Satire and Society in Wilhelmine Germany.* Lexington: The University Press of Kentucky.
Chandler, S.R.
1991   "Metaphor Comprehension: A Connectionist Approach to Implications for the Mental Lexicon." *Metaphor and Symbolic Activity* 6: 227-258.
Condor, S.
1997   " 'Having History': A Social Psychological Exploration of Anglo-British Autostereotypes," In: Barfoot:, C.C. (ed.) *Beyond Pug's Tour: National and Ethnic Stereotyping in Theory and Literary Practice and Preface.* Amsterdam: Rodopi, pp. 213-254.
Coupland, N. & A. Jaworski, (eds)
1997   *Sociolinguistics: A Reader and Course Book.* New York: St. Martin's Press.
Dews, S. & E. Winner
1995   "Muting the Meaning: A Social Function of Irony". *Metaphor and Symbolic Activity* 10: 3-19
Dirven, R. & R. Pörings (eds)
2002   *Metaphor and Metonymy in Contrast and Comparison.* Berlin: Mouton de Gruyter.
Dirven, R., R.M. Frank & C. Ilie
2001   *Language and Ideology.* Amsterdam: John Benjamins.
Dundes, A.
1962   "From Etic To Emic Units in The Structural Study of Folktales". *Journal of American Folklore* 75: 95-105.
Encyclopaedia Britannica
        Encyclopaedia Britannica Online; http://www.britannica.com/
Fauconnier, G.
1985   *Mental Spaces.* Cambridge: Cambridge University Press.
Fiebig-von Hase, R.
1994   "Der Anfang vom Ende des Krieges: Deutschland, die USA und die Hintergründe des amerikanischen Kriegseintritts am 6. April 1917". In: Michalka, W. (ed.), pp.125-158.
Forceville, C.
1994   "Pictorial metaphor in advertisements". *Metaphor and Symbolic Activity* 9: 1-29.
Freud, S.
1958   *Der Witz und seine Beziehung zum Unbewussten.* Frankfurt: Fischer.
Gernsbacher, M.
1990   *Language Comprehension as Structure Building*, Hillsdale, N.J.: Erlbaum.
Gibbs, R.W.
1994   *The Poetics of Mind. Figurative Thought Language and Understanding.* Cambridge: Cambridge University Press.
2000   "Making Good Psychology out of Blending Theory". *Cognitive Linguistics* 11: 347-358.

Glass, A.L. & K.J. Holyoak
1986²   *Cognition*. New York: Random House.
Gombrich, E.H.
1977⁵   *Art and Illusion*. London: Phaidon Press.
Grote, B.
1967   *Der Deutsche Michel*. Dortmunder Beiträge zur Zeitforschung 11 (1967). Dortmund: Rohfus.
Hammerton, J. A. (ed.)
n.d.   *Mr. Punch's Cavalcade, A Review of Thirty Years*. London: The Educational Book Company Ltd.
Hawkins, B.
2001   "Ideology, Metaphor and Iconographic Reference". In: Dirven, R., Frank, R.M. & C. Ilie, (eds), pp. 27-50.
Hewstone, M. & H. Giles
1997   "Social Groups and Social Stereotypes". In: Coupland, N. & A. Jaworski, (eds), pp. 270-283.
Hodge, R.
1989   "National Character and the Discursive Process: A Study of Transformations in Popular Metatexts". *Journal of Pragmatics* 13: 427-444.
Hodge, R. & G. Kress
1993   *Language as Ideology*. New York: Routledge.
1997   "Social Semiotics, Style and Ideology". In: Coupland, N. & A. Jaworski (eds), pp. 49-54.
Hofmann, W.
1956   *Die Karikatur von Leonardo bis Picasso*. Wien: Verlag Brüder Rosenbaum.
Hortmann, S.
1992   *Deutschland aus britischer Sicht: eine Untersuchung der Deutschlandbilder britischer Studenten in Nordrhein-Westfalen*. Universität Duisburg: Dissertation [PhD Thesis].
Hünig, W.K.
1974   *Strukturen des comic strip. Ansätze zu einer textlinguistisch-semiotischen Analyse narrativer comics*. Hildesheim: Olms.
2001   "Discourse Analysis". *Studies in Linguistics* 5: 66-114.
2002   *Political Cartoons*. LAUD paper no. 557, Series A.
Kennedy, J.M.
1980   "Metaphor in Pictures". *Perception* 11: 589-605.
1990   "Metaphor - its Intellectual Basis". *Metaphor and Symbolic Activity* 5: 115-123.
1993   "Myster! Unraveling Edward Gory's Tangled Web of Visual Metaphor". *Metaphor and Symbolic Activity* 8: 181-193.
Kennedy, J.M., C.D. Green & J. Vervaeke
1993   "Metaphor Thought and Devices in Pictures". *Metaphor and Symbolic Activity* 8: 243-255.
Kielmannsegg, P. Graf
1968   *Deutschland und der Erste Weltkrieg*. Frankfurt: Akademische Verlagsgesellschaft Athenaion.
King, J.C. (ed.)
1972   *The First World War*. New York: Harper & Row.

Koreik, U.
1993   "Bismarck und Hitler, fleissig und arrogant. Eine vergleichende Untersuchung zu Stereotypen bei britischen Studierenden und deutschen Oberschülern vor dem Hintergrund des Fremdsprachenunterrichts". *Informationen Deutsch als Fremdsprache* 20/4: 449-458.

Kris, E. & N. Leites
1947   "Trends in Twentieth Century Propaganda". In: Roheim, G. (ed.). *Psychoanalysis and the Social Sciences*, Vol.1. New York: International Universities Press, pp. 393-409.

Langacker, R.W.
1987   *Foundations of Cognitive Grammar.* Vol.1: *Theoretical Prerequisites.* Stanford: Stanford University Press.
1991   *Foundations of Cognitive Grammar.* Vol.2: *Descriptive Application.* Stanford: Stanford University Press.
1993   "Reference-Point Constructions". *Cognitive Linguistics* 4: 1-38.

Lakoff, G.
1987   *Women, Fire, and Dangerous Things: What Categories Reveal about the Mind.* Chicago: Chicago University Press.

Lakoff, G. & M. Johnson
1980   *Metaphors We Live By.* Chicago: Chicago University Press.

Lakoff, G. & M. Turner
1989   *More than Cool Reason: A Field Guide to Poetic Metaphor.* Chicago: Chicago University Press.

Langfeldt, H.-P. & M. Langfeldt-Nagel
1990   „Rekonstruktion und Validierung prototypischer Alltagstheorien agressiven Verhaltens". *Sprache und Kognition* 9: 12-25.

Lapp, E.
1992   *Linguistik und Ironie.* Tübingen: Narr.

Leland, C.G.
            Hans Breitmann's ballads, [Complete, unabridged reproduction of the edition New York 1914], New York: Dover Publications.
1999   *Hans Breitmann's party, with other ballads,* Philadelphia: T. B. Peterson & brothers, date of publication: [c.1871], publicly accessible text for non-commercial applications.
            < http://www.hti.umich.edu/cgi/t/text/text-idx?c=moa;idno=ABK1245 >

Levinson, S.C.
1983   *Pragmatics.* Cambridge: Cambridge University Press.

Lippmann, W.
1998   *Public Opinion.* New Brunswick: Transaction Publications.
(1922)

Mann, W.C. & S.A. Thompson
1987   "Rhetorical Structure Theory: Description and Construction of Text Structures". In: Kempen, G. (ed.). *Natural Language Generation.* Boston, MA.: Kluwer Academic Publishers, pp. 85-95.
1988   "Rhetorical Structure Theory: Toward A Functional Theory of Text Organization. *Text* 8: 243-281.

Michalka, W. (ed.)
1994   *Der Erste Weltkrieg.* München: Pieper.

240

Miller, G.A.
1979   "Images and Models, Similes and Metaphors". In: Ortony, A. (ed.) *Metaphor and Thought*. Cambridge: Cambridge University Press, pp. 202-250.
Mio, J.S. & A.C.Graesser
1991   "Humor, Language and Metaphor". *Metaphor and Symbolic Activity* 6: 87-102.
Morris, R.
1993   "Visual Rhetoric in Political Cartoons: A Structural Approach". *Metaphor and Symbolic Activity* 8: 195-210.
Oxford English Dictionary
        OED Online: http://dictionary.oed.com/
Press, C.
1981   *The Political Cartoon*. London, Toronto: Associated University Press.
Propp, V.
1968   *Morphology of the Folktale*. Austin: University of Texas Press.
(1928)
Punch
        Vol. CXLVI (January-June 1914) - vol. CLV (July-December 1918), London and Tonbridge: The Whitefriars Press.
Radden, G. & Z. Kövecses
1999   "Towards a theory of metonymy". In: Panther, K. & G. Radden (eds). *Metonymy in Language and Thought*. Amsterdam: John Benjamins, pp. 17-59.
Raskin, V.
1987   "Linguistic Heuristics of Humor: A Script-Based Semantic Approach". *International Journal of the Sociology of Language* 65: 11-25.
Reumann, K.
1969   „Die Karikatur". In: Dovifat, E. (ed.). *Handbuch der Publizistik*, Bd. 2, 1. Teil: *Praktische Publizistik*. Berlin: de Gruyter, pp. 65-90.
Rohkrämer, T.
1994   "August 1914 – Kriegsmentalität und ihre Voraussetzungen". In: Michalka, W. (ed.) pp. 759-777.
Rohrer, T.
2001   "Even the Interface is For Sale: Metaphors, Visual Blends and the Hidden Ideology of the Internet". In: Dirven, R., Frank, R.M. & C. Ilie, (eds), pp. 189-214.
Rosenberger, B.
1998   *Zeitungen als Kriegstreiber? Die Rolle der Presse im Vorfeld des Ersten Weltkrieges*. Köln: Böhlau.
Ruiz de Mendoza Ibáñez, F.J. & O.I. Díez Velasco
2002   "Patterns of conceptual interaction". In: Dirven, R. & R. Pörings (eds), 489-532.
Rutland, A.
1999   "The Development of National Prejudice, In-Group Favouritism and Self-Stereotypes in British Children". *British Journal of Social Psychology* 38/1: 55.
Sanders, M. L. & P.M. Taylor
1990   *Britische Propaganda im Ersten Weltkrieg: 1914 – 1918*. Berlin: Colloquium-Verlag.

Simplicissimus
    Founded by A. Langen & Th. Th. Heine. Biannual volumes: Vol. 19 (April -
    September 1914) - vol. 23 (October 1918 - March 1919). München:
    Simplicissimus-Verlag.
Sperber, D. & D. Wilson
1986   *Relevance: Communication and Cognition*. Oxford: Blackwell.
Stanzel, F.K.
1986   "National Character as Literary Stereotype. An Analysis on the Image of the
    German in English Literature before 1800". *Anglistik & Englischunterricht* 7:
    29-30.
Tajfel, H.
1969   "Cognitive Aspects of Prejudice". *Journal of Social Issues* 25: 79-97.
Tajfel, H.
1982   *Social Identity and Intergroup Relations*. Cambridge: Cambridge University
    Press.
Tajfel, H., Turner, J.
1979   "An Integrative Theory of Intergroup Conflict". In: Austin, W.G. & S. Worchel
    (eds). *The Social Psychology of Intergroup Relations*, Monterey, CA.: Brooks/Cole, pp.
    33-47.
Talmy, L.
2000   *Toward a Cognitive Semantics*. Vol 1: *Concept Structuring Systems*.
    Cambridge, MASS.: The MIT Press.
Turner, Mark
1987   *Death is the Mother of Beauty: Mind, Metaphor, Criticism*. Chicago:
    University of Chicago Press.
1989   "Categories and Analogies." In: Heiman D. (ed.) *Analogical Reasoning:
    Perspectives of Artificial Intelligence, Cognitive Science, and Philosophy*.
    Dordrecht: Kluwer, pp. 3-24.
1991   *Reading Minds: The Study of English in the Age of Cognitive Science*.
    Princeton: Princeton University Press.
1996a   "Conceptual Blending and Counterfactual Argument in The Social and
    Behavioral Sciences". In: Tetlock P. & A. Belkin (eds). *Counterfactual
    Thought Experiments in Worldpolitics*. Princeton, N.J.: Princeton University
    Press, pp. 291-295.
1996b   *The Literary Mind*. New York: Oxford University Press.
Turner, M. & G. Fauconnier
1995   "Conceptual Integration and Formal Expression". *Metaphor and Symbolic
    Activity* 10: 183-203.
2002   "Metaphor, Metonymy, and Binding". In: Dirven, R. & R. Pörings (eds).
    Metaphor and Metonymy in Contrast and Comparison. Berlin: Mouton de
    Gruyter, pp. 469-488.
Ungern-Sternberg, J. von & W. von Ungern-Sternberg
1996   *Der Aufruf "An die Kulturwelt!": das Manifest der 93 und die Anfänge der
    Kriegspropaganda im Ersten Weltkrieg;* mit einer Dokumentation. Stuttgart:
    Steiner.
Van Dijk, T.A.
1984   *Prejudice in Discourse - An Analysis of Ethnic Prejudice in Cognition and
    Conversation*. Amsterdam: John Benjamins.

242

Vicari, P.
1993   "Renaissance Emblematica." *Metaphor and Symbolic Activity* 8: 153-168.
Wagner, R.
1983   *Die Entstehung des Cartoon in seiner gegenwärtigen Form: dargestellt am Beispiel seiner Entwicklung in den Zeitschriften 'The New Yorker' und 'Punch'*. Universität Marburg: Dissertation [PhD Thesis].
Wenzel, A.
1978   *Stereotype in gesprochener Sprache*. München: Max Huber.
Wilson, T.
1986   *The Myriad Faces of War. Britain and the Great War, 1914-1918*. Cambridge: Polity Press.
Wilke, J.
1991   "Auf dem Weg zur „Großmacht": die Presse im 19. Jahrhundert". In: Wimmer, R. (ed.) *Das 19. Jahrhundert: sprachgeschichtliche Wurzeln des heutigen Deutsch*, Berlin: de Gruyter, pp. 73-94.

WWW:

http://209.211.248.99/exhibition/caricatures/intro.html
http://akmilitaergeschichte.de/links/firstww.html
http://www.boondocksnet.com/cartoons/mc05.html
http://cogsci.berkeley.edu/MetaphorHome.html
http://darwin.baruch.cuny.edu/biography/london/london.html
http://dictionary.oed.com/
http://homepage.tinet.ie/~lawe/LONDONCLUBS.htm
http://info.ox.ac.uk/departments/humanities/rose/chron.html#1914
http://rutlandhs.k12.vt.us/jpeterso/uboatcar.htm
http://store.german-usa.com/Books/German-American_Culture/hans_breitmann_s_ballads.html
http://www.bartleby.com/65/ku/Kuhlmann.html
http://www.dmalcolm.demon.co.uk/genealogy/raid.htm
http://www.encyclopedia.com/searchpool.asp?target=@DOCTITLE%20Arbuthnot%20%20Johoon
http://www.hti.umich.edu/cgi/t/text/text-idx?c=moa;idno=ABK1245
http://www.infoplease.com/ce6/people/A0828319.html
http://www.infoplease.com/ipa/A0001284.html
http://www.ku.edu/~kansite/WWI-L/2001/03/msg00213.html
http://www.lib.byu.edu/~rdh/wwi/1917/wilswarm.html
http://www.nlpb.de/04-pub/04-pub-pdf/gb.pdf
http://www.refdesk.com/
http://www.richthofen.com/ww1sum/
http://www.skalman.nu/worldwar1/1915.htm
http://www.spartacus.schoolnet.co.uk/FWWkitchener.htm
http://www.worldwar1.com/sfgarmy.htm
http://www.ww1-propaganda-cards.com/punch_cards.html